# Indian Vegetable Culture

## for

## Hills & Plains

W.W. Johnstone

2002

**ASIATIC PUBLISHING HOUSE**

**181/4-D, J. Extension, Street No. 5, Laxmi Nagar**

**DELHI - 110 092 (INDIA)**

*Published by :*
**Asiatic Publishing House**
181/4, Street No. 5, J.·Extn. Laxmi Nagar,
Delhi - 110 092 (India) Ph. : 2449904



**ISBN 81-87067-34-9**

Indian print : JANUARY 10 2002

*Printed at*
Santosh Offset,
40, Anand Nagar,
Delhi-110 035

# PREFACE.

IT has been a desire of mine for some years past, to publish a simple hand-book on Indian Gardening, which would be of use to the ordinary Amateur, and the following pages have been written, in the hopes that the hints given will be found useful by the many thousands who, in different-parts of this great land of India, try to make the land produce something better than can be done by the ordinary uninstructed Mali. Gardening is a most profitable and, at the same time, health giving hobby, and any simple instructions that will help in the producing of two plants where before only one was grown, cannot help but be a welcome addition to the library of those who, particularly on the Plains, try to relieve the monotony of existence by engaging in Gardening. Take my advice and do not be ashamed to use the spade or the hoe, for an occasional use of these health giving implements will do much to keep the doctor and his physic outside the door.

In a book of this size it is impossible to treat of all the plants grown in Indian Gardens, but I have done my best to select the most representative ones and those most commonly grown.

I am conscious of the many shortcomings in my effort and bespeak the kind indulgence of readers, and hope that, with all its deficiencies, my book will be of some practical use to those who are interested in the subject.

W. W. JOHNSTONE.

"WHYTBANK CASTLE"
Mussoorie, U. P. A. & O.,

# CONTENTS.

# GARDENING.

## A Guide for Amateurs in India.

MANY books have been written on the subject of "Gardening in India," but the writer is convinced that there is a demand for one which will give, in a simple way, without the many technicalities which mar the usefulness of so many of these works, practical assistance to the average amateur in raising good vegetables and beautiful flowers with the assistance of the ordinary native mali. The present work does not aim at taking the place of such standard works as Firminger's "Manual of Gardening," Woodrow's excellent "Gardening in India," Landolicus' "Indian Amateur Gardener" and such like much read books. The intention of the writer is to give to the Indian Amateur Gardener a work which will tell him or her what to sow, when to sow, how to sow, and a little on the after treatment of the plants. Gardening repays study of the subject, but most amateurs in India have not got the time to spare to wade through verbose treatises on the Botanical history, &c., &c., of the plants they wish to cultivate, so it is thought that this little hand-book will be welcomed.

### PREPARING THE SOIL.

To have a good garden it is essential that we should have good soil. Even a poor, unproductive soil can, with a little trouble, be converted into a paradise of beauty. Drainage for one thing, must be seen to. A waterlogged soil is all right for growing aquatics on, but for an ordinary garden it is worse than useless. When the garden ground is perfectly level, a certain amount of slope should be given to the soil. Personally, the writer is greatly in favor of terraces, which not only ensure good drainage, but also help to give a picturesque appearance to the garden. Where it is not possible to make terraces, fairly deep drains should be dug converging into one drain, or better still, any small stream that may be near and which can be utilised for carrying away the excess moisture from the garden. There is no use in my dwelling lengthily on this subject which has been very ably treated by numerous writers.

The next thing we have to consider is the soil. There is a great tendency in this country to take things as we find them, but this maxim does not, as a rule, hold good with garden soils. Many people seem to think that burying enormous quantities of manure in their gardens is sure to enrich the soil, and that they are then certain to have grand crops. Manure is all very good in its way, but we can have too much of a good thing. I maintain that the first essential in preparing ground for a garden is deep trenching. The whole garden should be turned over to a depth of two or three feet, say a couple of spades deep. The loosening of the soil ensures plenty of room for the roots to move in and get sustenance for the plants, and consequently the plants will be more healthy than those that have to force their way through a hard sub-soil, or as many have to do, content themselves with a shallow soil. The parable of the sower is very true to nature and shallow soil means, as a general rule, stunted, unhealthy, short lived plants. Well rotted stable manure should be well worked into the soil. Where the soil is very heavy the addition of a good dressing of sand, wood ashes or charcoal dust will be found very beneficial.

When the ground has been got into condition we must turn our thoughts to the kinds of seed we are going to sow. Get your seeds from a reliable firm with a reputation to lose, and you are fairly certain of having success with your gardening. The old adage of "cheap and nasty" is very applicable to seeds and the amateur will find that a few rupees extra given to a reliable firm for reliable seeds, is money well spent. The Mali is always anxious to be allowed to buy the seeds in the bazar on account of the dustoorie he can get from the native dealer, and it has often been found that he will deliberately spoil seeds obtained by his employer, in order to disgust him with the supplies, and so allow Mr. Mali to have the buying in future.

Well! we will suppose that you have got your supplies of seed and that you want some information as to how to sow, &c. In the following notes I have tried to give as simply as possible, the various points essential to ensuring that success which all gardeners strive after.

# The Vegetable or Kitchen Garden.

## ARTICHOKE, GLOBE.

### CYNARA SCOLYMUS. (Vern.—Hern, Hathichuk, Hurshuf, Kungor.)

Sow from August to October in the Plains, on a well raised bed in drills one foot apart; early sowings must be carefully protected from heavy rains. For successful cultivation a deep, sandy, well drained loam is the best soil, but they will do fairly well even in heavy soils; good drainage, however, is essential. As soon as the plants have made five or six leaves, they should be transplanted into rows four feet apart each way. They require a deep, well manured soil, and must always be kept well supplied with water and frequent doses of weak liquid manure. Sow March to end of May in the Hills. Of late years this most delicious vegetable has received much attention from the hybridiser, and many new and excellent varieties have been the result. Amongst the best varieties I would name the following :—*Artichoke of Modica* :—a very

GLOBE ARTICHOKE.

early variety, which bears an enormous quantity of fine heads. *Artichoke of Terranova* :—Without exception the very earliest variety in cultivation. *Remontant*:—heads very large, heavy, dark green and absolutely without spines. This variety will bear flower heads twice a year. *Large Flat Brittany ; Laon, or Paris Green ; Large Purple Paris, &c.*

## JERUSALEM ARTICHOKE.

(Helianthus Tuberosus.)

The Jerusalem Artichoke is largely cultivated in most parts of India, and is much used when Potatoes are not easily procurable. The tubers should be planted on the Plains at any time from the beginning of March, to the middle, or even end, of May. On the Hills, plant in March. This is by no means a gross feeder and any ordinary garden soil will suit it ; little or no manure should be given, as rich feeding tends to the formation of stem to the detriment of the tubers. On the Plains tubers fit for the table will be ready in November, while on the Hills good crops will be ready in August.

JERUSALEM ARTICHOKE.

## ASPARAGUS.

A. OFFICINALIS. (Vern.—Soot Moolee, Murchoba or Palagras.)

Sow from July to October in the Plains, in pans or boxes, or, if preferred on a well raised bed of light soil in drills a foot apart. Transplant when about 6 or 8 inches high into beds three or four feet wide, specially prepared for their reception, the plants one foot to eighteen inches apart. As the Asparagus is a most gross feeder, the soil must be rich, friable and well drained. Trench the ground two or three feet deep, and mix a heavy portion of

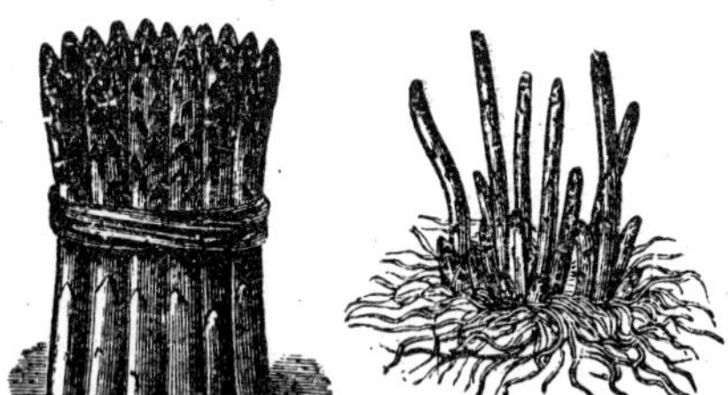

ASPARAGUS.

well rotted manure. The bed should be top-dressed once a year with well rotted manure, which should be lightly dug in with a garden fork. An application of half a pound of salt per square yard annually, when the plants first show signs of sprouting, will be found very beneficial. Asparagus must never be cut the first year, and but very sparingly the second season. By following this method strong plants will be secured, that will produce good crops for years, with but little attention beyond watering and manuring. Sow in the Hills, February to end of May. One ounce of seed for 60 feet of drill. Amongst the best varieties are the following :—*Palmetto* :—an American variety of enormous size. *New Giant* :—grows to mammoth proportions and yet retains its delicate flavour. *Connover's Colossal* :—one of the best known varieties, of large and vigorous growth. *Argenteuil* :—the finest of the purple varieties, &c., &c.

## Broad Beans.

FABA VULGARIS (VERN.—Bakla, Seem, or Sheem.)

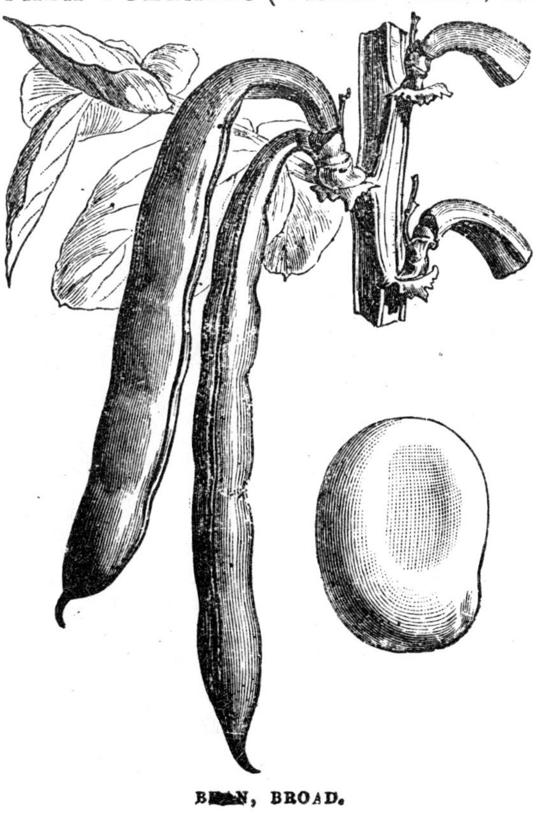

BEAN, BROAD.

Sow from September to November in drills about twelve inches apart. Seed should be planted about two inches deep with a space of four inches between them. They succeed best in a stiff, deep loamy soil, with a moderate amount of well-rotted manure. It is advisable to steep the seeds in warm water for some hours, and dry them before sowing; another favourite plan is, to flood the drills well immediately after sowing. Many growers, when the plants are about 3 feet high, and in full flower, nip off the point of each shoot, as this induces the plant more readily to set pods. Of the smaller sized seeds, 1 lb. will sow a row of 90 to 100 feet, and the same quantity of the large seeded varieties, a row of 70 to 80 feet. In the Hills sow from beginning of March to end of May. The following are perhaps the best of the many varieties now in cultivation :—LONG POD VARIETIES. *Bunyard's Exhibition* :—A very prolific variety and perhaps the best of this section. *Giant Seville* :—A very fine variety with pods from 10 to 12 inches in length and borne in great abundance. *Aquadulce Giant* :—One of the best kinds for the show bench, as the pods are of large size and the beans are of most exquisite flavour. *Early Mazagon* :—One of the earliest varieties in cultivation and consequently a valuable variety for the plains. *Mackie's Monarch*:—One of the best for general crop. WINDSOR OR LARGE SEEDED VARIETIES. In this section the two most grown varieties are *Harlington and Taylor's*. Both of these are excellent, the former bearing perhaps slightly larger pods.

# RUNNER BEANS.

## Phaseolus Multiflorus.

### (Vern. Lal Bakla.)

Culture the same as the preceding, except that as soon as the plants are about six inches high, they will require to be staked. Like the Broad Beans it is advisable to pinch off the point of each shoot as soon as it commences to flower, to induce the pods to set more freely. Sow on the Plains end of August to end of October; Hills April to June. Of late years many new varieties of the Runner Beans have been introduced, most of them good in their way. Amongst the best are, *Titan* :—a variety with enormous broad, straight pods, borne in clusters, almost stringless and very fleshy. *Giantess* :—a giant variety of the well known Painted Lady. *Hill's Prize* :—a grand Exhibition variety and a great cropper. *Veitch's Climbing French*:—a variety combining the best features of the two types—Dwarf French and Scarlet Runner—grows to a height of 6 or 7

BEAN, RUNNER.

feet, the plants being covered from top to bottom, with long, narrow, pulpy and brittle pods of most excellent flavour. The following are some of the best of the older varieties. *Carter's Champion* :—very large fleshy pods. *Girtford Giant* :—a very vigorous grower and heavy cropper. *Painted Lady* :—a variety which is also known as "York and Lancaster" and bears very handsome flowers. *White Dutch or Caseknife* :—this is the earliest of the Runner Beans and is very prolific and of good quality. *Ne Plus Ultra* :—one of the best Runner Beans in cultivation, and a variety which I can very strongly recommend. The pods grow to a length of 12 to 13 inches, are very thick and fleshy and of delicious flavour. *Flageolet Wax* :—a splendid variety of the Wax podded species. Is as early as most of the Dwarf varieties and remains in good condition for the table for a very long time. *Mont d'or or Golden Butter* :—pods of a golden wax colour, quite stringless and very productive. *Bulgarian Butter* :—a variety with long, fleshy, green pods speckled with black, &c., &c.

---

# Beans, Dwarf French or Kidney.

PHASEOLUS NANUS. (VERN.—*Fras Seem, or Chota Seem.*)

On the Plains sow from middle of August to beginning of November at intervals of ten to fifteen days. They require a moderately shaded position; if fully exposed to the sun, they rarely do well. Light, rich, well drained soils are the ones best adapted for growing this species in. Manure with well rotted stable manure. Sow in rows two to three feet apart, about three inches dividing the seeds, afterwards thinning out the plants to one foot apart. Sow from April to July in the Hills. 1 lb. will sow a row about 60 feet long.

Wax or Stringless Beans have now become established favourites throughout America and also on the Continent of Europe. In this country too, they are attracting considerable attention, and when generally known, will, I am sure, become exceedingly popular. They are entirely free from strings, the pods are of a beautiful waxy yellow colour, boil down as rich as butter, and taste more like a tender beefsteak than a vegetable. It is merely a question of time when they will supersede all other varieties. Culture and time for sowing same as the ordinary Dwarf French Beans.

BEAN, DWARF FRENCH.

Of the Dwarf French Beans there are very numerous varieties, many of them, we are afraid, differing only in name. Perhaps the following are the most distinct and best of the class:---*Canadian Wonder*:---the standard variety and one of the very best. *Negro Longpodded*:---of very robust habit. *Chevrier's Green Flageolet*:---a French variety of undoubted value; the pods and seeds are of a bright green and retain their colour when cooked. *Ne Plus Ultra*:---a distinct variety of very delicate flavour and comes into use very quickly. *William's Early Prolific*:---Very early and prolific, of excellent quality; the seeds and pods are marked with violet. *Earliest Red Valentine*:---an American introduction of sterling quality; is usually ready for picking in about 35 days after sowing. *Extra Early Refugee*:---enormously prolific, and from its earliness is almost certain to produce a crop, no matter how unfavourable the season. *Yosemite Mammoth Bush*:---the monster pods of this variety, which average from 10 to 14 inches, are of a rich golden yellow colour. *Golden Butter Wax*:---one of the very best of the waxpod varieties and more grown perhaps than any other of this class. *The Shah*:---

the most prolific of all the green pod varieties ; the plants will continue to bear all through the season, if care be taken to remove the pods as they became fit for use.

# LIMA BEANS.

**(Phaseolus Lunatus )**

It is strange that although a native of India, the Lima Bean is but little known. In America it is most popular and enormous crops are grown. Several of the varieties are most rampant growers and require stakes at the very least 10 feet high. A new dwarf growing variety has been introduced and this is taking the place, to a very great extent, of the tall growing sorts. The culture of the tall sorts is exactly the same as that required by the Scarlet Runner Beans, while the Dwarf variety must be treated in the same way as the Dwarf French or Kidney varieties. The pods of this species are not edible but the broad flat seeds should be shelled in the same way as the Broad Beans; when cooked these have a delicious flavour much resembling roast chestnuts. This species grows most luxuriously in the Hills, where they should not be sown before the middle or end of April. The two best of the tall growing varieties are:--*Challenger* (also known as Dreer's Improved or Potato Lima) and *Ford's Mammoth*. The Bush variety most in use is *Henderson's New Dwarf or Bush.*

LIMA BEAN.

# FLORIDA VELVET BEAN.

The Florida Velvet Bean though more properly classed as a forage or Fertilising plant, is very popular in America as a vegetable, and I have thought that it would be well to include it amongst the Garden Beans. The dry Bean is boiled and served in the same way as Haricot Beans. Sow the seeds about the same time as Maize and cultivate and treat in same way. When the Beans have been gathered the whole mass of foliage and stalk should be trenched into the soil which is greatly benefitted. Cattle will very greedily eat the green forage and also the dry bean, but it is more as a fertiliser that this is valuable.

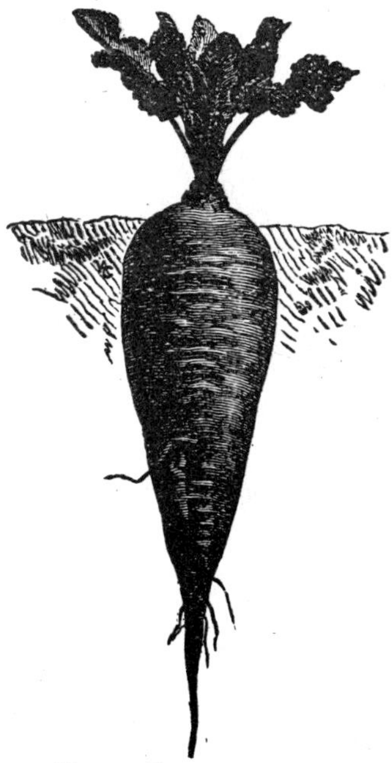

BEET, CHELTENHAM GREEN LEAVED.

# Beet.

BETA VULGARIS

(VERN.—*Chukandar or Mol Palang.*)

Sow from August to December on the Plains. Sow in an open position, well away from shade, in good rich, well manured soil. The manure, which must be thoroughly rotted, must be well incorporated with the soil. As soon as the plants are 3 or 4 inches high, they should be thinned out to a distance of 9 inches apart, in rows one and a half feet apart. Water liberally, and occasional dressings of liquid manure will be found very beneficial; care should be taken not to put the liquid manure too near the roots, as this is apt to encourage the growth of side roots. When lifting, great care must be taken not to bruise them or cut off any small shoots or outgrowths, or the colouring will be gone. In Hills sow from the beginning of March to the end of May. 1 oz. will sow a drill 30 to 40 feet long.

There are many excellent varieties of this favourite vegetable and I will try to give a list of those that really lead in the various classes. Of the turnip rooted varieties it would be hard to beat *Egyptian* and *Dewing's Improved.* Both of these are excellent sorts and well worth growing. Of the longer growing sorts the following are the best :—

*Cheltenham Green Leaved* :—Which is perhaps the very finest Beetroot in cultivation, having a beautifully shaped clean root and foliage of a splendid green. *Brydon's Exhibition* :—A very valuable variety for exhibition purposes; the flesh is of a dark colour and it comes to maturity very early. *Dell's Crimson* :—A variety which is useful both for culinary purposes and for flower garden decoration, as, besides having flesh of delicious flavour and excellent colour, the foliage is of a beautiful deep crimson colour, which makes it a most attractive object in the flower garden. *Covent Garden Red* :—A sort which is largely grown in England for the Market. *Veitch's Improved Black* :—A very fine variety of dark colour and good flavour; grows to a large size and is valuable for early use or may be sown late for general crop.

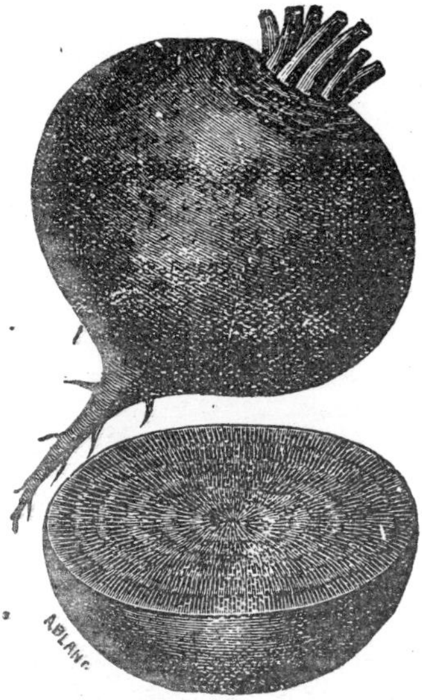

BEET, TURNIP ROOTED.

## BORECOLE OR KALE.

**Brassica oleracea acephala or fimbriata. (Vern.—Dal Kobee, Bari Khol.)**

A member of the Cabbage family which is but little grown in India. In flavour is inferior to the Cabbage or Savoy, but is much grown in Europe for Winter use, as it is very hardy and can be got in good condi-

BORECOLE OR KALE.

tion when no other variety of Cabbage is available. The culture required is identically the same as that for the ordinary Cabbage.

Amongst the best varieties are :—

*King of the Palms* :—a greatly improved variety of wonderfully vigorous growth, the plants frequently attaining a height of 5 feet. *Mosbach* :—a variety with beautifully curled foliage of medium size, rarely exceeding 2 feet in height. *Dwarf Erfurt* :—a very handsome sort of dwarf habit. *Phœnix* :—a valuable sort for India, as it will stand great extremes of climate.

# BROCCOLI.

## Brassica oleracea botrytis. Asparagoides.

(**Vern.**—Chota Phool Kobee.)

BROCCOLI.

The Broccoli is a very hardy class of Cauliflower and is very popular on this account in Europe. It requires a deep loamy soil, with good drainage, though even on any ordinary soil which has been well manured, the Broccoli will thrive and give good crops. The same treatment as recommended for Cauliflowers will suit this branch of the family equally well. The times for sowing vary, of course, in different districts. While sowings in Bengal should not be put in till the beginning of September, it is well to sow quite a fortnight earlier in the Punjab and United Provinces. In the Hills, sow in August and September and plant out as early as possible in October to allow the plants to get a good start. Transplant as soon as the plants have made their first pair of perfect leaves, into a bed of good rich soil, and transplant two or three times, at intervals of about a fortnight, before finally planting out where they are intended to grow. There are a great number of varieties now in cultivation, but for all practical purposes the following half dozen represent the pick :—*Sutton's Perfection* :—a very dwarf and handsome variety of excellent quality. *Veitch's Self Protecting* :—a variety which much resembles that well known and popular Cauliflower, Veitch's Autumn Giant, but which comes into use quite a month later if sown at the same time. *Carter's Champion* :—one of the largest and of fine flavour. *Covent Garden White* :—a very fine sort with firm white heads. *Leamington* :—this is an A1 variety with heads quite 8 to 9 inches in diameter. *Malta Early White* :—large, fine white heads which mature very early.

---

# Brussels Sprouts.

## Brassica oleracea bullata minor.

### (Vern.—Gooneegoon Kobee, Choke Kobee.)

BRUSSELS SPROUTS.

Sow from middle of August to end of October. To insure really good Sprouts it is necessary that they should be grown without a check, from the time of sowing, up to the period when they have made their full growth ; therefore sow thinly, and when transplanting, remove with a large ball of earth adhering to the roots, so that they are not injured ; place the rows about two feet apart. The after cultivation should be the same as that of the Cabbage ; except that, as, the lower leaves mature they should be carefully removed, which will induce the plants to sprout with greater regularity. Sow from end of February to middle of May in the Hills ; a small sowing should also be made in September. 1 oz. of seed will sow a bed 4 feet by 12 feet.

There are few vegetables that have been more improved during late years than the Brussels Sprout, and there are now a number of grand varieties in cultivation. Amongst the best are :—*The Bullet* :—Sprouts very solid and firm and of superior quality. *Paris Market* :—a semi-dwarf variety which seldom exceeds a height of two feet, the stems being densely clothed with small, very solid sprouts of the most delicious flavour. *Veitch's Exhibition* :—a Prize winner wherever shown. Is of medium height, bearing very large, fine flavoured sprouts. *President Carnot* :—a sort which has made a great name for itself and is well worth growing. This is a really excellent variety. *Covent Garden* :—the variety which is perhaps more largely cultivated than any other, as it produces sprouts of large size and good quality. *Sutton's Matchless* :—very productive, of sturdy and vigorous growth. *Reading Exhibition* :—one of the largest kinds in cultivation and an excellent show variety.

---

# CABBAGES.

## Brassica oleracea Capitata.—(Vern—Kobee, Banda Kobee.)

CONICAL OR POINTED CABBAGE.

Sow from end of August to December in the Plains at intervals of a fortnight. The ground in which the plants are to be grown can hardly be made too rich ; the manure best suited for the cabbage is goat or sheep manure, and where procurable, should be used in preference to any other. Where sowings are made in pans or boxes, transplant the seedlings into well raised beds as soon as they have made their first perfect leaf, putting them out six inches apart each way ; by this means, strong, healthy plants will be secured. In planting Cabbages and Cauliflowers it is most important that the plant should be set down to the first leaf, so that the whole of the stem is under ground. They may be planted out as soon as they have made four to six leaves, the small growing varieties in rows of two feet apart and 15 to 18 inches between the plants ; the large kinds should be at least three feet apart each way. In the Hills sow from beginning of March to end of May, also in Autumn. If Cabbages are grown on the same ground for some years, I would advise a liberal dressing of lime, previous to planting, in order to guard against club root. 1 oz. will sow a bed 4 feet by 12 feet. As the cabbage is a very gross feeder it soon exhausts the ground, so before planting out each crop a very liberal dressing of manure should be given. The Cabbage thrives best in land which has been well dressed with night-soil, but in India it is difficult to use this on account of the caste objections of the native cultivators. Failing night-soil, use plenty of sheep or goat manure. The mali should be instructed to frequently hoe between the rows as the crops will be greatly improved by this means. There are very many varieties of Cabbage now in general cultivation and it is difficult to select from the many, the few that should be grown by the ordinary amateur.

## CONICAL OR POINTED VARIETIES.

First in this class I must put that excellent variety *Early King*, which was introduced to India by me a few years ago and which has steadily made its way to the front. This is perhaps the earliest of the many early varieties now before the public and is well worth more extensive cultivation *The Charleston Wakefield:*—one of the largest of this class and does not sacrifice earliness for size, as it is also a very early variety. *Carter's Early Heartwell:*—Heads

DRUMHEAD CABBAGE.

extremely firm with few outside leaves. *Daniel's Defiance Giant Early Marrow* :—grows to a weight of from 10 to 20 pounds, very early and of delicious flavour. *Express* :—this is with the variety I speak of above—Early King—one of the very earliest sorts in cultivation. The heads are of medium size, very compact and solid and of a yellowish green colour. *Mein's No. 1* :—One of the largest and best early Cabbages in cultivation. As this variety does not bolt to seed quickly, it is well worth a trial, more particularly as it hearts very early and attains to a very great size and weight. *Large York* :—one of the largest of this class and an old favourite. *Early York* :—very early, small, round and slightly heart-shaped heads. *Filderkraut* :—A medium early variety with large sized heads, which are very hard and solid. Is very hardy and remarkable for its certainty to head. *Paris Market Early* :—A small growing, very early variety of great merit.

## Drumhead or Flat Varieties.

This class is, as a rule, grown for Cattle Feeding, but many people grow a few for table use on account of their usually delicious flavour. There are many excellent varieties now in cultivation-and it is difficult to select a few when there is such a large choice to select from, but the following are kinds I can very confidently recommend to those desirous of growing really good things.

Of the whole of this class it would be hard to beat that grand variety *Christmas Drumhead*, which combines with large size, most exquisite flavour and extreme hardiness. This variety has become of late years the most grown Drumhead Cabbage in India and a sure sign of its quality, the native cultivators buy large quantities of the seed every year. Varieties which run the Christmas very close are those two grand American sorts, *Surehead* and *Marblehead Mammoth.* Amongst enconiums passed on the former are such expressions as :— "The best Winter Cabbage I have ever planted ;" "I have heads of Surehead Cabbage that will weigh 18 to 20 pounds." "Surehead Cabbage is unexcelled in regard to size, quality and power to resist drought." The last expression of opinion will show that this is an excellent sort for India. Of Marblehead Mammoth little need be said, as it has proved its worth to the increasing number of cultivators who have sown it of late years. It is one of the very largest varieties in cultivation, as specimens have been grown to a weight of 60 pounds. As this kind grows, with ordinary culture, to a weight of quite 30 pounds, it is well to plant at least 4 feet apart. The illustration which I give of a Drumhead Cabbage, represents this variety. Amongst other really First Class Drumhead Cabbages are the following :— *Improved Brunswick* :—a greatly improved form of the old Brunswick Cabbage, which used to be very popular many years ago. Will grow to a weight of over 20 pounds. *Schweinfurt Quintal* :—We do not associate earliness with the Drumhead class of Cabbages, but in this variety we have earliness allied to size. It grows to a size of from one foot to eighteen inches in diameter; does not head very hard but is remarkably tender. *Warner's Drumhead* :—Very dwarf and compact and is one of the heaviest cropping varieties. *Mongibello Dwarf* :—The original stock of this excellent variety was raised in Italy. Is an especially useful variety for India as it is a great heat resister. *Hurst's Select Drumhead* :—Those who like plenty of flavour in a Cabbage will appreciate this variety, which is very large, hardy and productive. *Autumn King* :—An A1 American variety which was introduced by the famous firm, Peter Henderson & Co., of New York. Said to be the finest strain of late Cabbage that has ever been offered.

### Red or Pickling Varieties.

Of the Pickling varieties of Cabbage a great number have been introduced lately, but the few I give in the following list are amongst the best. *Mammoth Rock Red* :—grows to a weight of 10 to 12 pounds, but requires a good, rich soil for its perfect development. *Early Red Pointed Head* :—Much resembles in shape the Early York Cabbage. Is of splendid colour, medium size and very solid. *Blood Red Berlin* :—Of medium size and excellent quality. *Erfurt Blood Red* :—Very dark colour and one of the best pickling Cabbages in cultivation.

---

## SAVOY CABBAGE.

(Vern.—Kaffree Kobee.)

SAVOY CABBAGE.

The Savoy Cabbages are not nearly so extensivly grown as they deserve. They are peculiarly suited for cultivation on the Plains, as they keep in excellent condition right into the hot weather. Give the Savoy a good, rich, well manured soil and you will be surprised at the quantity of splendid Cabbages you will get. Cultivate in exactly the same way as the ordinary Cabbages but give plenty of water during the whole period of growth. There are a number of good varieties, but the following are the very best. *American Drumhead* :—One of the largest varieties. Of very robust habit, short stemmed and of most excellent flavour. *Large Aubervilliers* :—This may be described as the best Savoy Cabbage now in cultivation, as it combines heavy weight, large size and good quality. *Midsummer* :—The heads are beautifully netted and of a delicate light green colour. When cooked they are almost as tender as Cauliflowers. *Victoria*:—Extra fine. Leaves finely crumpled. *Early Dwarf Ulm* :—A very superior and distinct dwarf growing early variety. *Groots' Favourite* :—Medium size ; heads very firm, beautifully curled, and of very delicate flavour. *Erfurt Sugar-Loaf* :—A conical shaped variety of good size. Very quick growing and of splendid flavour.

# CAPSICUM AND CHILI.

## Capsicum Annuum and C. Frutescens—

## (Vern.--Mirich, Mircha, Lunka, or Kapsikam.)

On the Plains, sow at any time from March to October ; in Hills April and May. Sow in pans or boxes, and transplant when two to three inches high. When fruits of the larger kinds are required of extraordinary size, not more than four or six fruits should be left on a plant. They require a good, rich soil, and a fair quantity of water during dry weather. An occasional drenching with weak liquid manure will tend to greatly improve the crop. Many of the Capsicums form very pretty pot plants and thus become both useful and ornamental. We give an illustration showing the variety "Prince of Wales" thus grown. This illustration also gives an idea of the shape of the round growing kinds.

CAPSICUM, PRINCE OF WALES, AS A POT PLANT

CAPSICUM, LONG VARIETY.

Few vegetables have received more attention on the part of the hybridiser than has the Capsicum, and the result is that we have now got varieties such as our grandfathers never even dreamt of. Some of the larger kinds are so mild that they can be plucked off the plants and eaten like Tomatoes, while some of the small kinds are so very pungent that they will almost make one's hair curl. One of the very best of the large sorts is that favourite *Ruby King*, which is steadily displacing many of the older sorts The fruits grow to a length of 4 to 6 inches by 3 to 4 inches through. They are remarkably mild and pleasant to the taste, very productive, and extremely handsome in growth. Another kind which has lately gained a great name for itself is an American introduction which has been christened "*County Fair*." In quality and productiveness it has few, if any equals. The fruits are of medium size, very solid and meaty, and are entirely free from any biting or burning taste. A new variety which has become very popular lately is *Elephant's Trunk* (Capsicum Annuum Proboscideum). The fruits grow to a length of 10 to 12 inches and 3 to 4 inches broad. They are very fleshy and mild and agreeable in flavour. The illustration I give shows the form of this magnificent variety. *Golden Dawn*:–a variety of a beautiful golden yellow colour. Fruits are mild and of sweet flavour. *Japanese Bouquet or Cluster*:—The plants, which grow to a height of 12 to 18 inches, form dense compact bushes. As the fruits change while maturing from light green to bright yellow, and then to bright crimson-scarlet, the plants form very beautiful objects in the flower garden, more particularly as they have fruits of the various colours on them at the same time. *Prince of Wales*:—A variety which I illustrate grown as a pot plant. The fruits are of a beautiful pale citron yellow. *Procopp's Giant*:—One of the Goliaths among Capsicums. Fruits have been grown 9 inches long and 3 inches thick; the average length, however, under ordinary cultivation, being from 6 to 8 inches. The fruits, which are of a glossy scarlet colour with

CAPSICUM, ELEPHANT'S TRUNK.

very thick flesh, are wonderfully sweet and mild in flavour. *Red Cluster*:— Very prolific, hundreds of fruits being borne on a single plant. The fruits are a coral red in colour and very hot and pungent in flavour. Amongst other pungent varieties which are usually grown are, *Chili*, *Cayenne*, and *Long Red.*

# CARROTS.

## Daucus Carota.—

(Vern.—Gajur or Shoondar.)

Sow from August to December in the Plains, in drills 9 inches apart for the small kinds and 12 inches for the larger sorts. As soon as the plants are three or four inches high they should be thinned out to a distance of 6 inches between them. The crop must be kept clear of weeds, and the soil frequently stirred round the roots; they must be kept liberally supplied with water during the whole period of

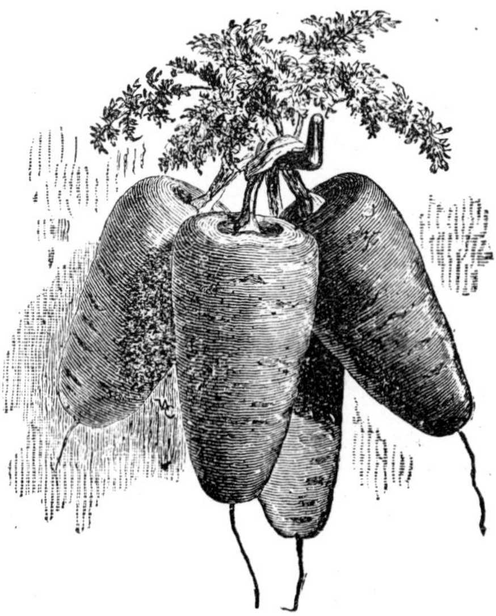

CARROT, MEDIUM SIZE.

their growth. This vegetable requires a deep, rich, light, sandy soil, and one that has been heavily manured the previous season suits it best ; in this case no fresh manure should be given, as this has a tendency to cause the roots to fork. As Carrot seed is somewhat slow in germinating, great care should be taken to "firm" the seed in the soil. Carrot seed is usually cleaned before sending out, and has all the beard removed so that much more seed is supplied in an ounce than is the case when bearded seed is supplied. Sow in the Hills from February to May. 1 oz. of seed will sow a row of from 60 to 70 feet.

The shorter growing varieties are as a rule much earlier than the long ones. and are usually sown about a month earlier. In order to have a continuous supply of carrots, sowings should be made every ten days. Many people soak the seed in water for about six hours before sowing, as this promotes early germination. There are several dozens of really first class varieties and it is rather difficult to select from the many, those that are the best, but I have attempted to do this in the following list. In order to help readers I have divided these varieties into two classes—early and general crop.

EARLY SORTS.

CARROT, EARLIEST PARIS

*Chantenay or Model* :—One of the finest varieties in cultivation. The Carrots are wonderfully uniform in shape. They are a little longer than the Horn varieties, but as they are much thicker at the shoulder they are much more productive. The illustration I give of a medium size variety, gives an idea of the shape of this really first class sort. *Earliest Paris* :—This is a grand sort for early crops as it will come into use in about 6 or 7 weeks from time of sowing. The roots are quite round, of good colour and delicious flavour. I give an illustration of this variety. *French, English and Dutch Horns* :—These

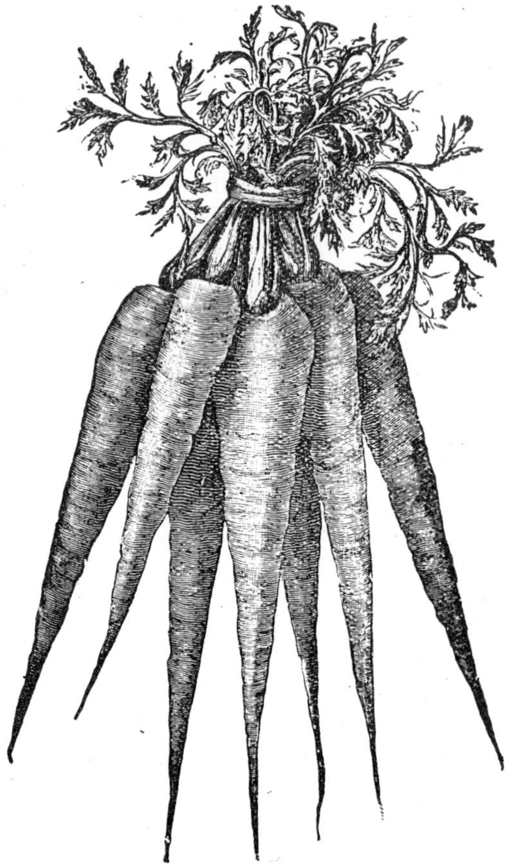

CARROT, LONG.

three kinds are all very quick growing and are much grown for early crops. *Danver's Half Long Scarlet*:--This is a very fine shaped variety of the half long class, of bright orange red colour and very productive. *Half Long Luc*:—A French variety of beautiful half long shape and, like the preceding, of bright orange red colour. *James' Scarlet or Intermediate* :—One of the most extensively grown sorts in cultivation and one which is perhaps *the* best of the early Class for general growing. It is of medium length and really fine flavor. This is a kind I can very confidently recommend. *Scarlet Nantes* :—This should perhaps be put into a class by itself, as it is really a second early variety. The roots are almost perfect cylinders. *Sutton's New Intermediate* :—This is a somewhat larger form of James' Intermediate.

## GENERAL CROP.

First in this class I place that old Favourite *Altringham*, which has proved itself, after very many years trial, to be one of the finest Carrots in cultivation. As this is a very deep rooting sort it requires to be sown in good deep soil. The roots are of good shape, very clean and of good colour and flavour. The illustration I give of a long Carrot gives an idea of the shape of this very valuable sort. *Long Red Surrey* :—This is another sort which is largely grown and is a really first class variety. The roots are very long and narrow gradually to the bottom. *Golden Barletta* :—A variety which I introduced from Italy some years ago and which is proving itself to be a useful sort; in colour a beautiful golden yellow and in flavour very sweet and delicate. *Long Red Coreless* :—This is a great improvement on the majority of the Carrots, as it is almost entirely free from heart; the heart is said to be the most indigestible portion of the Carrot. The roots grow to a length of about nine inches and are cylindrical in shape, that is, they are of the same thickness through their entire length. *Long Yellow Stump Rooted* :—This is another of the cylindrical family and is of French origin. The roots are long and of a true yellow colour. This variety is a splendid keeper and will be found useful for storing. *Ox Heart or Guerande* :—This is another French variety, of a peculiar shape. The roots are, as the name implies, shaped like an ox heart. They are intermediate in length between the Half-Long sorts and the Short Horns; they are much thicker than the latter, attaining at the top to a diameter of from three to four inches. *Saint Valery* :—A valuable sort on account of its productiveness, rich handsome colour and sweet tender flesh. The roots, which are of good size, grow very regular and smooth. They are of fair size, being from ten to twelve inches in length and from two to three inches in diameter at the top. *Henderson's Intermediate Red* :—A valuable American variety which is well worth growing. In size between the Half Long and the Long varieties. Colour deep orange red; the roots are very smooth and straight and are remarkably free from roughness.

# CAULIFLOWERS.

## Brassica oleracea botrytis Cauliflora.

*(Vern.—Phool Koobee or Phool Gobi.)*

The first sowings should be made about the same time as that mentioned for the Cabbage, and as soon as the seedlings are large enough to handle they should be planted into a bed of light, rich soil, at a distance of four inches apart each way. As soon as they have made three or four perfect leaves, they should be again transplanted into a bed of richer soil than the one first employed; here they should be placed at least six inches apart, and

CAULIFLOWER.

may then remain until they are strong enough to be planted out in the quarters where they are intended to be grown. Should, however, time and labour be available, a third transplanting would be beneficial to the plants. The object gained by frequent transplanting is, that it prevents a too luxuriant growth of the foliage and induces them to heart more freely and quickly. Sow from February to July in the Hills, and also in the Autumn. 1 oz. of seed will sow a bed 4 feet by 12 feet or will produce about 1,000 plants.

As the Cauliflower is one of the most delicate members of the great Brassica family, it requires considerable care and attention. One great essential is perfect drainage, and in order to ensure this, it is advisable to have the seed beds raised 6 or 8 inches. A good manure for Cauliflowers is broken mustard cake, the *Khullee* of the natives. This should be applied when the plants are about half grown. About half a pound of the cake per plant will be found ample.

There have been an enormous number of varieties of Cauliflowers introduced during the past few years, and from the many I shall try to select a few of the very best. For convenience of reference I have divided these into three classes according to the season of maturing.

### EARLIEST.

First in this class I must place that now standard variety "*Mussoorie Prize.*" This has during the past few years proved itself to be one of the very finest varieties ever introduced. The heads are large, one was grown in Upper Burma a few years ago which turned the scales at 17½ pounds; very firm, snowy white, and of the most delicate and delicious flavor. In earliness it is almost unsurpassed, as with good culture, plants may be had ready for use in about 14 weeks from time of sowing. *Early Snowball* :—Dwarf growing, fine white heads, ready for cutting in four months from time of sowing. *Henderson's Early Snowball* :—This is an improved form of the preceding and is described by the raisers as, "the earliest, the surest header, the most profitable, the best variety for either market or family gardens." This is a variety I can very confidently recommend. *Early Como* :—In this variety the heads are of good size; as they come to maturity are pure white, but as they fully develope become suffused with bright violet. *Primus* :—This is an Italian variety which bids fair to make a great name for itself. It is very early, heads large, white and solid. A really excellent sort. *Haage's* Dwarf Earliest :—This is one of the most expensive varieties which I import, the seed costing much more than its weight in silver. It is a very handsome sort, the heads being very dwarf, large, pure white and solid. This is one of the very best. *Early Paris or Small Solomon* :—One of the best known of the early sorts; very tender and delicious. *Early London* :—I do not suppose there is another variety in cultivation which is more extensively grown than this. The heads are large, very white and tender. Another first class early variety is *Early Erfurt or Dwarf Mammoth* which produces a very large, firm, white head.

MEDIUM EARLY.

It is rather difficult to decide which variety in this class is deserving of first mention, but I think *Veitch's Autumn Giant* deserves that position. This is one of the oldest but one of the best varieties in cultivation. It is very distinct; the heads are snowy white, large, firm and compact, and as they are thoroughly protected by the foliage they remain longer fit for use than any other sort. *Lenormand's Short Stemmed*:—This is a really superior variety with fine large, well formed heads. *Half Early Paris or Nonpareil*:—This variety is equally popular under both its names. It is equally good for an early or late crop. The heads are very white and compact. *Eclipse*:—This is a perfectly distinct variety which comes into use about the same time as "Veitch's Autumn Giant." The heads are somewhat larger than those of that standard variety. As it stands dry, hot weather perhaps better than any other variety, I strongly recommend it for growing on the Plains. *Half Early Italian Giant*:—An extra fine variety which produces magnificent large white heads; very fine and close.

LATE.

*Giant Malta*:—The largest variety in cultivation, heads of good shape and very solid, pure white when young, but suffused with violet when fully matured. *Asiatic*:—A very popular variety in India. Extra large and very fine flavoured. *Late Italian Giant*:—Similar to the Half Early variety I mention, but comes into season much later; if sown at the same time as that variety it forms a good succession crop to it. *Algiers*:—The heads of this variety remain firm and solid for an exceptionally long time. As it heads well, it is well worth cultivating. *Walcheren*:—Perhaps the best known of the late varieties. Is very hardy and produces large, white, firm heads of uniform closeness.

---

# CELERY.

**Apium Graveolens**—(**Vern.**—Shalaree, Ujoadar, Sildhere, Kurufus, Kurass.)

On the Plains the first sowing should be made in seed pans or boxes early in August; the seed at this period will, however, frequently take from five to six weeks to germinate. Main sowings should be made from end of August to end of October; in the Hills February to April.

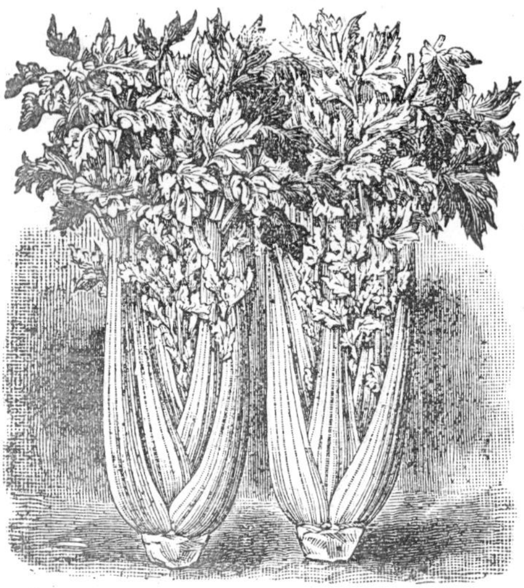

CELERY.

The tops should be shorn once or twice before transplanting so as to ensure "stocky" plants. The lower half of the root should also be cut off before transplanting. As soon as the plants are large enough to handle, they should be transplanted to a nursery bed, where they may remain till large enough to be planted in the trenches. They must, however, be carefully protected with mats during the continuance of heavy rains. The seed at this time will germinate more quickly, and the plants will not be more than ten days or a fortnight behind the first sowing. When the plants are five or six inches high, trenches must be prepared to finally plant them into. Dig trenches from 9 to 12 inches deep and about 15 inches wide, the soil from which place evenly on each side; then add four or five inches of thoroughly decomposed rich manure; dig in well and thoroughly incorporate with the soil; the plants may now be planted at once. The principal attention they will require for the next two months will be to supply them with water and rich liquid manure as frequently as it is possible to do so. Earthing up should not be commenced until the plants have attained a height of at least 18 inches. A dry day should be selected for the operation. 1 oz. of seed will produce from 2,000 to 3,000 plants.

Many market gardeners instead of earthing up entirely with soil, tie up the stems with a plantain leaf as soon as the plants reach maturity. Others place an ordinary earthenware drainage pipe over each plant as soon as it has made its full growth. I do not however advise either of these plans, as I do not think any treatment can beat the old earthing up.

## WHITE VARIETIES.

*Johnstone's Champion White*:—This is one of my own introductions, and is, I consider, one of the very best whites now before the public. It was selected from a crop of Bibby's Defiance and possesses all the good qualities of the parent, being pure white, and very solid, with a splendid nutty flavour. As it is very hardy and stands any amount of heat, it will be found a valuable variety for the Plains *Golden Self Blanching*:—The ribs are perfectly solid, crisp and brittle and of a most delicious flavour. The stalks are a very handsome fresh yellowish white colour. The heart is large, solid and of a beautiful golden yellow colour. This is a variety I very strongly recommend. *Giant Arezzo:* —An Italian variety of excellent quality. When well grown the plants attain a height of 40 inches with a circumference of 12 to 15 inches. The flavour is very sweet and nutty and the stalks are perfectly solid and of the purest white. *White Plume* :—An A1 American sort which has gained a great name for itself. Like the "Golden Self Blanching" this requires but little earthing up, as it blanches itself naturally; all that is required is to close the stalks by drawing the soil up against the plants and pressing it together with the hands. *Bibby's Defiance* :—A grand variety with rich nutty flavour, stems very stout and crisp, vigorous in growth and stands heat well. *Sandringham Dwarf* :—An old favourite of good quality; very solid and of compact growth. *Sutton's White Gem* :—A first class Celery, being of exceptionally fine flavour, crisp, solid and a good keeper. *Wright's Giant Grove White* :—A good early variety; very crisp and of excellent flavour. *Golden Dwarf* :—Hearts large, of a waxy golden yellow; very solid, of fine flavour and keeps well. *Haywood's Queen* :—A very compact growing sort, of superior flavour and remains fit for use very long. *Dickson's Mammoth* :— A really first class sort which often attains to a height of three feet, but although so large it is equal in flavour to most of the Dwarf kinds.

## RED VARIETIES.

*Covent Garden Red* :—This variety was awarded an "Award of Merit" by the Royal Horticultural Society in 1900. It is a very select sort, being large, very solid, of good colour, and excellent flavour. *Prizetaker Red* :—A variety of most excellent quality. Very large, solid, crisp and of fine flavour. *Standard Bearer* :—Another grand sort. Of superior quality, heavy weight, perfectly solid, crisp, juicy and of a fine nutty flavour. *William's Matchless Red* :—A variety of medium size, with fine large heart, crisp, juicy and solid. *Major Clark's Red* :—One of the standard varieties. Very solid, crisp and of delicate flavour. Recommended for an early crop. Other good sorts are :—*Cole's Superb Red, Sulham Prize Pink, Wright's Grove Red, &c.*

# CELERIAC.

## (TURNIP-ROOTED CELERY.)

**Apium graveolens, var. rapaceum.**—( Vern.—Knole Shalaree.)

Cultivate the same as the ordinary Celery, only these require no earthing-up except to draw a little soil around the roots as they increase in size. When planting out put the plants about one foot apart. The soil can hardly be too rich and a fair amount of water should be given. The roots can be stored in dry sand for use when Celery plants are not available.

CELERIAC.

The best variety in cultivation is *Apple Shaped* which has small, perfectly round and smooth roots. The flavour is almost equal to the best varieties of Celery. Other good sorts are :--*Giant, Prague*, a very large growing sort and *Erfurt Sweet* which is a medium sized variety with a sweet nutty flavour. The turnip like root is cooked, or it is sliced and used with vinegar, making a most excellent salad.

---

# Chervil.

## Anthriscus Cerefolium.

An aromatic sweet herb ; the young leaves are used in soups and salads. As only the young leaves are used, successional sowings should be made fortnightly, in the Plains from end of September to end of February, in the Hills from middle of February to end of August. Sow either broadcast on small beds, or in shallow drills about 8 inches apart. As this plant will not stand transplanting, the seed must be sown where the plants are to be grown. The leaves are ready for cutting in from six to eight weeks from date of sowing. The best variety and the one usually grown is *Extra Curled.*

# Chou de Burghley.

Raised by Mr. R. Gilbert, of Stamford, combining the good qualities of the Cabbage and Broccoli. It is as hardy as a Cabbage, which it resembles, but differs inwardly, having miniature Broccoli heads enveloped in the leaves, and has the rich flavour of Cauliflower and Sea Kale; very tender and delicious. The culture is the same as that recommended for Cabbages.

# Chicory.

Cichorium Intybus.—(Vern.—Kasni.)

The young leaves are used as pot herbs, or when blanched, like celery, as a salad; but perhaps its most common use is to mix with coffee to bring out the flavour. For the latter purpose, the roots are grown as large as possible, thoroughly dried, roasted and ground. In addition to the other uses mentioned, the variety which I illustrate is largely used as a Vegetable in Belgium, cooked whole like parsnips. On the plains sow during September and October; in the Hills, March to May. Sow in drills one foot apart, in well manured deeply dug soil. A number of varieties are grown but the one most extensively cultivated is the Brussels Witloof.

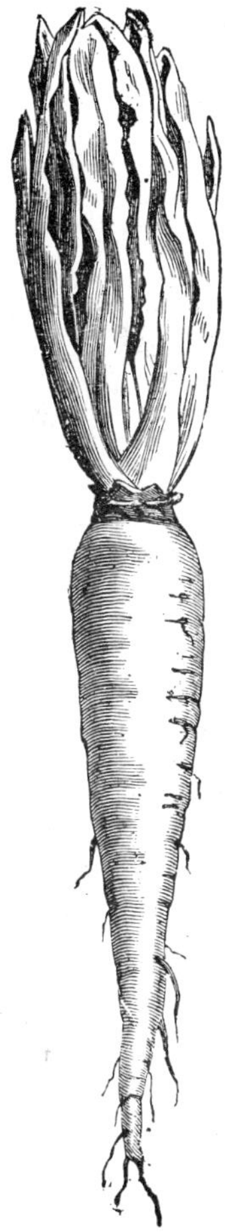

CHICORY, BRUSSELS WITLOOF.

# Chives or Cives.

**French Ciboulette.**—(Allium Schœnoprasum.)

Firminger in his "*Manual of Gardening*" (St. John Jackson's edition, page 130) speaks of the Chives as being little known in this country. These words are still applicable to the present time. On the Plains, sow in October and November; in the Hills March to end of May. Sow in pots, say 7 or 8 inch size, in light soil, and when the little plants form a dense mass, break up into about a dozen pieces and plant out in beds, in rows, leaving the clumps about a foot apart. Is used in Salads and Soups instead of young Onions. For use, cut the long, tender, Onion-like stalks close to the ground, leaving the roots undisturbed; the produce will be found more tender after each cutting.

## CORN SALAD, LAMB LETTUCE, OR FETTICUS.

### Valerianella Olitoria, or Fedia Olitoria.)

On the Plains sow during October and November; in the Hills beginning of March to end of June, and also in the Autumn. This should be treated the same as Spinach, but for early crops it is advisable to sow on well raised ground, as it is very sensitive to any excess of moisture. The corn Salad is most useful as an ingredient in Salads as it is free from the intensely bitter taste which detracts from the usefulness of so many varieties of Lettuce. The best varieties are. *Cabbaging* :—Forms small Lettuce-like hearts. *Italian* :—A sort which is very much grown in Europe. *Large Leaved* :—This variety if forced makes an extremely tender, delicately flavoured salad.

CORN SALAD.

---

# Cress or Pepper Grass.

### Lepidium Sativum.—(Vern.—Haleem, Chansur.)

Sow at intervals of eight to ten days all the year round. It requires a good rich soil. Sow from February to September in the Hills. I advise sowing in seed pans or shallow boxes at intervals of about ten days. The seeds should be very thinly covered with

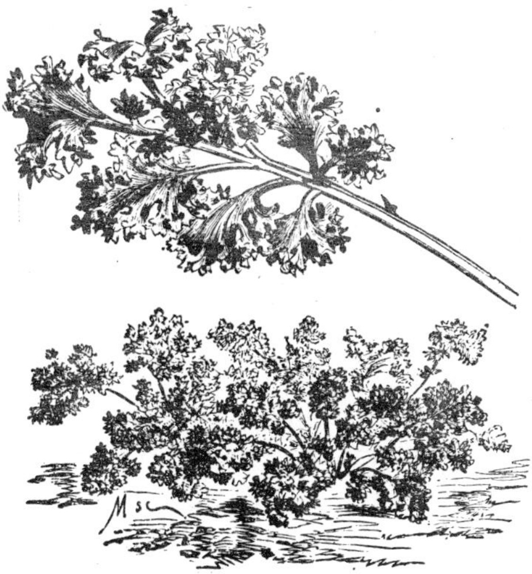

CRESS OR PEPPER GRASS.

soil, in fact it is just as well not to cover them at all, merely sprinkle thinly on the surface of the soil. To encourage quick growth give plenty of water but shade from the direct rays of the sun. The tender plants will be ready for cutting in a very few days after sowing. Sowings can also be made in the open ground but I much prefer pans or boxes as they are easily moved under shelter. This is a vegetable that is seldom grown in quantity, so that not more than half a dozen seed pans or three or four boxes need be sown at a time. There are several varieties grown but the best are:—*Extra Curled*, *Common or Plain*, *Moss Curled* and *Australian* or *Golden*.

## CRESS, AMERICAN.

(Barbarea Prœcox.)

CRESS, AMERICAN.

Many people who like the flavour of the Water Cress and who do not want to have the trouble of growing it, will welcome this substitute. Although possessing much of the flavour of the Water Cress it is inferior to it, so I would advise those who have conveniences for growing the Water variety, to sow some of both, while to those who have not got a stream or tank the American kind will be a very fair substitute. Sow the seeds at the same time as the ordinary garden Cress, but select, if possible, a shady, moist corner of the garden where you may happen to have sandy soil.

# CRESS, NEW UPLAND.

(Barbarea Prœcox variety.)

CRESS, NEW UPLAND.

Hundreds are deterred from growing Water Cress owing to the care and trouble it entails, but in this novelty, we have some thing so much resembling it in taste, that the difference is scarcely discernible. Its use should become general as it is as easy to grow as Spinach, indeed easier, for it is a perennial plant and in most districts, can be grown easily for two years without re-sowing, yielding enormous crops. Sow in October on the Plains, in drills about one foot apart.

---

# WATER CRESS.

**Nasturtium Officinale**

*(Vern. Pani Haleem, Jol Haleem.)*

WATER CRESS.

Sow from July to December in the Plains, either in pans of light soil or trenches; if the former method is adopted, the plants must be transplanted as soon as they are about two inches high into other pans three-fourths filled with a compost of equal parts of sand, coarsely broken brick, and leaf mould. These should be placed at the edge of a tank, the tops of the pans being kept just above the surface of the water. On the Hills the Water Cress will be found growing wild at altitudes from 5000 to 8000 feet. Sow the seed in

March or April and in about six weeks transplant, preferably at the side of a stream, but where a stream is not available transplant into any shady corner of the garden, taking care to have the plants thoroughly drenched every day during dry weather.

---

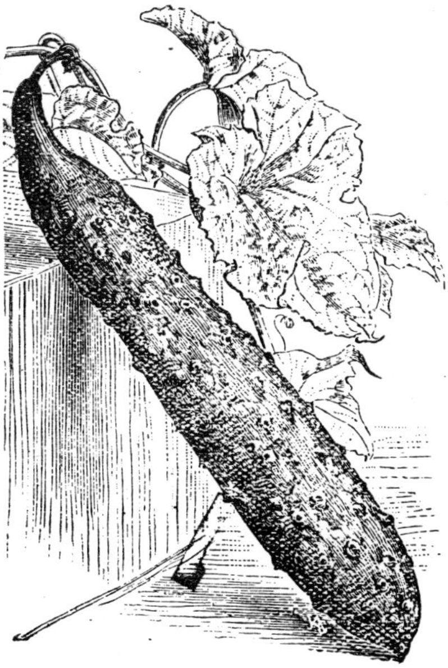

CUCUMBER, RIDGE.

# CUCUMBERS.

## Cucumis Sativus.

## (Vern. Kheera, Khira or Sakasa.)

On the Plains sow from end of April to beginning of June, also from October to December; in the Hills sow from beginning of March to middle of June. A fairly rich soil is the best, an occasional watering with liquid manure will be found beneficial. Train the plants on a rough bamboo frame, or stake like Peas. Care should be taken to remove the fruit as they become large enough, whether required for use or not, as, if left to ripen on the vines, it destroys their productiveness. If particularly fine fruits are wanted, only two or three should be allowed to grow on each vine.

It is not advisable to give the Cucumber a great depth of soil. Transplant into a shallow soil and give frequent top dressings, of rich soil. I do not advise planting in a greater depth of prepared soil, than say, 9 inches at the most. The soil used for topdressing should consist of quite half fresh stable manure; a small quantity of old mortar or brick rubbish mixed with the compost improves it greatly. Frequent waterings with weak guano water will stimulate the plants and will not affect the flavour of the fruits. Prepare the water by mixing a table spoonful of Pure "Ichthemic" Guano in a gallon of water. Allow this to stand for a while giving it an occasional stir. Before using, stir the mixture thoroughly. Cucumbers can hardly have enough water, and I advise watering alternately with the Guano water and fresh water.

CUCUMBER, FRAME.

There are very many varieties of Cucumbers now before the public, and it is by no means an easy task to select those that are really the best, but I will try to do so for the convenience of those who have not got much space to devote to Cucumber culture, and who may desire to grow only a few of the very best. I will divide into two classes calling the first

FRAME

VARIETIES.

These are kinds which are more or less delicate and I advise those only who can give careful cultivation to grow any of the following.

*Lockies' Perfection* :—Fruits produced in great abundance; medium in length, quite straight, short necked, without ribs and only a few black spines. The flesh is very crisp and solid with scarcely any seeds. A really splendid sort. *Covent Garden Favourite* :—A very prolific variety which is largely grown for the London markets. *Carter's Model* :—An excellent sort, which is becoming a great favourite. *Cardiff Castle* :—Medium size, prolific and of good quality. *Dreadnought* :—Very dark green, long and prolific. *Duke of Edinburgh* :—Grows to a length of thirty six inches; a grand variety for exhibition. *Marquis of Lorne* :—A very handsome and prolific variety, with little or no neck. *Rollisson's Telegraph* :—A very free bearer producing fruits from 20 to 26 inches long; of excellent flavour. *Tender and True* :—A prolific variety of good quality. *White Arnstadt Giant* :—Very prolific. The handsome fruits are milky-white coloured and of good quality. *Swan Neck* :—A variety bearing very delicately flavoured fruits which are often over a yard in length. *Goliath* :--As this variety requires a good deal of heat to bring it to perfection it should do well on the Plains. The fruits are very large and of good quality.

My second class I will call

### HARDY OR RIDGE VARIETIES.

This class can be grown on the Plains at all seasons. Plant in very rich soil as they are more gross feeders than the frame varieties.

*New Giant White or Parisian Long White Ridge* :--This variety grows almost as long as its name. The fruits are of gigantic size and of a pure waxen white from the time they are first set until matured. In length from 12 to 16 inches by 2 to 3 inches in diameter. A splendid exhibition sort. *Giant Pera* :-A very prolific variety with large fruits often 20 inches long. Very early and of delicious flavour. *Japanese White Climbing* :--A very distinct variety and very prolific. The fruits grow about 12 inches in length and are splendid either for pickling or slicing. *Bedfordshire Ridge* :--One of the standard varieties Of medium size and good flavour. *Bismarck* :--Fruits 15 to 18 inches long ; prolific and of good quality. *Green Long Prickly* :--This is perhaps the best of the ordinary Ridge varieties and one I can strongly recommend. Fruits are long and of excellent flavour. *Long Athens* :--One of the easiest varieties to grow. Of medium size and fine flavour. *Paris Gherkins* :--The variety which is most commonly grown for pickling.

# DANDELION.

### Leontodon Taraxacum.---(Vern. Rujul Ulgurab.)

As a salad, the Dandelion, when well grown and properly blanched, is certainly superior to Endive. The roots are sometimes dried, roasted and ground, and used to adulterate coffee, or as a substitute for it. In the Plains, sow at the same time as Lettuces, in good rich soil, thin out to a distance of 12 inches apart each way, and as soon as the plants are fully grown blanch in the same way as recommended for Endive. The flowers must be picked off frequently to prevent the ripening and distribution by the wind, of the seed. Sow from February to April in the Hills.

DANDELION

# EGG PLANT or BRINJAL.

**Solanum Melongena var. ovigerum.—(Vern.—Baigoon).**

On the Plains, sow from middle of September to end of October; also sow at the commencement of the rains and during the Spring. Is not grown above an altitude of about 3,000 to 4,000 feet. Sow broadcast in beds and when the plants are strong enough, plant out in well-worked richly manured soil in rows about 18 inches apart, putting the plants from 12 to 15 inches apart in the rows. The fruits are fit for use from the time they are the size of turkey's eggs, until they are full grown. In America the egg plant has become very popular and several of our very best varieties come from that country.

Amongst the best of the varieties now in cultivation are the following.

*New York Purple* :—I give an illustration of this excellent sort which shows its splendid form. It grows to an enormous size, fruits often turning the scale at 12 lbs. each. *New York Spineless* :—A form of the preceding, lately introduced. The plants are low and

EGG PLANT, ROUND.

branching, while both the plants and the calyx of the egg are quite free from spines. One of the earliest sorts in cultivation, as fruits can be gathered from it quite two weeks before the majority of the other kinds are in bearing. *Dwarf Nagasaki* :—A dwarf variety which,

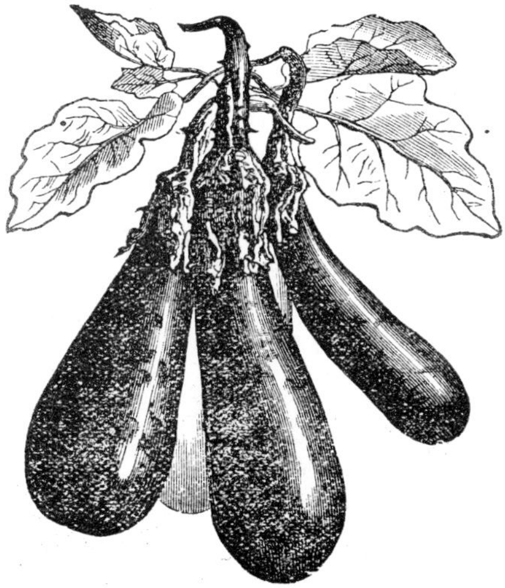

EGG PLANT, LONG.

unlike the majority of that class, bears large, well formed fruits. Is very thin skinned and of excellent quality. *Pekin Black Giant* :—Plants 3 feet high with handsome blackish violet leaves and round fruit; the fruits, with good culture, will often weigh 7 or 8 pounds. *Dwarf Earliest Purple* :—A small fruited but very early variety. *Long Purple* :—The fruits are from 6 to 8 inches in length. As this variety is very hardy it may be sown at all seasons. The two best of the white fruited sorts are, *White China Giant* and *White Naples*. The fruits of the former are very large and of good quality, while in the latter they resemble the old Long Purple, but are of a pure milk white colour.

# ENDIVE.

**Cichorium Endivia** (Vern.—Kasni, Kuru Saladh, Hundba.)

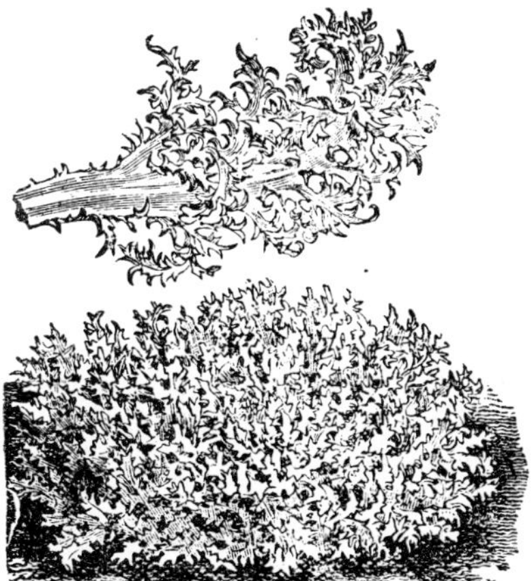

ENDIVE, CURLED LEAVED.

Sow from beginning of September to end of November in the Plains. In the Hills from beginning of March to middle of June and in Autumn. Water freely; they like rich soil and plenty of liquid manure, but bear transplanting badly. When full grown, in about two or three months, tie leaves together when perfectly free from moisture, in the afternoon, and they will be blanched in a fortnight, but do not blanch too many at a time. Mr. Gollan, in his excellent little book, "The Indian Vegetable Garden," gives rather a novel plan for blanching Endives, which is well worth a trial :—" There is a saucershaped earthenware vessel, found in all bazars under the name of *Rakabi* or *Sainak*, much used by the lower castes as a food dish, which answers admirably for blanching Endive. If a large size of it is obtained, and rested over the plants in an inverted position on small pieces of brick, the blanching is performed to perfection. Before placing the vessels in position, the leaves should be carefully flattened out with the hand, and the brick rests so adjusted as to allow of rather less than an inch of space between the edges of the vessels and the ground." There are two very distinct types of Endive, one with curled leaves, the other with broad leaves much like those of a Lettuce. 1 oz, of seed will sow a bed 8 square yards, or a drill 100 feet long.

ENDIVE, PLAIN LEAVED.

Amongst the best varieties are :—

*Large Ruffec* :—A green curled, extra fine sort. *Moss' Curled* :—A very beautiful variety, which, when well grown, resembles a tuft of moss. *White Curled* :—This resembles the preceding except in colour. The foliage is light green which blanches pure white. *Digswell Prize* :—A large green curled variety. Other fine curled varieties are:—*Courte a Cloche, Green Curled, Louvier, Rouen or Staghorn.* One of the best of the broad leaved sorts is *Batavian Broad Leaved,* which is a very compact growing variety, which forms a nice heart and blanches easily.

---

# HERBS

# SWEET, POT AND MEDICINAL.

I have thought it best to put the many varieties of herbs into one section with the above heading. In the following list I give those usually grown and have added a few notes on their uses.

Care should be taken to harvest the herbs properly. This should be done on a dry day, just before they come into full bloom. Dry quickly and pack closely, entirely excluding from the air.

On the Plains sow from September to November ; in the Hills during April and May, except where noted otherwise. Sow in shallow drills, one foot apart, and when well up, thin out, or transplant to a proper distance apart.

## ANGELICA (Archangelica Officinalis).

### (Vern.—Sumbul Khutaee.)

Mid rib eaten like Celery, or when candied makes an excellent confection. This is a perennial, but can only be grown as an annual on the Plains. Sow in October.

## ANISE. (Pimpenella Anisum).

### (Vern,—Soonf, Uneesoon.)

Cultivated principally for garnishing and seasoning or for Salads. In appearance this much resembles Celery, but the leaves are more finely divided. The seed is used in the manufacture of liqueurs and is also employed in Italy for flavouring bread.

BALM.

## BALM. (Melissa Officinalis).

### (Vern.—Badrunk, Mukeh Subzeh).

Principally used for making balm tea or balm wine. Grows to a height of some 18 inches. On the Plains must be treated as an annual, but in the Hills will last for years and may be increased by dividing the clumps in Winter.

## BASIL, SWEET. (Ocymum Basilicum).

**(Vern.--Reehan, Balungoo, Gulal Tulsi.)**

The leaves and tops of the shoots are the parts gathered, and are used for highly seasoned dishes, as well as in soups, stews and sauces ; a leaf or two is sometimes introduced into salads. On the Plains sow from about the middle of October to the middle or end of November ; in the Hills from middle of March to end of May.

BASIL, SWEET.

BORAGE.

## BORAGE. (Borage Officinalis).

**(Vern.-Chota Kulpa.)**

The young leaves are used in salads and for claret cup. This is a plant of annual duration and should be treated as such both on the Plains and Hills. It produces pretty bright blue flowers and is well worth growing for these alone. Plant out at a distance of 18 inches apart.

## CARAWAY. (Carum Carui).

**(Vern,--Zira, Jira).**

Seeds used in confections and for flavouring. On the Plains sow in October and from March to end of April in the Hills. Thin out the plants to a distance of 9 inches apart.

DILL. (Anethum Graveolens.)

(Vern.--Sooee Chooka, Sooa.)

The leaves are used in soups and sauces, and to put along with pickles. As the plants will not stand transplanting, seed should be sown where the plants are to remain. The plants grow to a height of 2 to $2\frac{1}{2}$ feet. Sow from middle of October to middle of November on the Plains ; Hills, March to end of May.

FENNEL. (Fœniculum Vulgare).

(Vern.--Sunf, Badeean, Shumrut.)

Used in fish sauce and for garnishing. On the Plains sow from middle of October to end of November ; Hills, middle of March to end of May. This is a hardy perennial which is well known in India. Sow in drills $1\frac{1}{2}$ feet apart and, when large enough, thin the plants out to 12 inches apart.

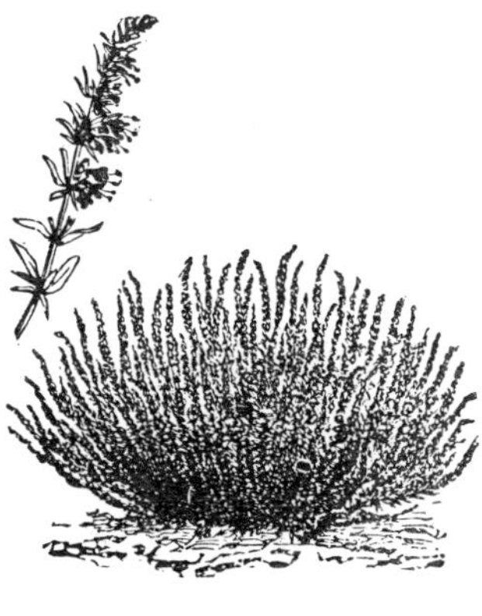

HYSSOP.

HOREHOUND. (Marrubium Vulgare).

A remedy for Asthma, coughs, &c., an excellent tonic. Can only be grown on the Hills.

HYSSOP. (Hyssopus Officinalis.)

(Vern.--Zooface eeabus, Uzoofa).

The leafy tops and flowers are gathered and dried, for making Hyssop Tea, &c.

LAVENDER. (Lavendula Spica).

(Vern.--Nurd, Nardeen).

A popular aromatic herb. By distillation it produces the scent Lavender Water. Sow on the Plains in October ; Hills, end of March to end of May. Can very seldom be induced to flower on the Plains but the leaves are useful for seasonings. Sow the seed in seed pans or boxes and transplant, when large enough to handle, into pots. They should be repotted once or twice into larger pots and when the plants are a year old they should be planted out in thoroughly drained soil. Thrives and flowers well on the Hills, but the plants should be protected during the rainy season as they are very apt to damp off.

LAVENDER.

MARJORAM, SWEET. (Origanum Marjorana.)
,, POT ( ,, Onites.)

(ern.--Murzanjoosh, M urooa, Ssatur.)

MARJORAM.

For seasoning soups and stuffings. Plants of very rapid growth. Sow in October on the Plains in the place where the plants are to remain; Hills from March to June.

MINT. (Mentha Viridis).
(Vern.—Podeena).

The Spear or Garden Mint of English Gardens. Used in the preparation of Mint sauce, a tasty adjunct to roast mutton or lamb.

Where roots are obtainable, plant in October on the Plains; any time during the Spring on the Hills. Seed may be sown at the same times.

PEPPERMINT. (Mentha Piperita).
(Vern.—Nana.)

A well known medicinal herb. Sow at the same time as recommended for the Spear Mint.

ROSEMARY. (Rosemarinus Officinalis.)
(Vern.—Akleel-ul-Jubul, Akhzzur, Hussalban.)

An aromatic herb, the leaves of which are used in summer drinks, it is also useful for garnishing. Sow on the Plains in October; Hills March to April. Sow in pots and transplant, when large enough to handle, into single pots and repot into larger pots as the plants increase in size. On the Hills the plants should be transferred into a garden border instead of pots.

ROSEMARY.

RUE. (Ruta Graveolens.)
(Vern.—Sudab, Suturee, Sundub, Suzub, Kheel.)

Used for medicinal purposes, also given to fowls for the croup. On the Plains sow in October; Hills March to May. This is a perennial and may be propagated by dividing the old plants, or by cuttings.

SAGE. (**Salvia Officinalis**) (**V E R N.— Seestur, Sufakus.**

The leaves and tender tops are used in stuffing and sauces, also used in making Sage cheese. This must not be confounded with the so-called Bengal Sage

SAGE.

(Meriandra Bengalensis). On the Plains sow in October; March to May on the Hills. Does well on the Hills but is not very easy to grow on the Plains. When the plants are large enough to transplant they should be taken from the seed boxes and planted out in a bed of rich light soil. Plant in a shady spot.

SAVORY, SUMMER (Satureia Hortensis.)

The tops of these being very aromatic are used in soups, salads, and seasoning.

SAVORY, WINTER. (Satureia Montana).

Sow on the Plains in October; March and April in the Hills. By no means common in India, but even on the Plains, can be grown with a fair amount of success. The Summer species is an annual while the Winter kind is an evergreen perennial shrub, although on the Plains it can only be grown as an annual.

TARRAGON. Artemesia Dracunculus).

A plant with numerous branching stems, bearing lanceolate entire leaves, possessing a very delicate aromatic flavour, particularly valuable for seasoning, or in a green state, for mixing with salads.

TARRAGON.

THYME, BROAD LEAVED. (Thymus Vulgaris).

(VERN—HASHA, IRPA.)

For seasoning, etc.

On the Plains can only be cultivated as an annual and even then must be grown in pots and not planted out in the garden. The seeds should be sown in October on the Plains and any time from March to May on the Hills. On the Hills the Thyme does excellently.

WORMWOOD.

WORMWOOD.

(Artemesia Absynthium)

Used for medicinal purposes; aromatic and

intensely bitter ; is used in drinks as a tonic, is also beneficial to poultry, and should be planted in poultry grounds. The famous liqueur Absinthe is prepared from this herb. Treat in the same way as Thyme.

---

## Kohl Rabi or Kohl Kohl.

**Brassica Oleracea Caulo-Rapa (Vern.—Gauth Kobee.)**

KOHL RABI.

The cultivation is the same in all respects as that of the Cabbage, except that, when planted out, they should only be placed at a distance of eighteen inches between the rows, and about twelve inches from plant to plant. It is better to sow the seeds where the plants are to remain, and when large enough thin out to distance mentioned. The thinnings can always be used to plant any spare ground. The soil in which they are grown can hardly be made too rich. As soon as the plants commence growing freely they should be supplied with frequent dressings of strong liquid manure, the great object being to induce the plants to make a rapid vigorous growth, otherwise they invariably become tough and fibrous. They are best suited for the table when about the size of a cricket ball. On the Plains sow any time from the beginning of August to the end of October; Hills, middle of February to end of May.

The best varieties are :—

*Earliest Erfurt* :—This is without exception *the* earliest variety in cultivation. The skin is pale green, flesh pure white and flavour excellent. *Green and Purple Vienna* :—These are very early varieties, being excelled in earliness only by the variety I have just mentioned. Very tender and of good flavour. *Large, Giant* and *Goliath Purples* :—These three varieties differ only in size. While the *Large* sort attains to a weight of 5 or 6 pounds, the *Goliath* may be grown to 25 pound each, and although so large are wonderfully tender. SANDER'S GREEN SHORT TOP :—This is one of the very finest sorts in cultivation and is now more extensively grown than any other. Is not distinguished for its earliness but is superior to very many of the older sorts. The flesh is solid and free from the stringiness which is so disagreeable in many varieties. *Giant White* :—a large growing sort of excellent quality, the flesh is very tender, and flavour good.

---

# LEEKS.

## ALLIUM PORUM.—(Vern.—Sundun, Kundanee, Kirath, Kiras, Gunduna, Zaluk, Vilaiyti Peeaj.)

Sow during September and October in the Plains, in rich light soil. When the Plants are about six inches high, they should be transplanted into trenches in the same way as Celery, but the trenches need not be more than eight inches wide. The plants should be placed in the rows at a distance of not more than five or six inches apart. In planting seedlings, they should be placed at least 3 inches

LEEK.

deep in the soil, and as they increase in growth, should have some light, rich soil drawn round the stems to insure their being properly blanched. They must be kept liberally supplied with water, and are also much benefitted by frequent dressings of strong liquid manure. The Leek delights in a soil which has been well impregnated with thoroughly decomposed manure; fresh manure is practically useless.

Sow March to May in the Hills. 1 oz. of seed will sow a bed 4 feet by 14 feet, or a drill about 100 feet long.

There are a number of good varieties now in general cultivation, but the following are the best.

*The Lyon* :—In this variety the stems are very frequently 10 to 12 inches long by 3 inches in diameter; in colour almost pure white and exceedingly mild flavour. *Bangholm Prizetaker* :—Very hardy, easily grown, of enormous size and very mild and agreeable flavour. *Monstrous Carentan* :—An enormous variety of French origin. *Henry's Prize* :—a very fine sort which blanches well; is also known as "*Ayton Castle*". *Musselburgh Improved* :—One of the very best sorts for general crop. Is exceedingly hardy. *Broad or London Flag* :—One of the best known varieties. Is very early and of quick growth.

# LETTUCE.

**Lactuca Sativa.**—(Vern.—Saladh, Kahu, Khus, Kuma.)

Sowings may be made for an early crop in pans or boxes, in August or September, and as soon as the seedlings have formed four leaves, they should be transplanted into well raised beds. They must, however, be protected from heavy rains, otherwise they are liable to damp off. For main crops, after the rains are over, sowings should be made in the open ground in drills twelve inches apart. As soon as the plants are sufficiently strong, they should be thinned out in the rows, leaving nine to twelve inches between the plants of the Cos varieties, and fifteen inches for the larger kinds of Cabbage. The plants that are removed from the drills should be transplanted into a bed of rich soil and carefully shaded for three or four days. These will form a good successional crop to those left in the original beds, although they will not be equal to them in size, as the finest Lettuces are always produced from the plants that are allowed to remain in the place where the seed is sown. The Lettuce luxuriates in an open, deeply worked and well manured soil. Plenty of water should be given through the whole period of growth. When the plants are large enough, a few should be tied up every three or four days to blanch them. This should be done on a dry day, as the plants will certainly rot if they are tied up when damp. For the same reason, care must be taken not to water the plants overhead, but round the roots only. Sow in the Hills from March to September. 1 oz. of seed will sow a row 60 feet long, or produce something like 3000 plants.

## CLASSES OF LETTUCE.

There are three distinct classes of Lettuce, *viz*:—(1.) Cabbage Lettuce (Lactuca Sativa Capitáta.) This class is distinguished by its broad, rounded leaves, which form low, spreading heads close to the ground. The illustration I give shows the form better than any description can.

(2.) Cos Lettuce (Lactuca Sativa Romana.) These grow upright, and, as shown in the illustration, the leaves are of an oblong shape,

(3.) Gathering Lettuce (Lactuca Sativa Foliosa.) This class is entirely distinct from the other two, and usually grow to a very large size. The lower leaves, as they mature, are pulled off and furnish excellent salad throughout the entire season.

As there are many hundreds of varieties of Lettuce now in cultivation, it will be very difficult to select the few which really lead in the several classes.

LETTUCE, CABBAGE.

## CABBAGE VARIETIES.

First in this class I place *Mussoorie Giant.* This variety I introduced to India a few years ago and it has become most popular. It grows to an immense size, early, very solid, colour light green, and, a great advantage, it does not run to seed quickly. *Webb's Wonderful* :—This is one of, if not the largest of the Lettuces in cultivation, as plants have been grown which have turned the scale at 6 pounds each. With ordinary cultivation grows about 2 to 3 pounds each. Heart very solid, pale green colour, very tender, crisp and without a trace of the bitterness which is such a drawback in so many members of this family. As this variety stands heat remarkably well, it is sure to become popular for cultivation on the Plains. *Tender and True* :—Another splendid sort. Very crisp and of superior flavour. The leaves, which are curled, are pale green in colour. Very early and does not quickly run to seed. *Genezzano* :—A sure sign of the quality of this variety lies in the fact that it has been given several names in different countries. The variety was raised in Italy but has become very popular in England and America, where it is known as "Continuity," "Jewel" &c., &c. It forms large, solid heads, the outer leaves tinted with brownish red, while the inner ones are of a rich golden yellow. Tender and crisp and peculiarly sweet. It has the same merit as the preceding varieties, in that it will stand a wonderful amount of heat and drought. *Blonde Blockhead* :-Of delicious flavour and rich golden-yellow colour. Withstands heat well and is a good keeper after being cut. *Salamander* :—A grand kind which I cannot recommend too highly. Is also known as "Satisfaction." Forms good sized, compact heads, and will withstand heat and drought well. *Mignonette* :—This is an American introduction of really first class quality. It has been proved that it will resist both heat and excessive moisture with equal success. A splendid variety for the Plains. *New York* :—One of the giants of this class, as it will often grow to a weight of four pounds. One of the best varieties introduced of late years. *Blonde de Berlin* :—Crisp, sweet, and does not run to seed quickly. Leaves pale green with yellow edges, folding into a close and compact heart.

There are dozens of other Cabbage varieties all of good quality, but I will leave readers to the lists given in various Seedsmen's Price Lists, merely mentioning the names of a few, which, in addition to those mentioned in the preceding lines, are really distinct and worth growing. These are :—*Buttercup, Marvel or Red Besson, All the Year Round, Drumhead or Malta, Perpignan, Neapolitan, Stanstead Park, Tom Thumb or Tennis Ball, White Chavigny, Big Boston, Black Seeded Simpson, Early Prize Head, Hanson, The Deacon, Tomhannock, Yellow Seeded Butter or Solid Headed Yellow, &c., &c.*

LETTUCE, COS.

## COS VARIETIES.

In my opinion the best Cos Lettuce we have in cultivation is that grand variety *Kingsholm.* The plants grow to an extra large size and are of splendid quality. A sort which will be found to be a prize taker by those who go in for exhibiting. *Bath or Brown Cos*:—One of the most popular varieties at home and is now largely grown in India, where it does well. *Paris White* :—One of the largest of this class, as specimens have often been grown to a weight of 6 pounds each. It hearts and blanches well without tying; is crisp and of excellent quality. *Paris Green* :—Very similar to the preceding, but does not grow to such a large size; the foliage is a dark green colour. *Leviathan* :—A very large growing sort but requires a rich soil for its proper development. *Jefferies' Little Queen* :—Very early, compact growing, solid and crisp. *Alexandra* :—Large, very crisp and solid. *Balloon* :—Heads very large, rather flat on the top ; firm, crisp and solid. *Crystal* :—One of the best flavoured of the Cos Lettuces. Heads large and full, but require tying to blanch well. Other good sorts are :—*Florence or Magnum Bonum, Victoria White, &c., &c.*

**LETTUCE, GATHERING OR CURLED.**

## GATHERING VARIETIES.

*American Gathering or Curled* :—Exceedingly tender and fine flavoured. *Australian Curled* :—Leaves light yellow and of good quality. *Californian Curled* :—Very hardy ; leaves darkish yellow. *Quercusifolia* (Oak-Leaved.):—A very distinct variety, the leaves of which are shaped like Oak leaves. In flavour very sweet and delicious *Laciniated Beauregard* :—A French variety of most excellent quality.

In order to keep the gathering Lettuces in condition fit for use, care must be taken to remove the leaves as quickly as they mature.

# MAIZE OR INDIAN CORN.

**Zea Mays.** (Vern. Bhuta, Kookree, Mukka.)

Both Plains and Hills sowings should be made just before the rains, say during May and June. The Maize requires very richly manured and well worked ground, and plenty of water from time of sowing until the cobs begin to ripen.

In Northern India sowings are often made at the beginning of the cold weather but it is rather risky trying to grow at this season, as the plants are very often killed by frost before the cobs have time to fill.

The seeds should be sown about 9 inches apart in rows about 2 feet apart, and when large enough thinned out to a distance of about 18 inches to 2 feet. When a little more than a foot high the plants should be slightly earthed up, and this should be repeated when the plants have attained a height of about 3 feet; after this second "earthing up" the ridges should be about a foot high. The great essential in Maize growing is to see that the plants are not stinted with water; even during breaks in the rains water must be given.

There are numerous varieties, mostly raised in America, and the following are amongst the best :—

*Country Gentleman* :—This is one of the finest of the sweet Corns, retaining its delicate tenderness and flavour, even when a little old. The ears are of good size and are produced in great abundance, the plants frequently bearing four good ears, while the average is three to a stalk. The cob is very small, giving great depth to the kernels, which are of pearly whiteness. *Ne Plus Ultra* :—This is pre-eminently an epicure's variety. The ears are short, but the cob is very small, and kernels of extraordinary depth, pearly whiteness and irregularly crowded together on the cob. *Early Marblehead* :—Until the introduction of the Cory, this was the earliest variety of Sugar Corn in cultivation. Its stalks are about four feet high, ears of medium size, and set low down. Roasting ears have been picked in sixty one days from time of planting, while the ordinary time required for maturing is seventy days. *Early Minnesota*:—The standard early variety ; eight-rowed, ears of good size, sweet and fine flavoured. A desireable variety alike for market or family garden, being highly productive and of good quality generally. *Extra Early Adams or Burlington.*—This variety is not a sweet Corn but is largely grown for table use. It is very hardy, with white grain, and short ear, and matures in sixty days. "*Golden Beauty*":—The

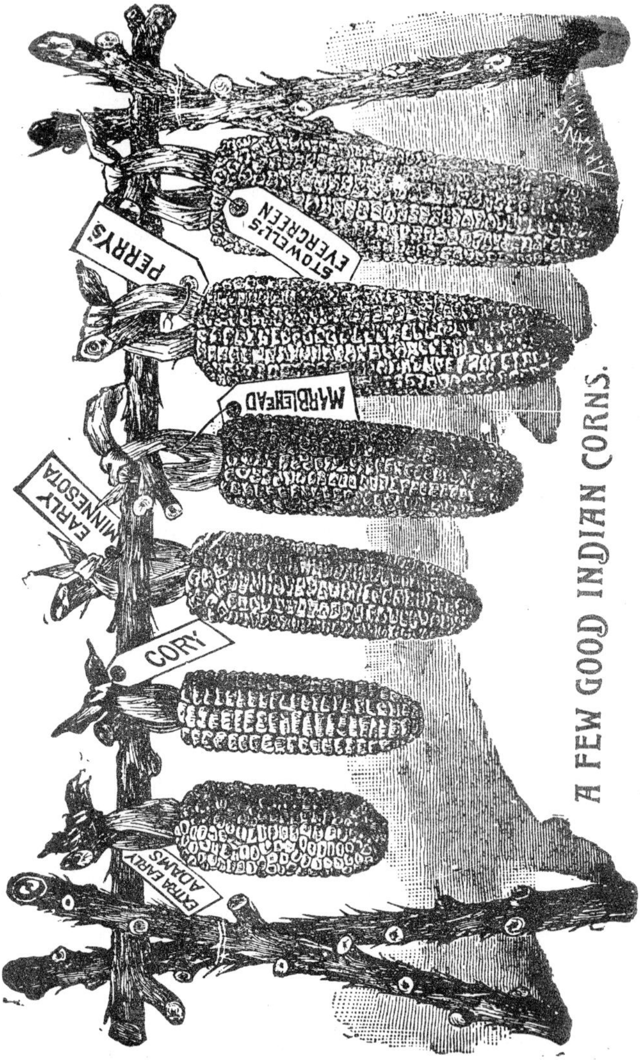


A FEW GOOD INDIAN CORNS.

productiveness of the Golden Beauty is due to the economical shape of the ears, and to the fact that a large proportion of the stalks produce two fine ears. It is one of the largest grained and handsomest yellow Corns in cultivation. The ears are of perfect shape, with from ten to fourteen straight rows of brightest golden yellow grains, of remarkable size, and filled out completely to the extreme end of cob. The cobs are unusually small, when broken in half the grain will always reach across. The richness of colour and fine quality of grain make it very superior for grinding into meal. The ears are easily shelled, although the kernels are firm on the ear. The stalks take a strong hold in the ground and grow vigorously to a height of eight to ten feet. "*Hickory King*":—Is entirely distinct from all other varieties, having the largest grains, with the smallest cob ever introduced in a White Corn. The stalks bear two good sized ears each, and occasionally three, are never barren no matter how thin the soil, and both ends of the ear are filled full out. A single grain will completely cover the cob section of an ear broken in half. It both shells and shucks easily, and will make more shelled corn to a given bulk of ears than any other variety. *Mammoth Late*:—A single ear sometimes weighs as much as two to three pounds. It ripens a little later than the "Evergreen" and the cobs are larger, the kernels being flatter, not horse-tooth shape. *Perry's Hybrid*:—A fine variety, nearly as early as the Minnesota, bearing ears much larger, which are well filled to the end. The cob is red and has twelve to fourteen rows of large white kernels. The ears are set low down and bear two to a stalk. *Roslyn Hybrid*:—Is a very large growing medium early variety, the quality of which is excellent. *Stowell's Evergreen*:—The most popular variety for a late sort in cultivation. One that is more largely planted than any other, it being the favourite with canners and market gardeners for late use. This variety is a necessity for every garden for a succession. The ears are large, grain deep, sugary and tender. *The Cory*:—The earliest sweet Corn in cultivation ; it is a week to ten days earlier than the Marblehead, much sweeter and of finer quality. Ears are larger than either the Marblehead or Minnesota. *The "Henderson."*—It is surprising how this variety continues to grow in popular favour. In the green condition, when ready for the table it is always pure white, and of a remarkably sweet and rich flavour. The Henderson ripens about 10 days earlier than Stowell's Evergreen, and the experience of those who have grown it is, that it is one of the most valuable sorts in cultivation.

POP CORN, *Early Amber Rice*.—This is a very distinct variety. The ears mature very early and the seeds are of a beautiful amber-yellow colour. The dry seeds are used for making that delicious American sweetmeat "Popped corn," which has now become so popular in Europe.

# MUSK MELONS.

## Cucumis Melo.–(Vern. Khurbooza, Karbuz.)

MUSK MELON.

The soil most suitable for the cultivation of Musk Melons is a rich, deep, sandy loam, fully exposed to the sun. Many growers sprout the seed before sowing. This is done by soaking for about twenty-four hours in warm water, then covering with damp ashes till the seeds sprout, when they should be sown in the places where they are to remain, as the Melon bears transplanting but badly. A plan which I think most growers would find very successful, is to sow in small pots, two or three seeds to a pot, and when the young plants have attained a height of 6 or 8 inches carefully plant out, taking care not to break the ball of soil in the pots and so disturb the roots; perhaps the safest plan would be to carefully break the pot, the roots will soon find their way through the breaks. The Melon is a gross feeder and requires a soil in which plenty of well rotted manure has been mixed and during the time of growth an occasional watering with liquid manure will be found very beneficial. I advise planting on "hills" raised about 6 inches above the ground level, the young plants being placed in the centre. On the Plains sowings may be made right on from January to the beginning of March; on the Hills sow in April.

The delicious English Melons can never be raised with any measure of success in India, but fortunately the many fine American sorts all do well. The following are the best of these:—*Perfected Delmonico*:—This Melon since its introduction some years ago, has given great satisfaction. The flesh is an orange pink color, ripens thoroughly to the rind, and is sweet and luscious beyond description. The Melons are of oval shape, and very deeply netted. The vines are hardy and thrifty in growth, and very prolific. *Early Hackensack.*—This is a selection or improvement almost equal in size to the Hackensack, and at least ten days earlier. Several years thorough trial have proved it to be the best as well as the earliest of all the netted Melons. The fruits weigh from four to ten pounds each, and are of delicious flavour. *Emerald Gem*:—A distinct and deliciously flavoured Melon; verly early and prolific. Skin ribbed, yet smooth, and of a deep emerald green. The flesh, which is thick, is of a suffused salmon colour, exceedingly sweet and delicious and very thick meated. *Miller's Cream*:—Most delicious. The flesh is a rich salmon colour, very thick, sweet and rich ; rind very thin and finely netted. Vigorous grower, very productive. *Montreal Market*:—Excellent variety of the largest size; can be grown over 20 lbs in weight. In shape almost round, flattened at ends, deeply ribbed, skin green and netted. Flesh green, very thick.

# WATER MELONS.

## Cucurbita Citrullus or Citrullus Vulgaris.

## (Vern. Turbuz, Turbuza, Kurbuj.)

On the Plains Water Melons should be sown during February ; in some districts even from end of January to middle of March. A rich, rather sandy soil is the one *par excellence* for Water Melon growing, failing which, select a well drained loam. As the Water Melon is a more rampant grower than the Musk, it should be planted further apart. Make large, well drained hills about ten feet apart. Into the compost used for each hill, thoroughly incorporate a couple of shovels full of well rotted manure. On each hill sow 8 or 10 seeds about three or four inches apart and about an inch and a half deep. Sow the seeds with the eye down. As the Water Melon is a gross feeder, growth should be hastened by plentiful applications of liquid manure. In the mornings when the leaves are wet with dew, dust them well with dry ashes, which will effectually protect them from the ravages of most insect pests. When the plants are well up, all should be removed, except one, or two at most, to each hill.

WATER MELONS.

There are almost innumerable varieties of the Water Melon and most of the best have been raised in America. I do not advise readers to sow any of the varieties ordinarily grown by the native cultivators, the seeds of which are obtainable in any bazar; but, as only a few plants need be grown, would advise the sowing of one or more of the following, all of which I can guarantee to be really good kinds.

*Cuban Queen*:—This is a large variety often weighing eighty pounds and upwards. The rind is marked with regular stripes of light and dark green. It is a very showy variety of fair quality. *Florida Favorite*:—Oblong in shape, growing to a very large size ; rind dark, with light green stripes ; flesh light crimson, crisp, and deliciously sweet; seed small and of a creamy white colour, Earlier than Kolb's Gem. *Hungarian Honey*:—This superb variety ripens early. The flesh is of a brilliant red colour and a very rich honey flavour ; colour of skin, medium dark green ; uniformly of medium size. *Kolb's Gem*:—Largely grown, particularly in the South States of America, for shipment to Northern markets. The fruit is nearly round ; rind dark green, somewhat marbled with lighter shades. Weight, 25 to 50 lbs. *Seminole*:—One of the best Water Melons grown ; excellent in flavour, and solid, ripening clear up to the rind. In shape it is oblong, slightly tapering at the ends. I can strongly recommend this variety.

---

# MUSTARD

## Sinapis Alba.--(Vern.---Raee, Sursoo)

Same culture as common Cress. Sow during Spring and Summer only in the Hills, at frequent intervals ; on the Plains sow practically all the year round. During the rains should be sown under cover. 1 oz. will sow a bed of 3 square yards.

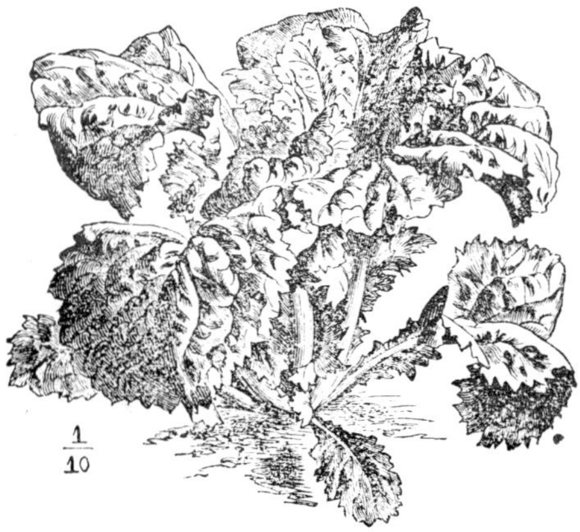

1/10

MUSTARD, NEW CHINESE.

The ordinary *White* variety is too well known to need any description. This is the kind that is always associated with the garden Cress. There is a new variety, however, which is deserving of much more extensive cultivation This is known as *New Chinese*. The leaves are of enormous size, often 12 to 15 inches long. Not only is it a most excellent salad plant, but it is a very valuable vegetable when cooked in the same way as Spinach. On the Plains the seed should be sown in October, and, when large enough, the plants thinned out to a distance of about 18 inches apart ; on the Hills sow during March and April.

---

## OKRA OR COMBO—(Ladies' Fingers.)

### Abelmoschus or Hibiscus Esculentus.

(Vern.—Bhindee, Ram-Torooee, Dhenroos.)

OKRA.

On the Plains sow any time from the beginning of March to the end of July ; is not grown much on the Hills, where it should be sown during May and June. Any good, well manured garden soil suits the Bhindee. During the sowing periods I mention, sowings should be made every two weeks, in order to keep up a supply of the pods.

The Okra will not thrive on the Hills above 5000 feet.

There are several varieties in cultivation but the following two are about the best and are the only ones I recommend.

*Dwarf Prolific or Density*:—A very fine variety, much dwarfer than the ordinary dwarf Okra and more productive. The long, slender pods are tender, of fine quality, and produced very early.

*White Velvet*:—Is very distinct in appearance, and, unlike other varieties, the pods are not ridged, but are perfectly round, smooth, of an attractive white velvet appearance, and superior flavour and tenderness. The plants are comparatively dwarf and of compact branching growth ; the pods are of extra large size and produced in great abundance.

# ONION.

## Allium Cepa.—(Vern.--Peeaj or Peeyaj.)

The Onion is a very gross feeder, and requires deep cultivation ; a light, rich, sandy soil suits it best ; the ground should be trenched to a depth of at least two feet, adding at the same time a heavy dressing of manure. On the Plains sowings may be made from the middle of August to November, in drills nine inches apart. After covering up the seed, the beds should be trodden or beaten down firmly. As soon as the plants are six inches high, they may be thinned out to a distance of six inches apart in the rows. They must be kept plentifully supplied with water, and frequent dressings of liquid manure will materially conduce to the production of a good crop. The thinnings should be transplanted into other beds, taking care not to plant too deeply ; these will form almost as good bulbs as those left in the original beds. Sow from end of February to beginning of June in the Hills. 1 oz. of seed will sow a bed 4 feet by 12 feet, or a drill 80 to 100 feet long.

ONION.

There are a great number of distinct varieties of Onions, but in the following list I describe, as a rule, early maturing sorts, as on the Plains it is advisable to sow only early varieties.

*Mammoth White Victoria.*---Skin silver white, but sometimes of a delicate light rose-colour ; flesh juicy, sweet and milky white. In other particulars this variety has the same qualities as the "*Red Victoria* ;" it generally grows equally as large, and is of the same distinct oval round shape. It delights in frequent hoeings of the soil, and watering in dry weather. *Mammoth Red Victoria* :—Of distinct oval round shape, weighing from 2½ to 4½lbs. each, with capacity of still larger growth under extra cultivation. Skin very dark red, almost blood red in colour ; flesh light rose coloured; flavour mild and sweet ; a good keeping variety. It grows best in loam or heavy soil, which may even be stony, and must be well worked. Properly cultivated, this variety, uniformly larger in size than any Onion hitherto known, produces an enormous crop. Bulbs of this wonderful variety have been produced in America weighing 5½ lbs. each. *Neapolitan Maggiajole*:—A large silver-white skinned variety. Of handsome flat shape, very fine flavour and quality. Its great merit, however, consists chiefly in the rapidity with which its large, handsome bulbs are formed, surpassing in this respect all other varieties, the bulbs being fit for use within three months from the time of sowing. *Portuguese Delicacy*:—A splendid large, globular variety ; flesh pure white ; flavour mild and delicious. This is one of the most handsome varieties in cultivation. *Giant Red Garganus, or Mammoth Pompeii*:—This variety was raised in Italy and sent out under the first name given above, but on arrival in America was re-named and sent out as the "*Mammoth Pompeii.*" Under whatever name it may be grown, it is undoubtedly a wonderful variety, excelled in size only by the two new Mammoth Victorias. Bulbs of the enormous weight of 5 lbs. have been grown in America, but the average weight, under good culture, is from 2 to 4 lbs. each ; notwithstanding their gigantic size, they retain their perfect shape and fine quality. The skin is very thin and delicate in appearance, of a reddish brown colour ; flesh pure white, fine grained and mild in flavour. *Giant White Garganus, or Mammoth Silver King*:—This variety has the same origin as the preceding, and its second name originated in America. If there is such a thing as a delicate flavoured Onion, we have it in this variety. It is very rapid in growth, attaining an enormous size, frequently measuring when full grown, 5 to 7½ inches in diameter, and weighing from 2 to 4 lbs each ; of a beautiful silvery white colour. Independent of its fine qualities, it is really a wonder in appearance, and also very attractive for exhibition purposes. Every cultivator of a garden should grow it. *Prizetaker*:—This is a very fine, large variety, and much grown in America, where it is becoming extremely popular, on account of its rich straw colour, enormous size and excellent keeping quality. Although of such large size, the flavour is extremely delicate, which makes it an excellent salad variety. *Bedfordshire Champion*:—Fine shape, and excellent keeper ; one of the best. *Blood Red*:—Medium size, strong flavour, excellent keeper. *Danver's Yellow Globe*:—An excellent sort ; good cropper, very fine and invaluable for general use. *Giant Zittau*:—An excellent keeping variety, of handsome shape and clear yellow colour. *Giant Red Zittau*:—A new variety of the preceding, of same size and shape, but of a bright blood red colour. *Giant Rocca of Naples*:—A very fine, large variety, of globular shape, light-brown skin, and very mild flavour; will frequently attain, under favourable circumstances, two pounds in weight. *Golden Queen*:—A splendid variety, of good size and flavour, very hardy and an excellent keeper. *James' Long Keeping*:—A fine, distinct, pear-shaped variety. Very popular in Europe. One of the best keepers. *Large Red Italian Tripoli or Bassano*:—A very large-growing variety, of blood red colour; flatter in form than the Rocca, and of mild flavour. *Large White Italian Tripoli*:—A very superior variety, of flat form, and large size, with a beautiful silvery white skin, and of mild flavour. *Magnum Bonum*:—One of the best varieties in cultivation, very hardy, good cropper, and will keep longer than any other. *Silverskin*:---The best variety for pickling; for this purpose they should be sown very thickly. *White Globe*:—A large globe-shaped onion; firm, fine grained and of mild flavour; keeps well. This is one of the most handsome onions grown, of beautiful shape, and clear white skin. *White Lisbon*:—The Onion that is grown so much in Europe for pulling when young, for salads. This is the variety that is usually known as "Spring Onions." *White Queen*:—A fine, early, silver skinned variety, of beautiful form and rapid growth, possessing good keeping qualities. *White Spanish, Portugal or Reading*.---Splendid selected stock. Well known as a large and excellent variety; pale straw colour, mild in flavour, and one of the best for general use.

# PARSLEY.

Carum Petroselinum.---(Vern.--Petercelee, Randnee, Ajmud.)

On the Plains sowings may be made in pans under shelter in August; by the end of the rains, these will have formed strong plants, which should then be planted out into beds of well manured soil at a distance of six inches apart. Further sowings may be made in the open ground from September to

PARSLEY.

end of November. These will not require to be transplanted but the plants should be thinned out to the distance mentioned above. Parsley succeeds best in a rich, mellow soil. A slightly shaded situation suits it best. The seed will be found to germinate much more freely if it is steeped in water for three or four hours, and then well mixed with dry ashes or sand before sowing. After rain, care should be taken to protect the plants from the sun, otherwise the leaves will become discoloured. In the Hills sow from March to September. 1 oz. of seed will sow a row 80 feet long.

There are a fair number of good varieties of Parsley grown, many of them, I fear, being only old sorts with new names. As few people want more than a small patch of Parsley, I mention half a dozen of the best and most distinct sorts.

First I must place one of my own introductions, which I consider by far the best variety now in cultivation. This is known as *Perennial Moss Curled.* It is very select, late to run to seed and intensely curled. I only introduced this variety in 1893, but it has already become the standard sort and is perhaps more grown than any other. A lady wrote to me a short time ago saying she had grown Perennial Moss Curled with *branches* almost as long as her arm, and although so long, they were covered with beautiful green, densely curled foliage. *Enfield Matchless or Myatt's Garnishing*:—Beautifully curled. *Extra Curled Dwarf*:—This is a most beautiful and valuable variety. The moss-like leaves are finely crimped and curled, and of a bright green colour For garnishing, no variety is more attractive. *Fern Leaved (Carter's.)*—Exquisitely perfect in form and colour, this beautiful variety is pronounced on all sides, to be not only the best for garnishing purposes, but also specially valuable as an ornamental foliage plant, for table decoration and the flower border. *Hurst's Improved Moss Curled* :—A magnificent stock. I can strongly recommend it, both for colour and quality. *Henderson's Emerald* :—I wish to call special attention to this Emerald Parsley, for the reason that it is altogether distinct in appearance from any of the other varieties, being of a lighter and more brilliant shade of green. The plant is of dwarf habit, with leaves finely cut and curled.

---

# PARSNIPS.

## Pastinaca Sativa.-(Vern.-Pastinac. Istufeen).

It is a great mistake to sow Parsnip seed too early on the Plains as it will almost invariably fail to germinate. I would not advise sowing before the first week of November. Many people are deterred from growing this favourite vegetable on account of the difficulty in getting the seeds to germinate, but this difficulty is being overcome by some of the leading Seedsmen, who specially import their stocks of seed from England and Australia, and thus are always in a position to supply fresh seeds, as the seasons of ripening in

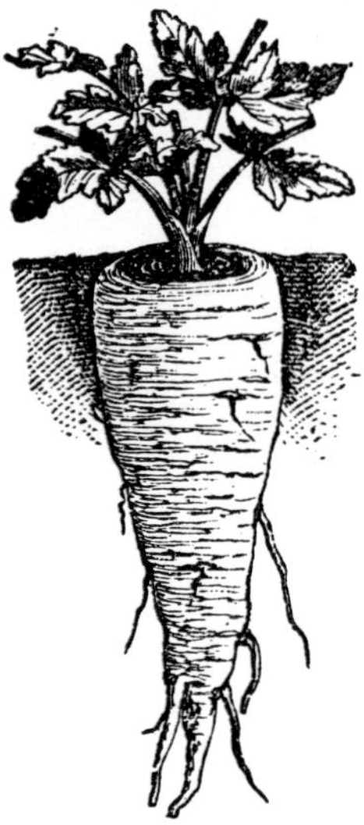
PARSNIP.

these two countries are quite different times of the year. The soil most suitable for the Parsnip is a light, rich, friable one. The seed can either be sown broadcast or in drills. If the latter style of cultivation is decided on, the drills should be about 9 inches apart. When large enough the plants should be thinned out about the same distance—9 inches apart. Give plenty of water and an occasional drenching with liquid manure. On the Hills sowings may be made any time during March, April and May. One ounce of seed will sow a row 100 feet long.

There are a number of varieties of Parsnip, some of them being quite late introductions, which are great improvements on some of the old sorts we used to be familiar with. A few years ago I brought out to India a variety which I had had some experience with at home, and this has taken the place of some of the older sorts. This variety is known as *Improved Marrow*. I can strongly recommend this to growers as is has a very clean, handsome root. In flavour I do not think it can be beaten, as it is very sweet, without the mealy taste of most sorts.

Other good sorts are :—

*Lisbonnais* :—This is a great improvement on the old "Hollow Crowned," but is quite distinct from it. A good looking variety which is being greatly grown by Market Gardeners at home. *Elcombe's Improved* :—A very heavy cropper, roots large and flavour good. *The Student* :—A very long variety which requires a good deep soil. *Guernsey or Jersey Marrow* :—An excellent variety which is much grown. The roots are of good size and excellent flavour. *Turnip Rooted* :—This variety differs from all the others, in that the roots are round instead of long. The flavour is very fine and this is a particularly useful sort for growing in shallow soils.

# PEAS.

## Pisum Sativum.—(Vern.—Mutter or Mater, Butanee, Kursuneh.)

The Pea delights in a rich, deep, light soil ; one that has been well manured for the previous season's crop suits it best. Should however, the soil be poor, it may be enriched with a good dressing of very old cow manure or leaf mould, which, when possible, should be

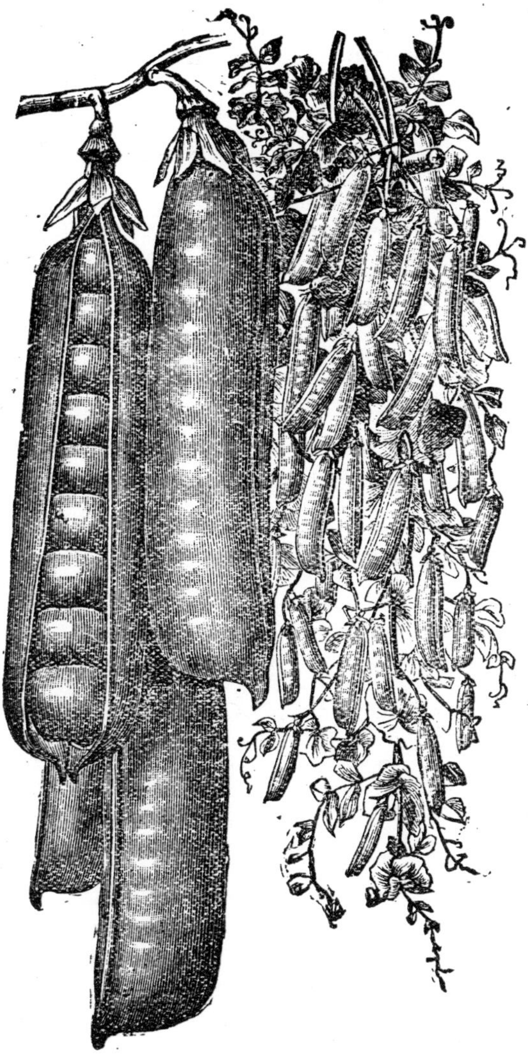

PEA.

applied a month or two before sowing. On no account use fresh or half-rotted manure; this being too stimulating in its action, causes an unnatural production of stem, to the detriment of the crop, and also frequently causes the plants to become infested with mildew.

Sow from August to December in the Plains, commencing with the dwarf early varieties, and where space is available, this should be followed by successional sowings at intervals of a week or ten days. Before sowing, in dry weather, the seed should be steeped in water for three or four hours, and then allowed to dry for about the same time before being put in. The dwarf kinds may be sown in rows about eighteen inches apart, and the seeds, about 1 inch apart, covering them with about an inch of soil. The taller growing sorts require a space of at least three feet between the rows, and should be planted two inches deep. As soon as they are about six inches high, they should be staked, planting the sticks so that they should be firmly tied together. The situation best adapted for the Pea is one where it receives the full morning sun, but is partially shaded during the remainder of the day. When the pods are well set, pinch out the leading shoot, so as to check the growth of vine, and throw the entire strength into the pods. Sow from February to May in the Hills, also in Autumn. 1 lb. of seed will sow a row of from 40 to 50 feet.

I do not think there is any vegetable in cultivation of which there are more varieties than the Pea, but many of the so called "varieties" are merely old sorts under new names. It is extremely difficult to select from the immense number given in Seedsmen's Catalogues, but in the following list I give those only which I consider really worth growing. I give the heights so that readers will know what size of sticks will be required, but I would draw attention to the fact that it is impossible to say exactly how high any particular variety *may* grow under special culture; if grown in very rich soil the heights I give may be greatly exceeded. I have marked with an asterisk (*) the *Wrinkled varieties*, and have divided all into three classes, EARLIEST, MAIN CROP and LATE CROP varieties.

## EARLIEST VARIETIES.

| | Height. |
|---|---|
| * **American Wonder**:--- This is one of the very earliest wrinkled Marrows in cultivation, deliciously flavoured, and an extremely heavy cropper. Its most distinctive feature is its very dwarf and compact growth, being only 12 inches in height, literally covering itself with pods. | 1 ft. |
| **Early Morning Star.**---Where earliness, productiveness, large sized pods and sweetness of flavour are desired, this is the variety to grow. In a favourable season will be ready for market in 42 days and the entire crop can be taken off in two pickings. Is much hardier, more productive, and withstands greater changes of weather than any other variety. Is not only the Largest Podded Extra Early, but is entirely free from runners. ... | 1 " |
| **Early Sunrise** (Day):---Large-seeded, first early dwarf white wrinkled Marrow, of strong and robust habit. It is very hardy and extremely prolific, the haulm being covered with large well-filled pods, while the peas are large and very sweet when cooked ... ... | 2½ " |
| **Earliest of All** (Laxton.):---A round, blue-seeded Pea, of excellent and rich flavour, dwarfer than Ringleader, more prolific (averaging eight peas in a pod) and fit to gather a week sooner. ... ... ... | 2 " |

| | Height. |
|---|---|
| * **Exonian** (*Veitch.*) :---A first early Wrinkled Marrow Pea. Messrs. Robert Veitch and Son, of Exeter, who send it out, write that "it is earlier than "William the First," bears a heavy crop of good sized pods, each containing six to eight and even nine large dark green peas. The flavour is unique for a first early variety and partakes of the character of "Veitch's Perfection and similar sorts." The Royal Horticultural Society, after testing it at Chiswick, awarded it a First Class Certificate ... | 3½ feet. |
| * **Extra Early Premium Gem**:---A very fine dwarf Pea, large pods and very productive ... ... | 1½ " |
| **Henderson's First of All** :---It is fully six inches dwarfer than the "Improved Sangsters' No. 1" or "First and Best," and produces pods of good size, which are well filled with round, smooth, white peas of splendid flavour. It is a prodigious bearer, and ripens up so evenly as not to require more than two pickings to clear off the crop. ... ... ... ... | 2½ " |
| IMPROVED SANGSTER'S NO. 1 :---Prolific and early ; one of the best ... ... ... ... | 3 " |
| **Lightning (Carter's)** :---A good cropper and of fine flavour ... ... ... ... | 2½ " |
| * **McLean's Little Gem** :---A dwarf green wrinkled marrow, very early and of fine flavour ; an excellent cropper ... ... ... ... | 1 " |
| **Ringleader (Sutton's)** :---Also known as "Carter's First Crop." One of the best white varieties in cultivation, very prolific and of fine flavour. ... ... | 3 " |
| * **William Hurst** :---A dwarf blue wrinkled marrow, with well-filled medium sized pods ... ... | 1 " |
| **William the First**, SELECTED STOCK :---One of the finest early green marrows, combining flavour, earliness and productiveness. ... ... ... | 3 " |

## MAIN CROP VARIETIES.

| | |
|---|---|
| ***Abundance** (*Bliss*):—Plant half-dwarf, fifteen to eighteen inches high ; foliage large, thick, full and dark green. Pods three to three and a half inches long, roundish and well filled, containing six to eight large wrinkled peas of excellent quality ; it ripens second early | 1½ " |
| * **Autocrat** (*Veitch*) :—First Class Certificate, Royal Horticultural Society. Robust, branching habit, and dark green foliage. Very productive, and of strong constitution | 4 " |
| * **Best of All** :—A highly recommended variety ; pods large, well filled and of exquisite flavour | 3 " |

| | Height. |
|---|---|
| * **Boston Hero**:—A very heavy cropper, the pods nearly all coming in pairs ; they are very large and well filled with fine sweet peas | 5 ft. |
| * **Celebrity**:—For appearance, flavour and cropping, I can confidently recommend this variety | 5 ,, |
| * **Champion of England.**—Good bearer, delicious variety ; one of the best | 5 ,, |
| * **Conundrum** :— A grand new medium and late wrinkled marrow Pea, of exceptionally robust habit and growth, extremely prolific either for garden or field culture. When comparatively old it retains its flavour. The pea is large and pods are long and well filled | 7 ,, |
| * **Daisy** :—A dwarf wrinkled marrow. Bears large, well-filled pods and is a heavy cropper | 2 ,, |
| * **Dr. McLean** :—A splendid wrinkled Pea, of finest quality ; produces an abundant crop ; one of the finest main crop varieties in cultivation | 3 ,, |
| * **Duke of Albany** (*Abbott.*):—Very productive, bearing a profusion of extra large, well-filled pods, borne in pairs, which being dark green in colour, are very handsome, and contain from 9 to 12 fine peas each ; the flavour and quality are also excellent ; of vigorous and branching habit, and should therefore be sown thinly | 5 ,, |
| * **Duke of York** :—This may best be described as an *earlier and dwarfer form of "Duke of Albany,"* possessing all the good qualities of that standard variety but maturing two or three weeks earlier, and producing an equally large crop on a plant growing to a height of only | 3½ ,, |
| **Fillbasket**:—Is a second early, round seeding variety, very heavy cropper, and of excellent flavour | 3½ ,, |
| * **George Clelland** :—A grand main-crop wrinkled marrow Pea, growing from 3 to 3½ feet high. It produces a heavy crop of large, well-filled pods, which grow in clusters and usually contain from 10 to 12 peas each of delicious flavour | 3½ ,, |
| * **G. F. Wilson**:—A main crop, green wrinkled Pea, somewhat resembling "Veitch's Perfection," but about a week earlier | 3 ,, |
| * **Hair's Dwarf Mammoth**:—A light wrinkled variety, of very delicate flavour, and very productive | 2½ ,, |
| * **Henderson's Midsummer**:—This is a white wrinkled, second early variety, attaining a height of 2½ feet. The pods are produced in pairs, and it is a most abundant bearer. The quality of this Pea, when cooked, leaves nothing to be desired | 2½ ,, |
| * **Henderson's Heroine**:—The "Heroine" is a medium early, green wrinkled pea ; very prolific, pods long, | |

heavy and pointed, containing eight to nine peas of rich, buttery, marrow-like flavour — Height, 2½ feet.

**Market Favourite**:—A splendid round-seeded white variety; the pods are large, well filled, and are borne in immense profusion — 4½ „

***Market Garden** (*Horsford's*):—The vines are uniformly two feet high, and very even and regular in growth. It is a prolific bearer, and has been known to yield more per acre than any other variety. The pods are literally packed with peas of a deliciously sweet flavour — 2 „

**Pride of the Market**:—A splendid variety for Market or Exhibition purposes, bearing grand pods, well filled with large, fine flavoured peas. First Class Certificate R. H. S. — 2 „

* **Prince of Wales**:—An excellent wrinkled marrow; large, well filled pods produced in pairs; fine flavour and heavy cropper — 3 „

* "**Sensation**" (*De la Bere*):—A new wrinkled marrow of exceptional excellence, described as surpassing any variety in cultivation, both as to size, flavour, and its extraordinary yielding powers. It grows 3 feet high, and owing to its vigorous habit, half the quantity of seed usually sown will suffice — 3 „

* **Sharpe's Queen**:—A splendid dwarf wrinkled marrow. The pods are of extraordinary size and well filled with enormous peas of the most delicious flavour — 2½ „

**Sir Harry Atkinson** :—A splendid Australian variety which has gained a great name for itself. Is said to be one of the finest Main crop Peas introduced in late years. Grows to a height of 3 feet, and bears, in vast profusion, fine deep green pods filled with rich sugary peas of large size — 3 „

* **Stratagem**.—This is admitted to be one of the best dwarf wrinkled peas in cultivation, the plants being literally covered with immense pods, many measuring from five to six inches long, and containing nine to eleven peas in each pod; unsurpassed as an Exhibition variety — 2½ „

***The Duchess** (*Abbott.*):-This pea was sent for trial to the Royal Horticultural Society under the name of "Abbott," and awarded a First Class Certificate. The *Gardening World* says of this fine variety:—"*New Seedling Pea*:-A beautiful sample of a new Pea comes to us from Messrs. Hurst and Son. It is described as a second early—something in the way of "*Duke of Albany*," but rather earlier and a heavier cropper, growing to a height of 5 feet. The pods sent us measured about 4½ inches in length, were quite straight and well filled throughout with an average of nine large, sweet peas in each. The latter, when perfectly matured, are deep green and wrinkled. As an exhibition variety it will, no doubt, take a leading place, owing to the fine appearance of the pods, well filled character and first class quality" Height 5 feet

* **The Stanley** (*Horsford.*):—The raiser says of it :—

"In offering this to the public I do so in the full belief that it is superior to any other variety of its class, and will prove of great value as a garden Pea."

He claims for it the following advantages :—

1st. It has a beautiful, large, well filled pod, larger than those of "Stratagem," and nearly as large as "Telephone."

2nd. It is a tremendous cropper.

3rd. It has a dwarf, stocky vine, and needs no sticking.

4th. It is very sweet, inheriting from both parents ("American Wonder," and "Telephone") their delicacy of flavour.

In rich soil, it grows about 18 inches high, and the full grown pods often measure four inches in circumference. Eight green pods weighed a quarter of a pound. They mature very evenly, so that almost the entire crop can be taken at one picking 1½ "

**Telegraph** (*Culverwell.*):—Immense pods, the peas often forming apparently a double row; when cooked, they are of a fine deep-green colour, and of good flavour 5 "

* **Telephone**:—A splendid wrinkled variety ; very prolific, pods long, broad, and well filled ; good for exhibition or table use 5 "

* **Triumph** (*Sharpe.*):—A grand free-cropping, blue wrinkled marrow variety of exquisite flavour ; pods large, very much curved, and well filled with extra large peas 3 "

***Veitch's Perfection**:—An extra fine wrinkled marrow of excellent quality. It is a wonderful cropper and the flavour is delicious. The demand for this valuable Pea increases every year 3 "

* **Walker's Perpetual Bearer**:—A variety of robust branching habit and a continuous bearer. It is an immense cropper and of first rate flavour; very free from mildew 3 "

* **Yorkshire Gem**:—Long, round pods, closely filled with large, luscious, wrinkled peas ; of extra fine quality and very productive 3 "

* **Yorkshire Hero**:—An old favorite variety, of excellent quality and a good cropper 2½ "

## LATE CROP VARIETIES.

*British Queen:—This sterling late wrinkled variety has proved a marked advance on any sort offered in its class. It is of most robust habit, and should be sown very thinly. ... ... ... 6 "

| | Height |
|---|---|
| *EMPEROR OF THE MARROWS:---A choice wrinkled marrow, producing handsome dark green pods, well filled with large exquisitely flavoured Peas ... ... | 6 ft. |
| *NE PLUS ULTRA, SELECTED:--Also known as 'Payne's Conqueror." Fine dark green, abundant bearer, of rich flavour; a first class wrinkled marrow, and one of the best late peas... | 6 ,, |
| *OMEGA:---A very prolific variety of delicious flavour, quite distinct; keeps in condition a long time after being fit for use ... ... ... | 2½ ,, |
| *SANDERS' MARROW:---A tall, very late and big cropping variety. The pods are produced in pairs, and are well filled with fine, large. wrinkled peas. The individual peas are about the largest that I have ever seen, and in quality, when cooked, sweet and delicious. It has the peculiarity of retaining its deep green colour when dished for the table, a characteristic that I need hardly say is most desirable. ... | 5 ,, |
| *THE "GLADSTONE":—Obtained XXX, Chiswick June, 29th 1896; also Award of Merit, R. H. S., August 25th 1896. This fine late variety is of robust and branching habit, and should be sown thin. *Extract from report of Peas tested at Chiswick, 1896*:—" The Gladstone (XXX, unanimous award June 29th.)---Excellent cropper, pods in pairs; haulm, pods and peas very dark green; pods very long, often containing eleven peas of large size in each; of fine flavour. | 4 ,, |

# PUMPKINS.

### Cucurbita Pepo.(Vern.-Kuddoo, Meethee Kuddoo, Koondha, Seetaphul.)

Sow any time from June to October in the Plains; March to end of June in the Hills. Support plants on a strong bamboo trellis or allow to run over out-houses or other buildings. They require a very rich, highly manured soil, with plenty of water during dry weather; an occasional drenching with liquid manure will help the growth of the plants materially. There are very many varieties in cultivation the best of which I name and describe in the following list:—

*King of the Mammoths or Jumbo*:---The largest growing variety, frequently attaining a weight of 200 lbs. Specimens have been seen weighing 250 pounds. The colour of the skin is a deep yellow, the flesh being of a lighter shade. Notwithstanding its enormous size, it is delicious in quality and generally desirable. *Large Tours*:---A very large French variety, frequently attaining a weight of upwards of 100 lbs. *Mammoth Etampes.*:---A fine French sort, said to attain a

weight of 100 to 150 lbs. "*Jonathan*":—A splendid variety. When cooked it has somewhat the appearance of a Sweet Potato but is more delicious. For flavour in pies and custards it has no equal; flesh thick, creamy white and exceedingly fine grained. Hardy, productive, sweet and delicious, one of the best for cooking purposes ever introduced. Its hard shell makes it an excellent keeping variety. *Golden Oblong* :—The fruits of this variety grow to a very uniform size of from fifteen to twenty inches in length; the outer colour is a rich golden-orange or old gold. The fruit, when young is dark green, and changes to rich golden yellow as it ripens. The flesh is light yellow in colour, of very rich, fine quality, and has been pronounced by lovers of pumpkin pies the very best they have ever had for this purpose. *Japanese Pie* :—The illustration correctly shows the shape of this variety which is of extra fine quality. The seeds are distinct in appearance, being curiously sculptured in the manner of Chinese letters. It is a very productive variety; the pumpkins ripen early, are of medium size, good keepers and weigh 15 to 20 lbs. each. As to their quality, one enthusiastic grower says :—"No other pumpkin or squash that has ever been introduced can vie with the "Japanese" for its excellent qualities, and exceedingly fine flavour when cooked." The flesh is a rich salmon colour unusually fine grained, and when cooked or stewed, is almost as dry and mealy as a sweet potato. For making pies, custards, etc., it certainly has no equal. Containing but little water, can easily be cut and dried, like dried apples and makes excellent pies, or sauce for Winter use. *Quaker Pie* :—This very distinct and valuable variety hails from Washington County, N. Y., where, for many years, it has been in the possession of a family of Quakers or Friends. It is of peculiar shape, being distinct and unlike any other Pumpkin or Squash, as it is oval, and tapers toward each end. It is of a creamy colour both inside and out. The vines are very hardy and prolific, always yielding a certain crop. It is early and keeps late. Its chief value is for "Pumpkin Pies." Being fine grained and rich flavoured it makes a superior quality of Pie. It has none of the coarse and stringy character so common to many varieties.

Amongst other good sorts I would mention :—*Large Green, Large Yellow, Cashaw Crook Neck, Connecticut, Large Cheese* (also known as *Sweet Cheese* or *Kentucky Field*), *Small Sugar, Tennessee Sweet Potato*, &c., &c.

PUMPKIN PLANT, SHOWING STYLE OF GROWTH.

# RADISHES.

## Raphanus Sativus.-(Vern.-Moolee, Mula, Turub, Fujul.)

Sow from August to January in the Plains at regular intervals of ten days or a fortnight. Radishes thrive best in a light, sandy loam. The seed should be sown in drills about five inches apart, and after lightly covering with soil, the beds should be well beaten down; which will ensure the roots forming of a good shape. As soon as the plants are large enough, they should be thinned out to a distance of four inches apart in the rows. If the soil is fairly rich and the plants are kept liberally supplied with water, they should be ready for drawing in about three weeks from the time of sowing. Care must also be taken to keep the soil well stirred about the plants. To ensure a supply of Radishes fit for use, seed should be sown about every eight or ten days ; this is essential, as the Radish remains fit for the table for but a very short time. Sow throughout Spring and Summer in the Hills. 1 oz. of seed will sow a bed of 3 square yards.

There are three great divisions into which the Radishes naturally fall and I will describe some of the best varieties in each.

## LONG VARIETIES.

*American Knickerbocker* :—This is a sort which has proved its value from the fact that it has been re-named in various countries and is now known as "Chartier," "The Shepherd" &c., &c. The roots grow to a large size, and for about two thirds of their length are of a crimson rose colour, shading off lighter, till towards the bottom they become pure white. They are of quick growth, very tender, and keep in condition for the table for quite a long time. This is a sort which I can strongly recommend. *Early Long Scarlet Short Top* :—This is, and has been for very many years, the standard long Radish. The roots average about half an inch in diameter at the top and gradually taper to the bottom, attaining generally to a length of some five inches. *Wood's Early Frame*:—This is *the* variety to grow when earliness is specially desired. The roots are not quite so long as the preceding but it is about 10 days earlier.

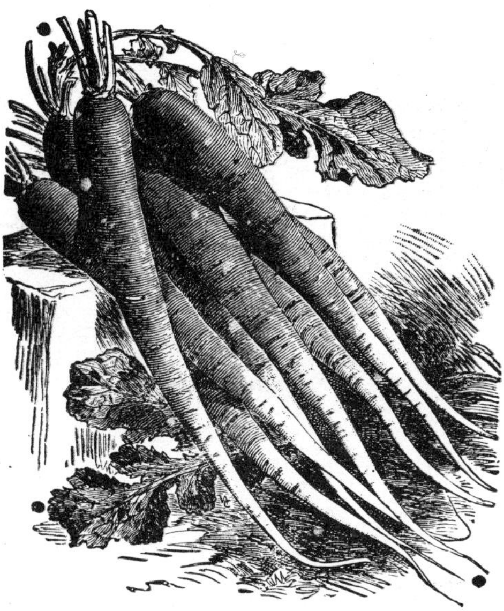

RADISH, LONG.

Many people like the long White Radishes which are so much grown by native cultivators, but if instead of the generally tasteless native varieties, they will grow one or more of the following, they will have

Radishes really worth eating. Perhaps the best of the white long kinds is *Long White Vienna* which is also known to many as *Lady's Finger.* It forms a splendidly shaped root, both skin and flesh being snowy white, while the flavour is excellent. Is very crisp and of rapid growth. *White Strasburg* :---This variety is of a tapering shape, much like the Intermediate Carrots. Very tender, quick growing and of fine flavour. *Long White Naples* :---Another A1 sort with white flesh. The roots are crisp and mild. Last but not least, of the white varieties, I will mention *Giant Stuttgart.* This is really the giant amongst the Radishes. It will stand any amount of heat and will grow to an immense size. Although so large, the quality is always of the finest, being firm, brittle and not pithy, so that it can be pulled fit for the table even when comparatively old.

A very peculiar looking Radish is *Black Paris Winter,* with its coal black skin and white flesh, but as it will stand greater extremes of temperature than any other sort, it is being very largely grown in districts where many of the ordinary kinds will not thrive.

RADISH, OLIVE SHAPED.

## OLIVE SHAPED VARIETIES.

As is shown in the illustration I give, this class forms roots of a shape between the Long and the Round varieties.

*Deep Scarlet White Tipped:*—This is one of the most handsome of the early varieties. The roots are regularly olive shaped, very even and have an extremely smooth skin ; in colour a rich scarlet shading off at the tips to pure white. Very quick in maturing, as perfect roots can often be pulled in 20 days from date of sowing *Early Scarlet Globe* :—A new German variety which is becoming very popular. Very early and of brilliant scarlet colour. *Red Rocket* :-This is perhaps the earliest Scarlet Radish in cultivation, as the roots will mature in little more than a fortnight after the seeds germinate. *French Breakfast* :—A variety very much like the Deep Scarlet White Tipped. Is of quick growth and a good forcer.

Other good kinds in this class are :—*Scarlet Olive, White Olive* and *Violet White Tipped Olive,* all of which are very similar, differing only in colour.

## ROUND OR TURNIP SHAPED VARIETIES.

RADISH, ROUND OR TURNIP.

This class of Radish is perhaps more largely grown than any other. The roots form very quickly, are of good flavour, and as they can be cleared off the ground very soon, a great number of successional crops can be grown. There are a number of really fine varieties in this class and amongst the best are :--

*Earliest Erfurt Scarlet Turnip* :--Matures in from 15 to 20 days from germination ; very crisp and tender. *Rosy Gem* :--Matures in about a fortnight ; of delicate flavour but will not remain long fit for use. *Extra Early Scarlet Forcing* :---A very early form of the old *Red Turnip* ; an excellent variety. *Golden Globe or Golden Yellow Summer* :--In colour a bright golden yellow. Of very fine quality and delicious flavour ; as it stands heat well, will be found a splendid sort for the Plains. *Earliest White Turnip* :--Very early, roots of good flavour, crisp and tender. *Large White Summer Turnip or Globe*:---A very large round variety. Pure white skin and flesh very crisp and brittle. It quickly grows to a large size and withstands heat well.

Other good varieties are the following, which differ but little, except in colour :---*Red Turnip, White Turnip, Scarlet White Tipped Turnip, Violet White Tipped Turnip, Yellow Summer Turnip.* Unless growers are particularly fond of any special variety, I advise them to grow the *Mixed Turnip varieties,* seed of which is offered by most Seedsmen.

HORSE RADISH.

## HORSE RADISH.

(Cochlearia Armoracia.)

I cull the following note on Horse Radish culture on the Plains from Firminger's "*Manual of Gardening*"---a book which should be in the library of every garden lover :---" Place round the sides of a flower-pot, filled with mould, well lightened with sand, pieces of the root of the thickness of a quill, and two inches long. These being kept watered, quickly sprout and form rooted plants. Dig holes a foot and a half deep, 10 inches wide and a foot apart, on a piece of high ground, fill the lower half foot with well manured soil, and the remaining upper foot with a light mellow soil, and put one of the plants in each. When they have been established about a week or two, remove the earth from the roots, and clear away all the small fibrous roots that have formed, leaving only one main root to proceed downwards. Repeat this three or four times at intervals, removing the earth deeper each time for the purpose. When the main root has descended about a foot deep, it will have reached the rich soil at the bottom of the hole. Remove then the uppermost foot of soil and fill in with sand. The water given to the plant will immediately sink down through the sand to the roots where it is alone wanted, and the main stem will not be induced to form fibres on its sides. The roots will be ready for use in about four or five months' time."

On the Hills the culture is much more simple. Cut the roots into pieces about an inch long and plant in a rich, fairly damp, deeply dug soil.

---

# RHUBARB.

## (RHEUM HYBRIDUM.)

It is practically impossible to grow Rhubarb with any success on the Plains. Firminger speaks of having succeeded in raising plants from seed sown in November. On the Hills sow from March to May, and when the seedlings are large enough to handle, plant out in very rich soil, about 3 feet apart. The Rhubarb requires a very shady situation with plenty of moisture but with good drainage. Every year a heavy top dressing of well rotted stable manure should be worked in amongst the the roots. Forcing can easily be done by placing small tubs or boxes over the leaves. Place the tubs or boxes on bricks so as to allow of ventilation and so prevent rotting the leaves.

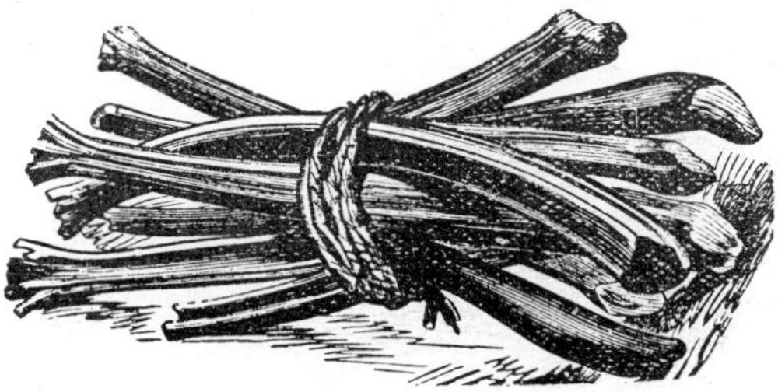

RHUBARB.

There are several good varieties of Rhubarb in cultivation but the following four will be ample for any ordinary grower:—

*Johnstone's St. Martins*:—This variety was raised by the writer's father at St. Martins, Perthshire, some 50 years ago, and the fact that it is still the most popular kind in cultivation, shows that it is a really good sort. It is immensely productive, one of the earliest and has a rich spicy flavour. *Prince Albert*:—Also known as *Albert* and *Royal Albert*. Very large and prolific. *Linnæus*:—A good early sort of fine quality, excellent for forcing. *Victoria*:—Stalks very large and thick, and of good quality.

# Salsify, or Vegetable Oyster.

(Tragopogon Porrifolius.)

Very generally known as the Oyster Plant. The roots are boiled like Carrots or Parsnips, or half-boiled and grated fine, made into small flat balls, dipped in a batter, and fried like oysters, which they greatly resemble in flavour. Salsify may also be eaten as a salad, sliced and dressed with vinegar, salt and pepper.

On the Plains sow from end of September to middle of November; on the Hills, March to end of May. The Oyster Plant succeeds best in light, well enriched, mellow soil, which previous to sowing the seeds, should be stirred to a depth of eighteen inches. Sow in drills fifteen inches apart; cover the seeds with fine soil, an inch and a half in depth, and when the plants are strong enough, thin out to six inches apart.

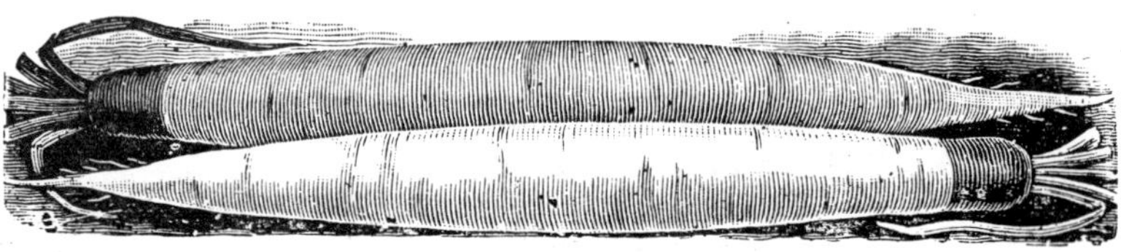

SALSIFY.

There are two varieties of Salsify in general cultivation, the ordinary *Selected French* and the *Mammoth Sandwich Island*. Until the introduction of the latter, the French was the only sort in cultivation. In the Mammoth the roots grow to quite double the size of the old variety, and are of very superior quality and delicate flavour.

# Scorzonera Hispanica.

This very much resembles the preceding, having the same habit of growth and requiring the same treatment. Produces larger roots than the French Salsify, and by some is preferred to it. This is known as the Black or Spanish Oyster Plant.

# Sea Kale.

(Crambe Maritima.)

When well grown, one of the most delicious of vegetables. On the Plains sow from end of September to beginning of November ; in the Hills, February to September. Requires a light, fairly rich soil. Blanch for use, by inverting large earthenware vessels over the plants. The young shoots, when cooked, have a flavour something between Asparagus and Cauliflower, but are much preferred to either. I do not advise the cultivation of the Seakale on the Plains, as it is most difficult to grow, but on the Hills it can be grown to perfection.

# SHALLOTS.

Allium Ascalonicum.—(Vern. Gundhan, Gundana.)

This is a very useful and popular member of the Onion family. The onion-like bulbs are much esteemed by cooks in Europe, where it is grown very largely. On the Plains sow from end of September to beginning of November ; in the Hills, March and April, Requires a light, well manured soil. When large enough thin out the plants to about 6 inches apart.

Shallots, Jersey.

The bulbs can be taken up, dried and stored, or may be left in the grouud and dug up as needed.

The variety usually grown is the *Jersey* which has much larger roots than the old common sort.

# SPINACH.

## Spinacea Oleracea.—(Vern.—Paluk, Isfanaj, Punees.)

On the Plains sow from the beginning of September to the beginning of December; in the Hills sowings may be made practically all the year round, except from December to February; late sowings, however, should only be made of the Prickly variety. Sowings should be made in succession, as the Spinach matures very quickly. Requires a rich but friable soil, and plenty of water should be given right through the period of growth. I think it is better to sow in drills than broad cast; the drills should be about a foot apart and when the plants are well up, they should be thinned in the drills to about a foot apart. To induce strong, healthy growth an occasional watering with liquid manure will be found useful. 1 ounce of seed will sow a row of about 60 feet.

SPINACH, PRICKLY.

The following are amongst the best of the varieties in cultivation. *Bloomsdale or American Savoy*:—I give an illustration of this sort which shows its splendid form. The leaves are large, thick, heavy and finely curled. In quality it is unequalled, while its productiveness is something wonderful. *Henderson's Savoy Leaved*:—An American introduction of excellent quality. Is of very fast growth, and remains in use for a long time before running to seed. *Monstrous Viroflay*:—A sort which is very largely grown in France. The leaves are round and extra large. *Victoria* (*Veitch*):—More robust and larger than the old *Round*. As this is a vigorous grower it requires rather more room in the drills than the ordinary sorts. *New Zealand Spinach* (Tetragonia Expansa.):—Very useful to supply the place of the ordinary Spinach during the hottest months of the year, or in dry, arid localities where the ordinary Spinach does badly. The seed is sown where the plants are to stand, on the Plains during October, in the Hills, March to beginning of June. The plants will continue to yield a supply of good leaves, of excellent quality, during the

entire summer, requiring hardly any attention. Other good sorts are :—*Long Standing Round, Prickly or Winter, &c.*

---

# SQUASHES.

### Cucurbita pepo or Melopepo. (Vern.-Kumra.)

On the Plains sowings can be made from the end of February to the beginning of April ; in the Hills sow from the end of March to the beginning of June. "Firminger" says that the seeds should be sown in Lower Bengal about the end of October. Sow the seeds in very richly manured soil. The Squash requires much the same treatment as the Pumpkin. The plants require plenty of water, and an occasional drenching with liquid manure is advisable.

Most of the varieties in general cultivation have been introduced in America and these are being added to yearly. In the following list I give some of the best of the varieties and all of them I can strongly recommend.

*Boston Marrow* :—Is of fine flavour and a good keeper. The Boston markets are completely stocked with this variety. Visitors to Boston are very liable to be impressed with the idea that the Bostonians live entirely on Squashes, from the enormous quantity to be seen in the markets. *Bush Summer Crookneck*: —Very early and of large size. Orange yellow colour covered with warty excrescenses. A much exteemed variety. The illustration I give shows the peculiar form of this most excellent sort. *Cocozelle Bush* :—This is a distinct type of Bush Squash. The plants grow very compact and uniform in height and the vines do not run. The Squashes are oblong in shape, green and white striped. A remarkable feature of this variety is, that the little green Squashes when still very small, only two to four inches long, are most delicious in flavour. They can either be boiled whole or sliced and fried like Egg Plant, and are nearly, if not quite, equal in flavour, while of course, they are more easily raised. *Delicata* :—The fruit is of most handsome appearance ; the ground colour is orange yellow, splashed and striped with very dark green. The "Delicata" is very early and extremely prolific ; from twenty-four plants one grower has gathered no fewer than 352 perfect fruits. Although of small size, this variety is wonderfully solid and heavy. The quality is splendid, being rich and dry, similar in this respect to the well known Fordhook Squash. *Essex Hybrid* :—A very productive Squash, of the finest quality and an excellent keeper. It is one of the richest flavoured, finest grained, and sweetest of all squashes, while at the same time it is one of the most productive, the fruits growing close together on the vines and averaging from eight to twelve pounds in weight ; of quick growth. *Henderson's "Golden Custard"* :—The beautiful illustration which I give on page 81 conveys a good idea of the appearance and manner of growth of this most excellent sort. This variety exceeds in size any of the scalloped-edged sorts, frequently attaining a diameter of 2 feet. In colour a dark, rich golden-yellow, while for quality it cannot be excelled. *Hubbard*:—The standard Squash

SQUASH, BUSH SUMMER CROOKNECK.

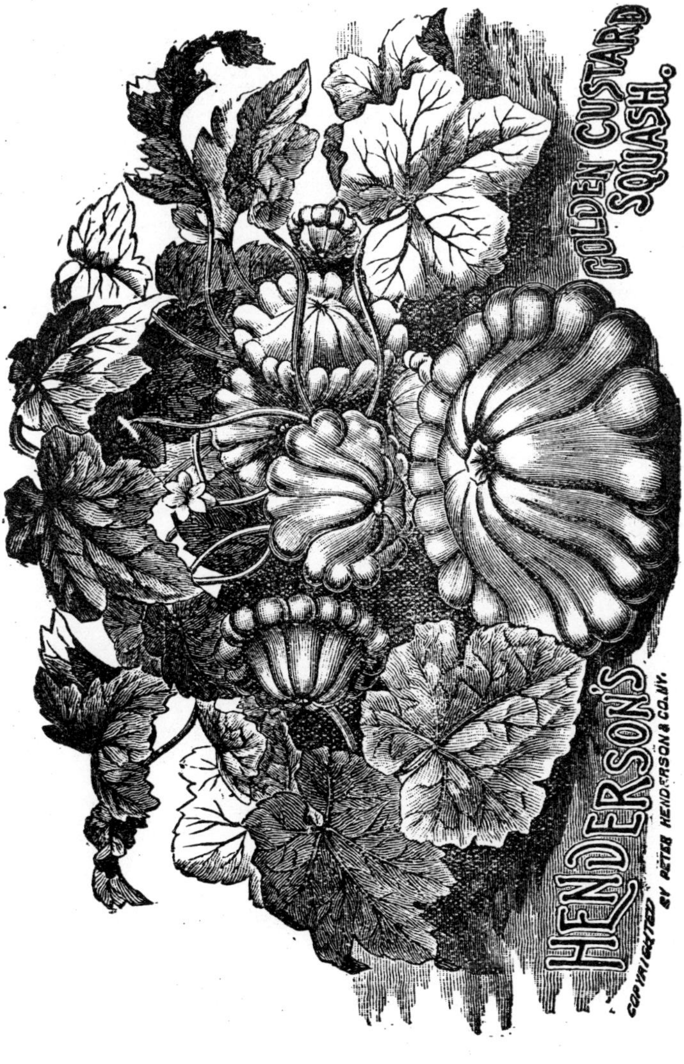
HENDERSON'S
GOLDEN CUSTARD SQUASH.
COPYRIGHTED BY PETER HENDERSON & CO. N.Y.

excellent for table use, of good size, dry, fine grained flesh, and a good keeper. *Mammoth Chili*:—This is the "*Jumbo*" of the Squash family, and all the so-called "Mammoth" Squashes, of different names, owe their capacity for large growth to this parent variety. The form is round, flattened at both stem and blossom end. The outer colour is a rich orange-yellow; the skin is quite smooth, with wide fissures. The flesh is very thick and of a rich yellow colour; the quality is good and very nutritious. They are most profitable to grow for stock feeding.

SQUASH, MAMMOTH CHILI,

**The Fordhook**.—The engraving, accurately reproduced from a photograph, shows the shape of the Squashes and the solidity of section. The size is most convenient for family use, and appearance extremely handsome, of a bright yellow outside and straw yellow within. The flesh is extremely dry and very sweet—making it one of the best in quality, of all Winter Squashes It seems incapable of rotting, and placed in a cool, dry room, keeps in perfect condition. With such a remarkable keeper the skin is so very thin and delicate that the Squashes are prepared for the table by simply cutting in half lengthwise and cooking skin and all. The meat is very thick, and the seed cavity small. Another feature which is altogether unique, is, that the green Squashes can be used at any stage of their growth; when sliced and fried they are of such consistency that they never fall to pieces, and in flavour are superior to any summer Squash. The "Fordhook" is thus really an "*all-the-year round*" Squash and must prove of great value, not only for the family garden but also for market, where its decidedly handsome appearance, unequalled flavour, and convenient size, will render it quickly saleable.

Other good varieties much grown are :—*Early Prolific Marrow, White Bush Scalloped, Marblehead, White Pineapple or White Turban, &c.*

---

# Tiparee or Cape Gooseberry.

## Physalis Edulis or Peruviana.

### (Vern.—Tiparee, Tupureea, Poopteh.)

PHYSALIS EDULIS (Tiparee.)

On the Plains sow at any time from the beginning of April to the end of June; on the Hills, April and May. The seed of the Tiparee is obtainable in any of the native bazars, but I advise readers to obtain a supply of imported seed, as the local varieties deteriorate very much and it is always advisable to get a "change of seed." The Tiparee is by no means particular as to the quality of the soil, but, of course, does best when it is given a little care. Plant in a rich, open soil, which has been well drained. The seeds can be sown broadcast in beds, and when the young plants are about 4 or 5 inches high, they can be transplanted into the prepared gound at a distance of about 3 to 4 feet apart. During warm weather give plenty of water.

The variety usually grown is *Physalis Edulis or Peruviana,* but a new variety has lately been introduced from Japan, with a great flourish of trumpets. I do not think the new kind is worth growing in the vegetable garden, as the fruits are not a patch on the old variety in flavour. This variety is called *Franchetti.* I do advise the planting of this kind in the flower garden, as it has a very handsome appearance with its enormous orange-red seed pods. The plants which grow to a height of about 2 feet, look well when grown in pots, and are useful for decoration.

---

# TOMATO.

## Lycopersicum esculentum.

(Vern.—Bilatee Baigan, Goot Baigan.)

Sow from June to beginning of November on the Plains. The first sowings are best raised in pans or boxes, and the seedlings put out when 6 or 8 inches high. They should be planted in well-manured soil, in rows three feet apart, with the same distance between the plants. When practicable, a bamboo trellis should be placed along each row, about three feet high, to which the plants may be trained. In England, it is customary to pinch out the point of each shoot to induce them to set their fruit; here, however, this is quite unnecessary; they require no care beyond an occasional watering and tying up. A drenching with liquid manure now and then will be found very beneficial, as the Tomato is a rather gross feeder. Sow in April or May in the Hills.

An enormous number of varieties of Tomatoes have been introduced of late years, but the following list comprises most of the best.

*Acme* :—Fruit of fine shape and smooth outline; purplish-crimson colour and very prolific. *Cardinal* :—Colour brilliant cardinal-red; fruit solid, of good size. The plants are very productive. *Challenger* :—Fruit of good size, very deep, solid and heavy; of bright scarlet colour, grand flavour, very fleshy, and with but little core; free setting, wonderfully prolific, and a continuous bearer. *Chemin Rouge* :—The vines are very healthy, vigorous in growth and of *marvellous productiveness,* bearing bunches of ten to fifteen fruits each. As shown in the illustration on page 85, the Tomatoes are very distinct in form, being almost perfectly *apple shaped* and of fine flavour, the roundness and bright scarlet colour making them very attractive in appearance. The

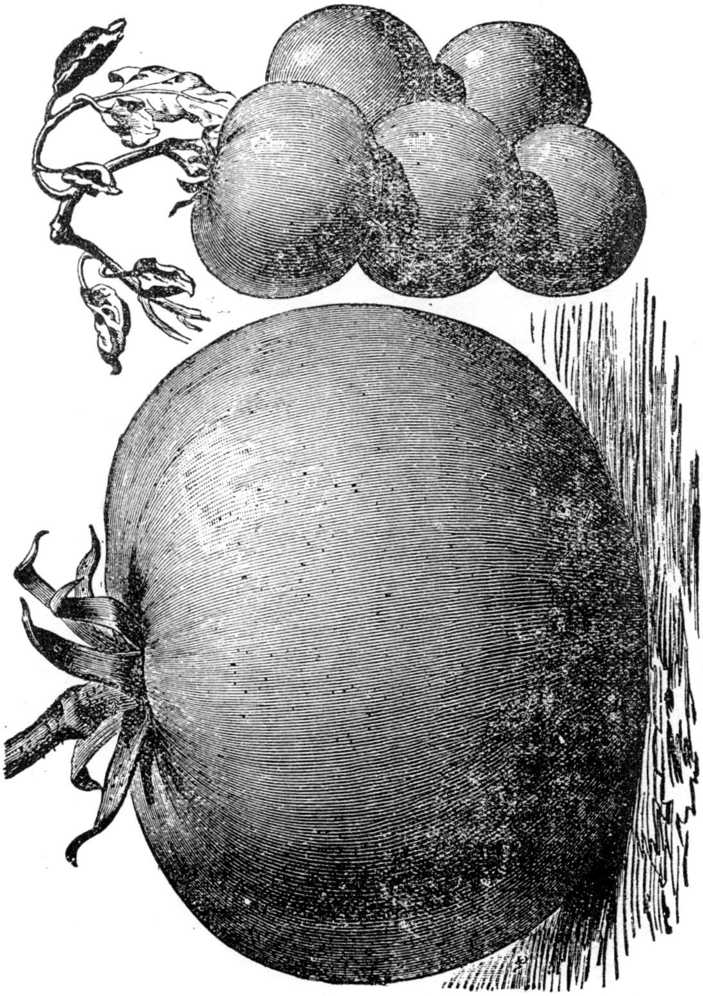

TOMATO, CHEMIN ROUGE.

fruits are *very solid,* without any hard core; they are borne early, and continuously throughout the season. A lady writing from Kumaon says of this variety :—"Out of the Tomato seed sown, from some of the plants I have taken Tomatoes weighing from 1 lb. to nearly 2 lbs. each. These were from the "Chemin Rouge' kind." *Conference* :—This fine Tomato was distributed privately to the Fellows of the Royal Horticultural Society and excited the admiration of all who saw it at the Vegetable Conference. It is very handsome, perfectly round and smooth, very firm and solid, of delicious flavour, and bright glossy red colour. *Crimson Emperor* :—This Tomato is a cross between the celebrated American variety "New Jersey" and "The Trophy." The colour of the fruit is a rich glossy crimson and the flesh very solid. The even shape of the fruit will make it a general favourite both in the market and private gardens. *Dunedin Favourite*:—This splendid variety will be found an invaluable acquisition to all who have to provide a continuous supply of this indispensable fruit, either for private or market purposes. It is one of the earliest and for quality and flavour cannot be beaten. The following description of this variety appeared in the *Gar-"dener's Chronicle.* Among fifteen varieties, "Dunedin Favourite" "was the earliest to ripen, and the first fruits were as perfectly symmetrical "as those that followed. The flesh is peculiarly rich, and contains "but few seeds; the colour is a very attractive combination of deep scarlet "and crimson, and the skin is glossy. In weight it exceeds all others, "being very solid, and with little or no core, whilst its level and re-'gular shape is a great advantage in packing for market." *Early Ruby* :—The great value of this variety lies in the fact that it is one of the earliest of the large sized Tomatoes, and combines good form, rich crimson colour and solidity. It is certain to prove itself to be one of the best varieties. *Empress of India* :—This is a cross between "Ham Green" and "Perfection," and is of exceptionally fine quality. The fruits are of a beautiful bright scarlet colour, very massive and solid, without ribs, well flavoured and wonderfully prolific, the plants carrying 9 or 10 bunches of fruit weighing $2\frac{1}{2}$ to 3 lbs. per bunch. *Goldfinder* :—Is of beautiful form, brilliant scarlet colour and exquisite flavour. The flesh is solid and contains very few seeds. It is specially remarkable for its profuse and continuous bearing. *Golden Queen* :—The tomatoes are of large size, handsome round shape, very smooth free from ridges and ripen up evenly. They are early and very productive, of good, substance and excellent for slicing, the handsome yellow slices making a beautiful contrast in a dish with red tomatoes. *Golden Sunrise* :—This splendid variety has all the good qualities of the red sorts but is of a beautiful golden yellow colour, making it invaluable for slicing and mixing with red varieties for table use. *Greengage*:—Rich citron-coloured, semi-transparent fruit. It is particularly early and prolific, and the deliciously piquant flavour, described as "a beautiful blending of the Apple and Tomato," has secured for it the most universal admiration. *King Humbert, Red*:—Smooth, glossy scarlet fruit, of the size and shape of a large plum, unsurpassed for productiveness, and one of the earliest sorts grown. This is one of the best varieties for early sowing on the Plains. *King Humbert, White*:—This remarkable kind also occupies a first place as an abundant bearer and for the excellent flavour of its fruits, which are of a wax-white colour. For mixing with the yellow and red Tomatoes this variety is certain to become extremely popular. *Mikado*:—One of the most remarkable features about this variety is that, notwithstanding it produces perhaps the largest fruit of any sort in cultivation, it is at the same time one of the very earliest to ripen; generally we find that we secure earliness at the expense of size, but the "Mikado" seemingly reverses the rule. The "Mikado" differs from all other Tomatoes, in its immense size and the fruits produced in immense clusters, are perfectly solid, generally smooth but sometimes irregular. The colour is purplish red, like that of the "Acme," while the variety has all the solidity that characterizes the "Trophy." It is not unusual for single fruits of this variety to weigh from 1 to $1\frac{1}{2}$ lbs. each. The foliage of the "Mikado" alone shows the distinctiveness of the variety, for it is whole or entire, while in all other varieties the leaves are cut or serrated. If I were asked to name the two best red Tomatoes in cultivation I would not hesitate in mentioning "Chemin Rouge" and "Mikado." *The Peach*:—A splendid variety, extremely ornamental, the ripe fruit exactly resembling a well-coloured Peach. The illustration I give shows better than any description could, the unique appearance of this sterling sort. "*Ponderosa*":—Messrs. Peter Henderson and Co.,—the introducers of so many grand novelties—a few years ago offered a number of large prizes for the best specimens of "The Ponderosa," and in response, some really wonderful fruits were sent, the first prize of 150 dollars being carried off by a fruit turning the scale at no less than 3 lbs; the first ten fruits ranging from 2 lbs. 6 ozs. to 3 lbs. The fruits of this wonderful variety are almost perfect in form, and so free from ridges or corrugations, as to appear as smooth as glass. A great peculiarity is that it is nearly seedless. Although of such enormous size, it is—unlike most abnormally large fruits—as early as most of the older sorts, whose only merit is that they are early. One grower writing of this giant says "*it is nealy as firm as an apple.*"

*President Garfield*:—A variety of extraordinary size, bearing fruit weighing from 2 to 3 lbs. each; very luxuriant and prolific. *Trophy, Selected*:—The popularity of the Trophy is equal to that of any other variety, and it will always be regarded with great favour by all growers. This variety is noted for its solidity and beauty. *The Shah*:—Identical with the Mikado in every respect except in colour (which is a dark, waxy yellow), having the same distinct foliage, the same enormous size, solidity and productiveness. Alternate slices of red and golden Tomatoes make one of the most ornamental dishes. *Flying Dutchman, (Veitch's)*:—The idea in naming this new Tomato "Flying Dutchman" is to indicate its marvellous earliness for a variety of *first class* quality. it is *very* early, of a splendid scarlet colour, and fruits at an early stage of its growth. By nipping off the top shoot, fine fruit can be had on a very dwarf plant. The size and weight of the individual fruits is very considerable, and the flavour first-rate. *Yorkshire Wonder*:—A tremendous cropper; ripens early. The fruit is very even in size, solid and of good quality,

Amongst other really first class Tomatoes I would mention the following, most of which are too well known to require any description :—

Champion, Optimus, Essex Early Hybrid, Favourite, Golden Trophy, Large Red, Mayflower, Paragon, Pear Shaped, Perfection, Prelude, Red Currant or Grape, Volunteer, &c.

# TURNIPS.

## Brassica rapa—(Vern.—Shalgum or Selgum.)

TURNIP, HALF LONG RED TOP VERTUS.

A rich, deep mellow soil, with a fair amount of moisture, is the most favourable for Turnips, although any good soil, well dug and manured, will grow them well. On the Plains sowings should be commenced in September and continued at intervals of a few days up to the end of November; in the Hills, March to end of June and after the rains. They should be sown in drills about twelve inches apart, and as soon as the plants are large enough, they should be thinned out to the same distance in the rows. The plants must be kept free from weeds, and the soil frequently loosened around them. They must also be kept freely supplied with water, and occasionally drenched with liquid manure. 1 oz. of seed will sow a drill 100 feet long.

In the following list I describe only sorts that have been grown in India and have done well.

TURNIP, EARLY SNOW-WHITE GLOBE.

*Chirk Castle Black Stone* :—Black skin, flesh pure white, sweet and juicy, hardy; a useful sort for late use. *Early Snow White Globe* :—This is one of the best formed varieties known, of pure snow-white colour, and almost as round as a ball ; a very desirable and productive early market variety ; is far superior to the White Globe for a general crop. See engraving for the form of this fine variety. *Early Red American Stone, or Strap Leaf* :—Very early, flesh white and firm, keeps well. *Early Snowball* :—One of the best whites, flesh sweet and tender ; very select stock, of beautiful shape. See illustration on page 91 *Early Purple Top Munich.*—A distinct and very early variety, one of the finest in cultivation. *Extra Early Milan Strap-leaf* :—The earliest variety, in cultivation, of fine shape and excellent quality. First Class Certificate Royal Horticultural Society. See illustration on page 91. *Golden Ball* (*Robertson's*) :—Rapid grower, excellent flavour, globe shaped, and of a beautiful bright yellow colour ; a good keeper, and has no superior for table use. See engraving on page 91. *Half Long White Forcing* :—A remarkably early white variety. The best for forcing (see cut.) *Half Long Red Top Vertus* :—A very popular French variety. The illustration gives a good idea of the form. *Large Red Top Globe* :—This is a variety of recent introduction, of large size and globe form. Is of rapid growth, very productive, and of the same character and habits as the Red Top Flat, differing only in its shape and leaves ; can be sown either broadcast or in drills. Flesh pure white, with a red or purple top. A very desirable variety and destined to become very popular. *Late*

*Auvergne* :—A splendid French variety producing fine, well shaped roots, quite 6 inches in diameter, and 3 to 4 inches deep; flesh solid and of fine flavour. I recommend this for a late crop. *Moore's Warwick or Early Green Top Stone*:—A very choice variety of quick growth and fine flavour; strongly recommended. *Scarlet Kashmyr* :—This variety is a "first early." Small, rarely exceeding three inches in diameter; shape inclined to flat. The leaves are few and small. The outer colour is rich crimson scarlet, the interior pure white; flesh crisp, tender, fine-grained and exceedingly solid. *Selected Flat White Dutch* :—This is a vast improvement on the ordinary Dutch variety; bulbs smooth and free from cracks, very delicate flavour, and the earliest of all varieties. *Selected Flat Red Dutch* :—Resembling the preceding in every respect except in colour. *Veitch's Red Globe* :—A useful sort for late sowing, remains fit for use a long time; handsome shape, very hardy and superior quality. *White Egg* :—Its shape is nearly ovoid or egg-shaped; flesh very firm and fine grained, skin thin and perfectly smooth; skin and flesh are of snowy whiteness. Its flavour is of the very best, mild and sweet. *Yellow Altringham* :-One of the best of the yellow varieties. *Yellow Dutch* :—This variety in appearance exactly resembles the White Dutch, except that the flesh is of a bright golden yellow.

TURNIP, HALF LONG WHITE FORCING.

*Yellow Montmagny* :—A very handsome variety; outer colour dark yellow below ground, and of a dark violet red in the portion above ground; roots about 6 inches in diameter, and 3 or more deep; flesh yellow, firm, tender and of good quality. The very striking contrast between the yellow and the red parts of the root, gives it a particularly handsome and pleasing appearance, which, together with its earliness and the superior quality of the flesh, are powerful recommendations in its favour. It is one of the most agreeably flavoured of all garden varieties of Turnip, especially when taken young before it has attained its full size.

THREE TABLE TURNIPS
GOLDEN BALL
Early Snowball
EXTRA EARLY MILAN

# TURNIP, SWEDISH or RUSSIAN.

### Brassica Campestris Var. Rutabaga.

These require the same culture as the ordinary Garden Turnips, except that they should be thinned out rather farther apart, as they grow to an enormous size. Very many people enjoy the flavour of the "Swedes" and a small patch in the garden will be useful, because if not wanted for table use, they are eaten greedily by horses and cattle.

The best sorts are the following.

*Dickson's Defiance Prize Purple Top* :—Is of globular shape, rind deep purple, clean shoulders, small neck and top. *Hurst's Monarch* :—The flavour is remarkably sweet, and the bulbs are formed very early. The tops are of a rich plum colour, more than purple, which gives the tubers a most marked and distinctive appearance. *Crimson King* :—Flesh very solid, of a deep golden-yellow; top of bulb bright crimson. *Laing's Selected* :—A very fine variety with rich golden-yellow flesh. *Lord Derby* :—A bronze-top variety of fine rich quality and robust constitution.

# VEGETABLE MARROW.

### Cucurbita Pepo.—(Vern.—Sufuree Koomra.)

On the Plains sow from beginning of February to end of April; in the Hills, beginning of March to end of June. Requires a very rich, well manured soil, and the same treatment as the ordinary Squash, of which this is really a variety. The plants must be given plenty of water throughout the entire period of their growth, while occasional waterings with liquid manure will greatly improve the crop.

VEGETABLE MARROW.

The following are amongst the best varieties :—

*Custard* :—A free bearing sort, of fine flavour. *Hibberd's Prolific* :—Small, well shaped fruit, of excellent flavour ; very early and prolific. *Italian Striped* :—Of fine flavour and very prolific. *King's Acre Cream* :—A distinct variety, recommended for its fine flavour. *Long White Ribbed*:—A very large, prolific variety. This sort I specially recommend. *Moore's Vegetable Cream* :—A splendid variety, one of the best for general use, very prolific and of delicious flavour. *Pen-y-byd* ("The best in the World." *Welsh*):—A very prolific and distinct variety. The fruits are very handsome, averaging about 6 inches in diameter, and are of a delicate creamy white colour, with thick, firm flesh, which when cooked, is of finest quality and delicate flavour. Highly recommended.

# Periods of Maturing of Garden Crops.

As many people enquire as to the time certain crops take to mature from time of sowing, I have taken the following particulars from a very useful American booklet entitled "*Vegetables for the Home Garden.*" The times given are, of course, taken from trials made in America and will be found practically correct with regard to gardening on the Hills, but for the Plains, readers may safely deduct some days, as crops mature more rapidly than they will in a colder climate.

| | Days. | | Days. |
|---|---|---|---|
| Artichoke, Globe, ... | 120 to 130 | Lettuce, ... | 40 to 65 |
| Beans, Dwarf, ... | 43 to 70 | Maize, Earliest, ... | 55 to 75 |
| ,, ,, Lima, ... | 78 to 90 | ,, Late, ... ... | 85 to 95 |
| ,, Runner, ... | 110 to 120 | Melons, Musk, Earliest, | 90 to 100 |
| Beet, Early, ... ... | 50 to 65 | ,, ,, Main Crop, | 115 to 140 |
| ,, Medium, ... | 60 to 70 | ,, Water, ... | 120 to 140 |
| ,, Late, ... ... | 140 to 150 | Okra, ... ... | 90 to 105 |
| Borecole, or Kale, ... | 100 to 130 | Onions, Earliest, ... | 100 to 110 |
| Bròccoli, ... ... | 120 to 145 | ,, Main Crop ... | 130 to 160 |
| Brussels Sprouts, ... | 140 to 150 | Parsnips, ... ... | 125 to 140 |
| Cabbage, Early, ... | 100 to 110 | Peas, Earliest, ... | 49 to 60 |
| ,, Late, ... | 140 to 160 | ,, Main Crop, ... | 65 to 88 |
| Capsicums, ... ... | 135 to 160 | Pumpkins, ... ... | 105 to 120 |
| Carrot, Early, ... | 70 to 100 | Radish, Earliest, ... | 18 to 22 |
| ,, Late ... ... | 110 to 120 | ,, Later Sorts, ... | 25 to 45 |
| Cauliflower, .. ... | 105 to 115 | Salsify, ... ... | 130 to 140 |
| Celery, ... ... | 140 to 175 | Spinach, ... ... | 21 to 30 |
| Corn Salad. ... ... | 60 to 65 | ,, New Zealand, | 40 to 55 |
| Cress, ... ... | 30 to 40 | Squash, Summer, ... | 55 to 65 |
| Cucumber, Earliest, ... | 50 to 55 | ,, Winter, ... | 115 to 125 |
| ,, Main Crop, | 65 to 75 | Tomato, Earliest, ... | 90 to 100 |
| Egg Plant, ... ... | 145 to 160 | ,, Main Crop ... | 125 to 150 |
| Endive, ... | 43 to 50 | Turnips, ... ... | 60 |

# The Flower Garden.

This part of my subject is a big one, but I will do my best to give information which will be of real practical use to my readers.

There are some points connected with the Flower Garden which require careful attention in order to ensure the beautiful flowers, which are the ambition of most amateur gardeners.

I think *the* point which cannot be to much emphasised is, that however good the mali may be, he requires constant supervision. Many gardeners have been very much disappointed when their seeds have failed to germinate, while in neighbouring gardens the plants are luxuriating. Probably the seeds have been got from the same dealer, but in one case the mali has been left to himself for the sowing, while in the other, the employer has stood over him while the work was being done. Often Mr. Mali is not averse to earning an honest (?) rupee by selling his master's seed to one of his brother malis.

However it is not only through the dishonesty of the gardener that employers are often disappointed, but also through the crass ignorance of the men. Seeds which should barely be covered with soil will be sown a couple of inches deep, the watering pot will be used much too freely, or else not at all. Personally I would prefer the latter, as almost enough moisture is given by the dew to keep the soil sufficiently moist for seedlings. A great fault I have had to find with gardeners, European as well as native, is that they like to have their seed beds as smooth as billiard tables. Before sowing, use a rake to loosen and roughen the surface of the soil and then rake after sowing and the seeds will, in most cases, have quite as much covering as they require. If we consider that in Nature the seed has to rely on the rain or the scratching of birds for what covering it gets, we will see how unnatural it it to *bury* seed inches deep. In sowing seeds of small seeded plants in pots I have followed the following plan, which I have found very successful. Seeds of such things as Begonias, Gloxinias, Petunias &c., which are very tiny, really require no covering with soil whatever, so when sowing such, I take the number of flower pots required, half fill them with crocks—broken flower pots, stones, &c.—cover this with a thin covering of moss, to prevent the drainage being blocked, then fill up to about a quarter of an inch from the top with good soil, composed of about equal parts of loam, sand and leaf mould. I leave the top of the compost rather rough, then thinly scatter the seed over, cover with a piece of glass and place in a green-house; a glazed verandah will, of course, answer just as well. I keep the soil just damp by dipping the pots for a minute or so into a can of water. I think this style of watering is infinitely better than the over-head style, however carefully it may be done. Readers must often have found their seed germinate all on one side of the box or pot and may have wondered why: I think it has only been through the seed having been washed to one side by the over-head watering. In addition to the piece of glass over the pots, readers will find a piece of newspaper an improvement, as seeds germinate more quickly in a fairly dull light than in bright light. The glass, of course, is used to maintain a fairly equable temperature and also to prevent too rapid evaporation, which would necessitate frequent watering. It is well in most cases to transplant the seedlings at least once, before the plants are finally planted out where they are to bloom. In the case of pot plants I like to give three or four shifts. First pot off the tiny seedlings into thumb pots, then when they have rooted well, shift on into larger pots, placing the whole of the contents of the thumb pots into the larger ones and filling up with fairly rich soil. This should be repeated three or four times till the plants are in the pots in which they are to flower. There are some varieties which will not bear transplanting. It is difficult to transplant things like Nasturtiums, Sweet Peas, &c., but a plan I have followed when I have wanted to get the plants for transplanting in special places, has been to sow two or three seeds in a thumb pot and then when the plants are well up, transplant by making a hole where I have wanted to put the plants, just large enough to contain the contents of the pots; then carefully knocking the soil and plants out of the pots, have placed the ball of earth into the hole, filled up with earth and firmed down round the plants. By this means even Sweet Peas or Nasturtiums can be safely transplanted. Care must be taken not to use fresh manure when preparing flower beds. The older the manure the better it is in most cases. I have often used manure which has been lying for ten years until it has become like black earth and have found it splendid stuff for potting or for beds. Liquid manure is very useful and is easily made, but as it is not very odorous, it is best to make it at some distance from the house. Get an old tub or barrel and about half fill it with fresh cow-dung or horse droppings, well cover with water and allow it to stand for a few days, giving an occasional stirring The liquid can be taken out and diluted with water, as it is a great mistake to give too strong liquid manure It is as well to put the manure in an old gunny bag before putting into the tub, as the liquid will then be free from solid matter A splendid liquid manure is made with "Ichthemic" Guano. Use one tablespoonful of the manure to a gallon of water. Allow to stand for a day or so and stir well before using. The solution should be given about three times a week. Readers will find "Ichthemic" a very reliable manure

In the following notes I have tried to give as much information as is necessary for the proper cultivation of the various plants treated of. In a handbook of this size it is quite impossible to give the exact times for sowing in the various districts, but in the Calendars I give at the end of the book, I have given information for as many districts as possible

## Abronia.

Nat. Ord.—Nyctaginaceæ.—(*Sand Verbena.*)

Very pretty creeping or trailing Annuals, the flowers of which are much like Verbenas. Make excellent pot plants and are also useful for bedding. On the Plains sow from end of September to beginning of November; in the Hills during April and May. Do not water too freely as they are apt to damp off. *A. Umbellata* has bright rose, sweet scented flowers, *A. Villosa,* which is a very free flowering variety, bears dark red flowers, while *A. Arenaria* bears dense clusters of lemon-yellow, honey scented blooms.

## Abutilon.

Nat. Ord.—Malvaceæ.—(*Chinese Bell Flower. Vern.—Jhoomka.*)

ABUTILON.

This is a very showy and free growing shrub which is deserving of much more extensive cultivation. As its common name implies the flowers are bell shaped and are borne profusely. On the Plains sow in seed pans during September and October; April and May in the Hills. When the seedlings are about 3 inches high they should be planted out in good rich soil. The Abutilon likes plenty of water, but care must be taken to give thorough drainage. An occasional soaking with weak liquid manure during the flowering period will be found very beneficial. There are a great number of hybrids of this beautiful shrub, but few gardeners out here will need more than a few plants, and it is much better to get a packet of good mixed seed, as from it a great number of fine varieties will be procured. A comparatively new variety called *A. Snowball* (Boule de Neige) is becoming very popular. The flowers are a beautiful snow-white, upwards of 3 inches in diameter and the plants are literally covered with them. In *A. Darwini* we have a very distinct variety with large, bright orange coloured flowers, which are deeply veined with shades of crimson. The plants grow to a height of about 4 feet and are of a good bushy habit. Most of the hybrid Abutilons have been obtained from *Darwini.* For those who want a mixture of colours, but do not feel inclined to invest in separate packets of different varieties, I can strongly recommend the *George's Hybrids.* In this strain will be found plants of very dwarf habit, free flowering, flowers of very large size and of almost every shade of colour.

——:o:——

# Acacia.

### Nat. Ord.—Leguminoseæ. (The Wattle.)

Belongs to the family of the Babool and Phulaee of the native.

Unfortunately the Acacia cannot be grown with any amount of success on the Plains of Bengal; in the Punjab however, they grow well, while on the Hills they, of course, luxuriate. There are several Acacias which are natives of India, such as *A. Farnesiana*, but they are very jungly looking plants and quite unsuitable for the flower garden. Amongst the prettiest of the many varieties are *A. Dealbata* and *A. Lophantha.* The former of these is commonly known as the Silver Wattle of Tasmania and grows to a height of from 10 to 20 feet. In *Lophantha* the fern-like foliage makes it very useful for decoration. Both these varieties are easily grown from seed, which should be sown in October on the Plains and April or May on the Hills. Plant in sandy soil with good drainage.

———

# ∴ Achimines. ∴

### Nat. Ord, Gesneraceæ.

This is one of the most beautiful of the gesneraceous plants and is very popular in India, where it grows well. They are most easily grown from tubers, which can be obtained from any Seedsman or Nurseryman. On the Plains the tubers should be started into growth in February or March; about the beginning of May on the Hills. I always grow my Achimines in shallow seed pans about 12 inches in diameter by about 3 inches deep. They are very pretty when grown in hanging baskets, or can be grown in balls of moss and soil wired round and hung from the roofs of verandahs. In potting the soil used must be very open, composed principally of sand, with a little fibrous loam and leaf mould added. Many people add cocoanut fibre to the compost, which is said to be an improvement. Achimines may also be grown from seed, which should be sown on the Hills at any time from February to April; on the Plains sow about the same time, where a sowing should also be made in October.

ACHIMINES.

---:o:---

# Acroclinium.

### Nat. Ord.—Compositæ.

This is one of the prettiest of the everlasting flowers and is well worth cultivation. The dried flowers retain their colour for a long time and are very useful for decoration when flowers are scarce. They look very pretty arranged in vases with dried grasses. Sow on the Plains in October or November: middle of March to end of May in the Hills. Sow in pots and plant out either in rows or beds. They luxuriate in a loamy soil. Cut the flowers when young, if required as dry flowers.

ACROCLINIUM FLORE PLENO.

There are two colours—white and rose—both single and double. In the single flowered varieties the flowers consist of a single row of petals with bright yellow centres. The doubles are particularly beautiful and are best adapted for drying. I give an illustration which shows the form of these very pretty flowers. I might say that the flowers of the Acroclinium are much used as Immortelles for making funeral wreaths.

---

# Adonis Flos.

Adonis Flos.

(*Syn.* **Flos Adonis**)

Nat. Ord.—Ranunculaceæ.

(Pheasant's Eye.)

This is a very pretty little annual, with dark green foliage and bright crimson flowers. Should be grown in masses, in a moist, shady situation. Grows best in very light soil. On the Plains sow in September and October; beginning of March to middle of May in the Hills. There are two annual varieties commonly grown :—*A. Æstivalis* with deep crimson flowers, and *A. Autumnalis* in which the flowers are of an intense blood-red with black centres. Each of these grow to a height of 1 foot

—:o:—

# Agapanthus.

Nat. Ord.—Liliaceæ.

(The Blue African Lily, or the Blue Nile Lily.)

This is one of the most beautiful of all the bulbous plants and is easily raised from seed, which should be sown on the Plains in October. The plant is very common in Hill gardens and bulbs can easily be obtained, as it increases quickly and can readily be divided. Where bulbs cannot be got, the seed should be sown in the Autumn as soon as it has ripened. The variety commonly grown is *A. Umbellatus* which grows to a height of some three feet and bears large umbels of handsome azure-blue flowers.

# Agathæa.

Nat. Ord.—Compositæ. (Blue Marguerite.)

The Agathæa is closely allied to the Cineraria and requires much the same treatment. It grows to a height of about $1\frac{1}{2}$ feet and the one variety, *A. Cœlestis*, has pretty sky-blue flowers. This is a Perennial of herbaceous habit. Although it has been in cultivation for many years, having been discovered in 1753 at the Cape, it is but little grown, but is well worth extensive cultivation, as it can be kept in flower practically the whole year round.

——:o:——

# Ageratum (Cœlestinum.)

Nat. Ord.—Compositæ. (The Floss Flower.)

AGERATUM.

The Ageratum is much used as a bedding plant on account of its free flowering habits ; the flowers remain on the plants for a very long season. It is quite hardy on the Plains, in fact is apt to become quite naturalised and plants spring up year after year from seeds cast by the preceding year's plants. On the Hills they also grow well, but are not so hardy as on the Plains. Sow the seeds in very light, rich, sandy soil, from August to October ; from the beginning of March to middle of May on the Hills. Although of very easy cultivation, it is best to sow in seed pans and transplant when strong enough. As the plants are rather delicate in the early stages of their growth, they should be shaded after transplanting till well established. There are numerous varieties, mostly originating from the old variety *Mexicanum*, differing but little except in colour. A variety which is very useful for an edging is *A. White Gem*, which only grows to a height of some 4 inches and is literally covered with pure white flowers. Other good sorts are :—*Swanley Blue*, very deep blue, 6 to 8 inches high ; *Lasseauxii*, flowers rose coloured, height 1½ to 2 feet ; *Little Dorrit*, a dwarf growing sort with azure blue flowers ; *Imperial Dwarf Blue* and *White*, differ only in colour and grow to a height of about 9 inches, the blue variety being covered with flowers of a delicate porcelain blue ; *Cœruleum*, pale lavender.

## Alonsoa.

### Nat. Ord.—Scrophulariaceæ. (The Mask Flower.)

These are very seldom seen in this country, but are peculiar and pretty, of pyramidal habit, densely covered with bloom As they do not do well when crowded together, they should be grown as single specimens, when they look very well. They are by no means particular about the quality of the soil and will thrive in any ordinary garden soil. On the Plains sow in October ; March and April in the Hills. Sow in pots and when large enough prick out into boxes or beds, transplanting as single specimens when about 3 inches high. There are several varieties differing in the colour of the flowers and habit of growth. *Grandiflora*, is the largest flowering of the species and bears scarlet flowers, but not so freely as some of the other sorts. *A. Linifolia*, the leaves of this variety are shaped liked the Linum (Flax). It grows to a height of some 1 to 1½ feet and is covered with bright scarlet flowers. *A. Warscewiczii compacta*, a dwarf growing sort with rosy scarlet flowers and one I can strongly recommend. *A. White Gem*, in this sort the flowers are of a pretty creamy white.

## Aloysia (Lippia.)

### Nat. Ord.—Verbenaceæ

The lemon scented Verbena is almost too well known to need any description. Few plants have got more names than this has, as it is equally well known as, Aloysia Citriodora, Lippia Citriodora, Verbena Triphylla and Lemon Scented Verbena. However, under whatever name it be known, it is always a welcome guest in the garden. In my garden I have it growing as quite large shrubs, year after year covered with the refreshingly sweet scented leaves. The plants are very easily grown from cuttings made in October on the Plains or in April and May in the Hills. It is also grown from seed which should be sown on the Plains in September and October and March to May in the Hills. As the Aloysia is a rich feeder, it is advisable to give it a top-dressing about twice a year with well rotted manure, while an occasional drenching with liquid manure will greatly improve the growth. The only variety in cultivation is *A. Citriodora*

— —

# Alyssum.

## Nat. Ord.—Cruciferæ (The Mad-wort.)

A very pretty dwarf growing hardy annual, which is much grown in Europe for edging beds. Is of the easiest possible culture, as once established it will grow on year after year from self sown seed. To be really effective should be sown either in fairly wide lines or, better still, in large masses. On the Plains sow from the middle of September to the end of October; Hills middle of March to end of May. Any ordinary garden soil will suit the sweet Alyssum. This is one of the best of the Bee-feeding plants. The variety commonly grown is *A. Maritimum*, which is the common Sweet Alyssum (also known as *Kœniga Maritima*) This variety grows to a height of from 6 to 9 inches. A dwarf form of *Maritimum*, called *Little Gem*, is becoming very popular, as it is much more free flowering than the original and only grows to a height of some 3 or 4 inches. The annexed illustration gives a good idea of the free flowering habit of this beautiful little plant. Readers should give the plants plenty of room, as each will cover a space of about 18 inches in diameter. One grower has counted as many as four hundred clusters of flowers on a single plant. I can recommend this as one of the very best of the dwarf growing hardy annuals

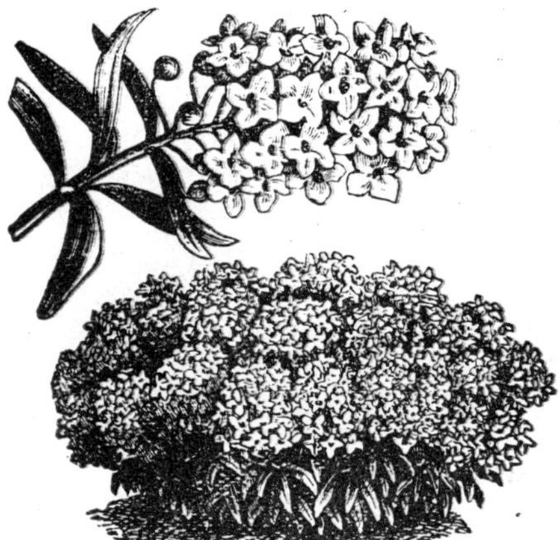

ALYSSUM, LITTLE GEM

# Amaranthus.

## Nat. Ord. Amaranthaceæ. (Amaranth. Vern. Sâg.)

AMARANTHUS, MARGARITÆ.

The *Sâg* is almost too well known to need any description, but there are several varieties now in cultivation which are very little known in India, and which are immense improvements on the old common sorts usually grown, and some of these I shall describe. On the Plains they can be sown both in June and July and also from September to November; in the Hills from the beginning of April to end of June. They can be sown either in the beds in which they are to flower, or better still, in seed pans or boxes and then transplanted into the garden beds when they are about 2 or 3 inches high. Many of the varieties make beautiful pot plants, but must be well fed, both by potting in a rich compost and also with a soaking with liquid manure every ten days. The following are amongst the best of the varieties, but most Seedsmen offer the seed in mixed packets, which will be found best for most gardeners who do not want any special variety. Of course where special beds of Amaranthus are wanted it is better to get separate varieties, as the different sorts vary a good deal in height. *A. Amabilis tricolor*, is a very handsome sort with beautifully coloured leaves of a fine purplish red or dark carmine at the stalk end of the leaves, the middle bright yellow merging off into green at the tips. Grows to a height of $1\frac{1}{2}$ feet. *A. Bicolor ruber*, leaves are of a brilliant shining scarlet which merges into dark reddish violet mixed with green. In *A. Caudatus* we have the old fashioned *Love Lies Bleeding*. A very free flowering variety, in which the flowers are of a dark purplish colour, borne in long, handsome, drooping spikes. This grows about 2 to 3 feet high. *A. Henderi* is one of the most beautiful of the comparatively new varieties and is now becoming very popular. The leaves are rosy carmine, sometimes golden yellow, orange, buff and olive green. Height about 3 feet. *A. Margaritæ* is a beautiful novelty which is entirely distinct from any of the other kinds. The illustration gives an idea of the form of this variety, but no illustration in black and white could possibly portray the beauty of the plants. The flowers are borne on upright spikes and are of the richest crimson, while the plants form dense bushes about 18 inches high and the same in diameter. When well grown the plants appear to be all bloom. *A. Melancholicus ruber* is a Japanese variety which grows about 1 foot high. The plants are very compact, the leaves being very dark shaded crimson. From its dwarf habit and brilliant appearance will be found very useful for bedding. *A. Princess of Wales* is a much taller growing sort, as with ordinary cultivation it attains to a height of 3 feet. The colour of the leaves is beautifully blended with carmine, orange, green and bright yellow. *A. Pyramidalis nobilis* is a very effective variety. Each plant is crowned with an enormous flower spike, from which branches spread in every direction, each bearing spikes of bright purple flowers, each spike being from 8 to 12 inches in length. *A. Salicifolius*, commonly known as the Fountain Plant, grows to a height of about 3 feet ; the leaves, which are of a beautiful willow leaf shape, are from 7 to 15 inches long and are very effective with their bands and tips of orange, carmine and bronze.

# Ampelopsis.

### Nat. Ord. Ampelideæ. (Virginian Creeper.)

This is a very popular creeper in Europe and is of very rapid growth. In 3 years I have seen a double storied house completely covered from top to bottom. It grows splendidly on the Hills, where there are several wild varieties. I fear it would not thrive in most places on the Plains, but as it is a really beautiful plant, it would be well worth trying. Is usually grown from cuttings which strike readily if made from the soft wood in the Spring on the Hills. One great advantage that this plant has over most climbers is, that when established it requires absolutely no nailing, as the plants are covered with tiny suckers, which cling to the stone of the wall and so support the plants. On the Hills seed should be sown in the Autumn under cover and the plants should be planted out about April or May. The variety commonly grown is known under several names, such as, *A. Veitchii*, *A. Japonica* and *A. Tricuspidata*. The first name is the most common one. I believe this variety was introduced from Japan by Messrs. Veitch and Co., of London some 30 or 35 years ago. On the Hills the leaves turn to most magnificent colours in the autumn before falling off. I should say that the plant is deciduous, that is, it casts its leaves in the autumn and throws out a fresh lot in the spring.

## Antigonon.

Nat. Ord.—Polygonaceæ. (Mountain Rose of the West Indies or the Sandwich Island Climber.)

A fairly common creeper on the Plains and one of the most beautiful in cultivation. Is very free flowering and remains in flower for a very long time. Propogate from layers or seed sown during the rains. The variety most grown is *A. Leptopus*, which, during the greater part of the year, is covered with its sprays of beautiful rose coloured flowers.

## Antirrhinum Majus.

Nat. Ord.—Scrophulariaceæ. (Snapdragon.)

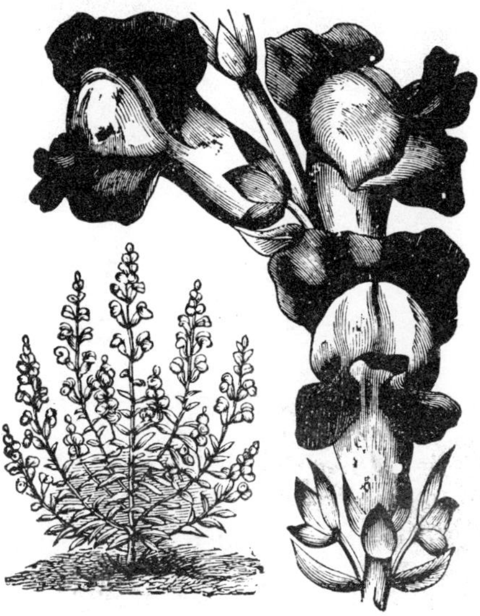

ANTIRRHINUM MAJUS.

There are very few more showy plants than the old Snapdragon and, besides being so showy as plants, they are most useful for cutting for decoration. There are almost innumerable colours and shades and, as the plants are very free flowering, they are deserving of wide cultivation. This is a hardy Perennial and will come into flower on the Plains the first season after sowing but, to improve the size of the flowers, I advise growers to cut off the flower buds as they form and only allow the plants to flower from the second season after sowing. The plants should be protected from heavy rain and will then grow on year after year. Sow on the Plains at the end of September or beginning of October; March to June on the Hills or in October or November. When the seedlings are about 2 inches high, plant out at a distance of 12 to 18 inches for the larger kinds, and 6 inches for the Dwarf or Tom Thumb sorts. Although the Antirrhinum will thrive in very poor soil it repays feeding, so have your ground as rich as possible. The Tom Thumb section is quite distinct from the old Majus varieties, as will readily be seen on comparing the two illustrations I give. These form compact globular bushes some 6 or 8 inches high. Although the flowers are not so large as those of the older variety, yet their dwarf compact habit of growth and masses of richly coloured flowers make them very useful and attractive For separate beds many people like to have distinct colours and the seed of Antirrhinum can be obtained in separate colours from most Seedsmen The following are amongst the colours thus obtainable, but for all practical purposes readers will find a packet of good mixed seed quite enough for any ordinary garden. *Album*, pure white ; *Album rubrum striatum*, white, striped red; *Brilliant*, scarlet, white and golden yellow ; *Crescia*, deep scarlet ; *Delila*, carmine with white throat; *Firefly*, scarlet with yellow and white throat; *Galathea*, crimson with white throat ; *Henry IV.*, cinnabar or vermilion red ; *Luteum rubrum striatum*, yellow with red stripes ; *Nigrescens*, purplish black ; *Papilionaceum*, purple and white ; *Roseum*, deep rose ; *Sulphureum*, sulphur yellow, &c., &c.

ANTIRRHINUM TOM THUMB

---

AQUILEGIA, DOUBLE.

# Aquilegia.

## Nat. Ord. Ranunculaceæ.

## (Columbine.)

The old Columbine of the home gardens is a well known herbaceous perennial, which grows fairly well in most places on the Plains and simply luxuriates on the Hills. On the Plains sow in October; Hills, October and March and April. During the hot weather on the Plains it is advisable to shade the plants during the heat of the day, otherwise is quite hardy and easily grown. There are a few distinct varieties but few people will care to sow more than a little mixed seed. There is a very beautiful yellow variety, *A. Chrysantha,* with large, bright golden yellow flowers, which have peculiar long spurs. and also a very distinct pure white variety called *Nivea Grandiflora,* with large single flowers.

## Arabis.

**Nat. Ord. Cruciferæ. (Rock Cress, or Mountain Snow).**

A very hardy and compact growing Perennial of great usefulness as a rockery plant. I have seen *Arabis Alpina* growing on large rockeries in England with flowers in such abundance that the rockeries looked just like banks of snow. Grows to a height of about 6 inches. On the Plains sow in October; Hills April or May. Does well on any dry soil.

## Ardisia.

**Nat. Ord. Myrsinaceæ. (The Spear Flower.)**

A plant which is even more useful than the Solanums for decorative purposes. The plants bear masses of pure white flowers, which are followed by numerous coral like vermilion berries, which will often remain on the plants till the new crop is ripe. The variety *Crenulata* grows to a height of from 3 to 6 feet. Make admirable pot plants or can be planted out in the open ground. On the Plains sow during the rains; early Spring on the Hills.

## Arnebia.

**Nat. Ord. (Boraginaceæ).**

*(The Spotted Golden Borage.)*

In *Arnebia Cornuta* we have a magnificent annual, forming profusely branched bushes, of about two feet in height and breadth, with narrow lanceolate foliage. The blossoms, three quarters of an inch in diameter, appearing on the whole length of each branch, are of a brilliant yellow colour with large black spots; the latter change into a coffee-brown shade on the third day of its bloom, so that pure yellow and spotted flowers are on the same flowering branch. The abundance of bloom of this novelty is an extraordinary one; each plant produces about 100 to 120 flowering

ARNEBIA CORNUTA.

spikes, which keeping up a constant succession of bloom throughout the season, present with their different coloured flowers, a charming aspect. This new species cannot be too highly recommended, being equally useful for flowering beds, as single specimens, or for cut flowers. On the Plains sow in October or beginning of November; Hills, October and again in March and April.

## Asparagus Plumosus Nanus.

### Nat. Ord. Liliaceæ.

A climber with exquisitely graceful and feathery, bright green foliage. It is extensively grown by florists for cutting purposes, the lace-like leaves being used for bouquets, baskets, and other decorations, the effect of which cannot be equalled. As the leaves keep fresh for a long time after cutting, this is a very valuable plant for growing for all kinds of floral work, while being so very light and feathery looking, it adds considerably to the beauty of a bouquet, wreath or any other form of floral design.

The plants are easily raised from seed or by division of the roots. On the Hills I find it best to sow in the Autumn, under cover of a glass frame, and the plants are then ready for transplanting into thumb pots in the Spring. Care should be taken when transplanting not to injure the delicate fleshy roots. As the Asparagus likes a damp warm climate, it should do well in many places on the Plains, where I would advise sowing in June and again in October. Grow in a moderately rich but open soil. A compost with a good proportion of sand will be found best.

Asparagus, Plumosus Nanus.

# ASTERS.

## Nat. Ord. Compositæ.—Callistephus hortensis.

### (Star Wort.)

Few annuals have been so much improved during the past few years as the Aster. Not only has it developed into a great variety of forms, both in the habit of the plants and the shape of the blooms, but at the same time the colours have been so diversified and brightened, that only those who are familiar with the recent progress of the flower can have any conception of the magnificent display it will now produce in the garden. The following selection embraces all the most distinct and beautiful classes of this popular flower.

Aster, as a Pot Plant,

On the Plains, sow during September and October; in the Hills, March to May, also in October. Sow the seed in boxes or pans of light, rich soil, covering very lightly, and after giving a slight watering, place in a sheltered position until the plants come up, when they should have the full benefit of sun and air. As soon as large enough to handle, they may be transplanted into pots or pans filled with very rich soil. The soil that suits them best is a compost of equal parts of leaf mould, old cow manure and good garden soil, with a small quantity of coarse sand added. Great attention must, however, be paid to their drainage, as the plants are very sensitive to damp. The healthy growth of the plant and the development of fine blooms, are greatly assisted by occasional applications of weak liquid manure up to the time of the plants showing flowers, when it should be discontinued. If particularly fine blooms are required, the buds should be carefully thinned out on each plant, leaving only three or four of the strongest. The taller growing varieties will require to be carefully staked before coming into flower. I give an illustration which shows how well the Aster looks as a pot plant, if well grown, while for bedding it is invaluable.

There are now very many varieties of the Aster, all of them pretty and useful in their own way ; but with such a variety to choose from it is difficult for the ordinary Amateur to select, from the many, the few which are really the best. Lately a new class has come into prominence—the single Marguerite—and I give an illustration which will give some idea of the form of this sterling novelty.

In the following list I give only those that have been proved to be really first class.

*Betteridge's* or *Reid's Quilled.* In this class the flowers are produced very freely. The extreme edge of the flowers is formed by one row of the ray florets. The plants grow to a height of 2 to 2½ feet. *Boltze's Dwarf Bouquet.* Single plants of this class have been seen with as many as 40 to 50 flowers, and this too on plants growing to a height of not more than 8 to 10 inches. *Cocardeau* or *Crown.* The flowers, which are about 3 inches across, are very striking on account of their flat petals, white centres and broad brilliant coloured margins, after the manner of a cockade. *Comet.* This is a new class which has become very popular and deservedly so. The flowers resemble Japanese Chrysanthemums and are often nearly five inches across. *Dwarf Chrysanthemum Flowered.* This is one of the most useful of the many varieties, as it does equally well for pot culture and edging beds. Growing to a height not exceeding 12 inches, and often no more than 9 inches, its low growth, stiff habit and great abundance of flowers, make it an exceptionally useful annual. The flowers are large, being often 4 inches in diameter and are borne 15 to 20 on each plant. *Dwarf Queen.* Grows to a height of 10 to 12 inches, and although branching very freely, the branches are upright, so making a dense compact bush. The flowers are of very large size. *Goliath.* Flowers of enormous size and perfect form ; plants 2½ feet in height. *Harlequin.* Flowers oddly spotted and striped. *Mignon.* Flowers very double and of extraordinary size. *Queen of the Market.* Very early flowering, generally being in full bloom a couple of weeks before any other Aster

ASTER, MARGUERITE SINGLE.

begins to blossom. *Triumph.* A grand variety of great merit, which only grows to a height of 7 or 8 inches. Very floriferous, plants generally bearing from 30 to 40 beautifully formed flowers, each from 2½ to 3 inches across. As this variety is very uniform in growth, it is well adapted for borders, groups, carpet bedding or pot culture. *Truffaut's Pœony Perfection.* The flowers in this section are very beautifully incurved and of the brightest colours. *Victoria.* The most showy and massive of all the Asters, bearing enormous flowers of great fullness. As the petals of this class curve outward instead of folding in, this variety forms a splendid contrast to the Pœony-flowered varieties. *Jewel.* A comparatively new class somewhat similar to the Pœony-flowered, but distinguished by its beautiful short petalled and perfectly round flowers, which are very much like the incurved Chrysanthemums. The plants grow about 2 feet high and the flowers measure from 2½ to 3 inches across. *Lady in White.* Very free flowering, the plants often producing from 40 to 70 pure white flowers, borne on long, slender stalks. *Queen of the Felibrés.* Another pure white variety of great value. Flowers very fine and without the open centre which spoils so many of the other varieties. It is very early, practically as early as the *Queen of the Market.* *Single Marguerite.* The illustration which I give shows the form of this splendid novelty but it is deserving of some description. I take the following remarks from the description published by the raiser and can strongly recommend this as one of the best novelties in this line of recent years.

ASTER, GROWN IN OPEN GROUND.

"The chief characteristics of these new Single Asters are a very floriferous habit, and brilliant coloured flowers. They are of great value for bouquets and floral decorations generally, and will be found to be a most desirable contribution to this class of Florists' flowers. The plants are of a globular form, and carry on stout and long stalks a mass of single star-shaped flowers, which appear early and last a long time. Planted out on beds or borders, they have a brilliant effect, and form a pleasing contrast to the many varieties of Double Asters. A bouquet of "Marguerite Asters" in different shades makes a magnificent table decoration, and is equally effective in vases, the flowers remaining fresh for ten days or more. It comes true from seed both as regards habit and colour, which latter varies from pale rose to deep carmine, and light blue to deep violet."

Many growers will find that a packet or two of *German mixed* Asters will give them a large number of plants of many good varieties and for those who require plants of one class for any special purpose, the list given of the best separate varieties will be found useful.

## PERENNIAL ASTERS.

### (Michaelmas Daisies.)

As this class is perfectly distinct from the German or China Aster, it needs a paragraph to itself. The Perennial Asters are commonly known as Michælmas Daisies at home, and are very popular as cut flowers. Sow as early as possible at the end of the rains on the Plains, and March to May on the Hills. As soon as the plants are large enough to handle, pot off in good rich soil and shift on into larger pots as they require. They need plenty of room and if they can be protected from excessive rain, I much prefer to plant out in the open garden. Lately some attention has been paid to this useful flower by hybridizers and we have now got a much improved strain in which the flowers are very much larger than in the old varieties.

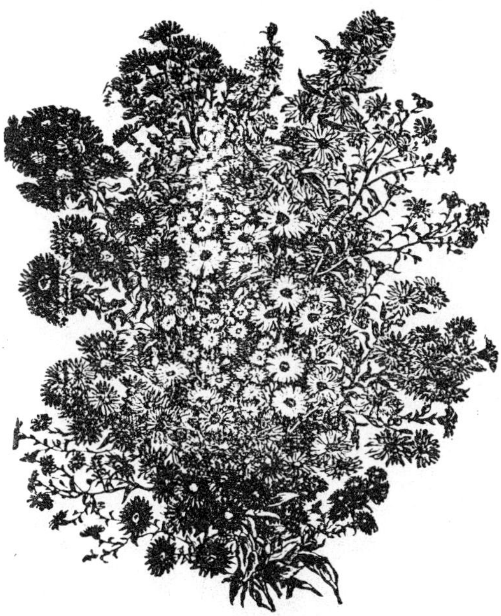

ASTER, PERENNIAL.

# AZALEA

## Nat Ord—Ericaceæ. (False Honey Suckle.)

This is a plant which it is practically useless trying to grow on the Plains, but on the Hills it is almost hardy, and with care, succeeds admirably. To grow Azaleas with any measure of success, it is imperative that the compost used shall consist of one-half peat while the other half should be composed of good fibrous loam, leaf mould and sand in about equal proportions. Thorough drainage is indispensable. I would advise growers to sow the seed in the autumn under cover and in the spring pot off singly in thumb pots, shifting on into larger pots as the plants increase in size. The plants look magnificent trained over wire balloons and form very decorative objects

# BALSAMS.

## Nat Ord.—Balsaminaceæ (Impatiens Balsamina, or Ladies' Slipper. Vern—Gool Mehndee, Doopatree).

On the Plains sow from end of June to beginning of September; in the Hills, April and June. Sow seed in pans or boxes and plant out when about two inches high. They also make very effective pot plants when grown in a good rich soil; for this purpose they should be first planted in 3 inch pots, and re-potted every fortnight, using pots a size larger on each occasion until they are in eight inch pots, which will be sufficiently large for them to flower in. At each shift they receive, the plants may be dropped lower in the soil, that the bottom branches may be pegged or tied down, so as to be level with the rim of the pot.

BALSAM, CAMELLIA FLOWERED.

There are several distinct classes of Balsams, all good in their own way, but the ordinary amateur will find a packet of good Mixed seed, which can be obtained from any Seedsman for about a rupee, ample for a fair sized garden. The following are all good sorts :— *Camellia Flowered.* Most brilliant coloured flowers, blotched and marbled with white. *Rose Flowered.* Extra double and of immense size. *Carnation Striped.* A very novel and distinct class in which the flowers are distinctly striped in various brilliant colours. *Solferino.* A new class with extra large flowers finely streaked and blotched.

Balsam, Rose Flowered.

## BARTONIA.—(Golden Barton's Flower)

Bartonia Aurea.

Nat. Ord.—Loasaceæ.

On the Plains sow in October ; in the Hills, March to May Requires a rich soil and plenty of water. Sow in a position well exposed to the sun, where the plant will open its beautiful buttercup-like flowers to the fullest perfection.

The variety I illustrate is the best known one, but a new dwarf variety has been introduced, which will be found useful for bedding.

# BEGONIAS.

## Nat. Ord.—Begoniaceæ, (Elephant's Ear.)

Begonia, Double.

The Begonia has become extremely popular of late years, not only as a pot plant, but also for bedding out. This is one of the most ornamental plants now in cultivation and is deserving of even more extensive cultivation in this country. The writer has taken a great interest in the cultivation of the Begonia and has been very successful in raising many most beautiful varieties. The compost I have found most successful is one composed of equal parts of good fibrous loam, coarse sand and very old and well rotted cow manure, together with a small proportion of cocoanut fibre and charcoal dust. This latter is a most useful article in the garden and the servants should always be given orders to save the dust when the charcoal go-down is cleaned out. I usually mix some charcoal ashes with my potting soil, and find this also a great addition. The Begonia is very easily raised from seed and it is most interesting to watch the plants in the various stages of their growth. For the Plains I advise readers to grow the Begonia from bulbs, which can usually be obtained from Seedsmen and Nurserymen. If you decide to get bulbs, they should be started into growth in September. Pot in the compost I advise, and place them under cover till the plants are well up. Start in small pots and repot as the plants require it, taking care not to injure the roots when doing so. Knock the whole contents out of the pots and place in the larger ones, filling up with compost. The leaves of the Begonia are very liable to be attacked by mildew, more particularly if grown under glass. I find that my plants grown in the open very seldom suffer, so advise readers to put their plants out in the rain for a time, whenever mildew makes its appearance. Sulphur is fatal to fungoid growths and a dusting over the leaves will soon clear them of the pest. In growing from seed, care must be taken to have the pots filled with good open soil, with plenty of drainage. I always raise my seedlings in 12 inch seed pans. These pans can be obtained from any native potter and should be about 3 inches deep, with a good number of drainage holes. Half fill the pans with coarse gravel or broken crocks, cover this with moss, to prevent the soil from percolating through the drainage and so clogging it, and then fill up to within quarter of an inch from the top with soil, which, as I say above, must be very open. Sprinkle the seed very thinly over the surface and then place a piece of paper over the top of the pan and cover all with a sheet of glass. This treatment prevents too rapid evaporation and consequent frequent waterings. In watering Begonias and all other small seeds, I never use a watering pot, but dip the seed pan into a bucket of water for a minute or so and allow the soil to absorb the water. When the tiny seedlings appear, give plenty of air and remove the paper and glass, otherwise they are very likely to damp off. As soon as the seedlings are large enough to handle, pot off into small thumb pots and pot on into larger ones as the plants increase in size. Plants from seed can be got to flower in about six or eight months from time of sowing. I would advise readers on the Plains to grow from bulbs, but it is by no means impossible to raise from seed. On the Plains seed should be sown just before the rains or in September ; on the Hills, April or May. There are many strains of the tuberous Begonia and almost as many growers who specialise with this plant. Messrs. Laing and Sons, of London, have, for very many years, been the recognised Begonia specialists and it would be hard to beat their magnificent strains. Some of the German growers have also introduced some fine novelties and amongst these I would mention the striped strain—tuberosa vittata. The Rex

BEGONIA, SINGLE.

Begonias do grandly in India, naturally too, as they are natives of the country. These can be raised from seed in the same way as advised for the tuberous section, but where leaves of a good variety are obtainable, it is a much quicker way to propogate from leaf cuttings. Take well matured leaves with about a couple of inches of the leaf stalks and bury the stalks in well drained pans of sand or very open soil. Cut open the ribs of the leaves and peg down, so that the cuts are under the soil; where the cuts are made roots will form, and in a few months a good stock of healthy young plants will be obtained The Begonia luxuriates in a moist climate, but thorough ventilation is an absolute essential.

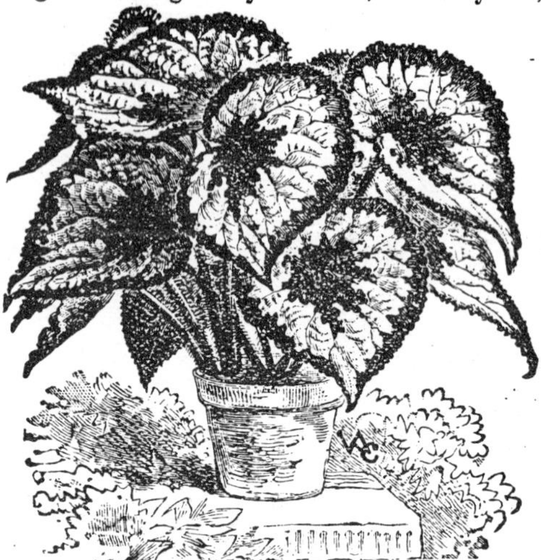

BEGONIA, REX.

## BELLIS PERENNIS.

### Nat. Ord. Compositæ (Double Daisy.)

### (Vern. Huzar-daneh.)

This old favourite of the home gardens is now very extensively cultivated in India, and as it is easy to grow, there is no reason why the plant should not be seen in every garden in the country. Of course on the Hills the Daisy grows quite as well as it does in Britain, but on the Plains it is usually grown as an annual, although plants can be kept alive during the hot weather if carefully shaded. Sow on the Plains in October; on the Hills in October, also at any time from the beginning of March to the end of May. Sow in good rich soil and prick out the seedlings as soon as they are large enough to handle. In order to prevent the plants from deteriorating, they should be transplanted very frequently, but always in rich

DAISY, DOUBLE.

soil. Most people sow the mixed double seed which, if of a good strain, will give a number of fine varieties and colours. When the plants are required for special purposes there are several varieties to select from, such as :—*Giant Snowball*, which bears very large, pure white flowers, carried on long stems, which makes this variety particularly useful for cutting ; then there is the ordinary *flore albo*, which has flowers smaller than the preceding, but is a useful kind for edgings or beds ; in *Longfellow* we have a very fine variety, bearing beautiful dark rose coloured, enormous double flowers.

## BIGNONIA.

### Nat. Ord.—Bignoniaceæ. (The Trumpet Flower.)

*Vern.* Soon.

These are very closely allied to the Tecomas, in fact many authorities group them together. They are perennial climbers and very easily grown from seed. The soil which suits them best is composed of two parts fibrous loam, one part peat, one part leaf mould and a good proportion of sand. Sow on the Plains in October and on the Hills in October or early Spring.

## BOCCONIA.

### Nat. Ord.—Papaveraceæ. (Plume Poppy or Tree Celandine.)

Bocconia Cordata.

A very handsome, hardy, herbaceous plant which does well in India. Is a native of China, varieties also being found in Mexico and South America. Grows equally well as a pot plant and in the open ground. The variety commonly grown is the Chinese variety *Cordata* or *Japonica*, which is also known as Macleaya Yedöensis. Grows to a height of some 5 to 8 feet. The flowers are buff-coloured and borne in great abundance. Sow on the Plains in October and on the Hills in October, also in March or April. The young plants should be planted out when large enough, in light, rich soil. The illustration gives a fair idea of the appearance of this useful plant.

# BRACHYCOME.

## Nat. Ord. Compositæ.—(Swan River Daisy.)

BRACHYCOME, IBERIDIFOLIA.

The illustration gives some idea of the beauty of these free flowering Annuals. Sow in October on the Plains and March in the Hills. The flowers, which resemble the Cineraria, are borne in great abundance, and as the plants are fairly dwarf, seldom exceeding a foot in height, they will be found useful for edgings. Plant out about 6 inches apart, or sow the seed where the plants are wanted to flower, and thin out to the same distance apart. The flowers are of various colours with dark centres.

# BROUSSONETIA.

## Nat. Ord. Urticaceæ.—(Paper Mulberry.)

A very ornamental deciduous tree, growing to a height of 10 to 20 feet. As this belongs to the same family as the common Indian Mulberry (Morus Indica), it should do well on the Plains, where seed should be shown in October. On the Hills sow in October and in Spring. Requires good open soil, well drained, and on the Hills should be planted in fairly sheltered position. *Papyrifera* (paper bearing) is the one usually cultivated, although there are several varieties varying in the shape of the leaves.

# BROWALLIA.

## Nat. Ord, Scrophulariaceæ.

A very pretty, free flowering annual of easy growth, which, if grown in masses, is very effective. Will flower in two months from time of sowing. On the Plains sow in October and March in the Hills, in pots or pans of rich, light soil. As soon as the seedlings are large enough to handle, plant out in well manured beds. The best known varieties are :—*B. Elata alba*, pure white ; *B. Elata Cœrulea*, bright blue.

Both the preceding varieties grow to a height of about $1\frac{1}{2}$ feet. *B. Elata Nana*, is a dwarf, growing form of *Elata Cœrulea*, with vivid blue flowers borne in great profusion. Very useful for edging beds and also makes a very fine pot plant. *B. Roezli*, of very compact habit, forming dense, compact bushes about 2 feet high, flowers very large and either azure blue or white with yellow tube.

BROWALLIA.

## BUXUS.

**Nat. Ord. Euphorbiaceæ. (Box Tree. Vern. Shumshad.)**

Unfortunately the old English Box cannot be grown with any measure of success on the Plains, but on the Hills grows splendidly. One of the most useful hedge plants in cultivation, as it can be pruned and trimmed to any shape. Grows best in a light, well drained soil. I have found it rather difficult to raise from seed, which I advise sowing in September or October on the Hills, or in early Spring. Cuttings put down immediately after the rains, strike readily and form fine strong plants. The variety commonly grown is *B. Semvervirens*, which is, as its name implies, an evergreen.

## CACALIA.

**Nat. Ord. Compositæ (The Tassel Flower.)**

An annual of no particular beauty, but useful in gardens on the Plains, as it is very hardy. Some readers may know this better under its true name of Senecio. The plant does well in any loamy soil and the seeds should be sown on the Plains in October and March to May on the Hills. There are two varieties, commonly grown :— *C. Aurea*. deep golden yellow and *C. Coccinea*, scarlet. The latter is commonly known as the Candle Plant, and botanically is synonomous with Emilia flammea and Cacalia Sonchifolia.

CACALIA.

Group of Cacti.

# CACTUS.

## Nat. Ord. Cactaceæ.

The many varieties of Cacti are most interesting and are well worth cultivation, more particularly as the majority of them require little or no attention, and are very easily raised from seed. The various kinds of Cacti are almost legion, comprising the following amongst others :— Cereus (torch thistle), Disocactus, Echinocactus (the hedge-hog or fly Cactus), Echinocereus, Epiphyllum (the leaf-flowering Cactus), Echinopsis (the globe-thistle), Leuchtenbergia, Mammillaria (the nipple-Cactus), Melocactus (the Melon-thistle or Turk's-cap Cactus), Nopalea (Cochineal Cactus or Nopal plant of Mexico), Opuntia (the Bastard Fig, Indian Fig or Prickly Pear), Pelecyphora, Pereskia (Barbados gooseberry), Phyllocactus, Rhipsalis, Umbilicus and a host of others. A group of Cacti, such as is shown in the illustration given, is a most interesting addition to a garden. Sow the seed in sand, or very sandy soil in October both on the Plains and Hills. Place the pots in a rather shady position till the seeds germinate, after germination pot off singly in small thumb pots, well drained and filled with a compost composed of one half fibrous loam, the other half made up of broken bricks (any old masonry may be used), old mortar and sand. Drainage is a very particular matter, and care should be taken to see that the plants do not become pot bound. Do not give much water, once or twice a week will be ample, but an occasional syringing will assist growth and healthiness of the plants. Cactus seed is usually stocked by retail Seedsmen in mixed packets only, but if the seed is obtained from a reliable dealer, purchasers can depend on a good selection being given them. As the seed varies very much in size, the seed of many of the finer sorts being very fine, readers are warned against throwing away what they may think is only dust, as a customer of mine did, much to his disgust when informed that he had thrown away most of the best seed.

# CALADIUM.

Nat Ord. Aroideæ.

The Caladiums are amongst the most ornamental of plants, and are very popular, as they succeed admirably on the Plains. The soil most suitable for the Caladium is one of equal parts of good fibrous loam, peat and thoroughly decomposed manure, together with a plentiful proportion of rough sand. As the Caladium requires a large amount of water, care should be taken in seeing that the drainage of the pots is good. On the Plains sow the seed in pans or pots at the beginning of the rains, or in October, while on the Hills the seed should be sown either in October or in early Spring under cover. When the young seedlings are large enough to handle, they should be potted off into thumb pots and shifted on gradually, till they are in 8 inch pots, when the plants should form fine objects in the grass-house or verandah. The plants should be given a slight shade during the hottest part of the day, but a fair amount of sunshine is essential to the bringing out of the gorgeous colouring of the leaves. When the leaves show signs of withering, withold water gradually and allow the plants to die down. Store the tubers in dry sand and start into growth again about the middle of March.

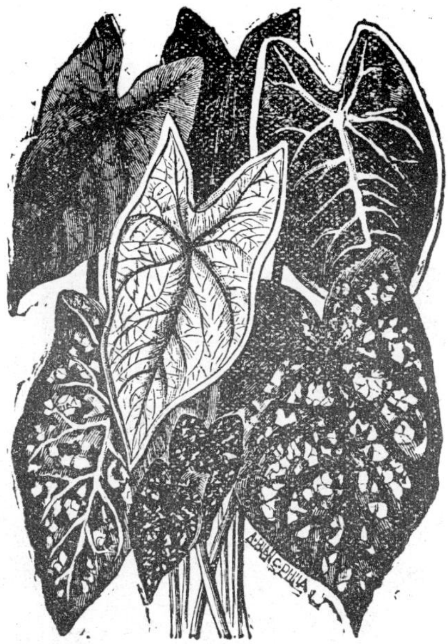

CALADIUM, HYBRIDUM.

# CALANDRINIA.

Nat. Ord. Portulacaceæ. (Rock Purslane.)

In Europe *Calandrinia Umbellata* is a hardy biennial, but on the Plains of India should be treated as an annual. Sow the seed in October where the plants are to remain, as they do not bear transplanting well. Like its cousin the Portulaca, the Calandrinia should be so n in a situation fully exposed to the sun, as the flowers will not open in the shade. Grow in light but rich soil, and give occasional waterings with weak liquid manure. The variety usually grown is *Umbellata*, which bears flowers of a bright magenta-crimson. The plants grow to a height of about 6 inches and are very free flowering. I would advise readers to grow in fairly large masses. Sow on the Hills in Spring.

---

# CALCEOLARIA.

**Not. Ord Scrophulariaceæ. (Slipper Wort or Slipper-flower.)**

The Calceolaria is a very popular plant at home, where it is now much used for bedding. Great improvements have been made in late years and well grown specimens form most beautiful pot plants. I do not advise the growing of this plant on the Plains, but on the Hills it does well. In Bengal it is practically impossible to grow it, but in portions of the United Provinces and in the Punjab, where the cold weather lasts much longer, it can be grown with moderate success. The seed should be sown in September or the beginning of October; in the Hills this is also the best time to sow, if the young plants can be protected in a glass house or warm verandah during the winter months. Sow under cover of paper and glass in a compost composed of equal parts of loam, leaf mould and sand. When the seedlings are large enough, prick out into pans or boxes and pot off when large enough to handle. Require a fair amount of water but plenty of ventilation. Do not expose to direct sunshine, but keep in a fairly shady situation. Support the flower stems with neat sticks, as otherwise the plants are apt to get untidy looking.

CALCEOLARIA.

# CALENDULA.

## Nat. Ord. Compositæ. (Cape Marigold.)

A member of the Marigold family, so dear to the Native Mali who, if he can grow nothing else, will be sure to have a most luxuriant patch of "ghendas." As the Calendula will not transplant well, the seed should be sown where the plants are to flower, in October on the Plains and April in the Hills. Do not sow in very rich soil, as the plants are very apt to grow straggly. There are a number of very fine varieties, of which the one I illustrate *Queen of Trianon* is one of the best. It is known

in France as the "Royal Marigold." The plants seldom grow more than a foot high and are literally covered with bright canary-yellow, dark, maroon centred flowers. Other good sorts are:—*Orange King*, intensely deep orange and free flowering; *Le Proust*, very double flowers of a bright nankeen yellow; *Meteor*, light orange striped flowers; *Pongei fl. pl.*, double white; *Prince of Orange*, deep orange striped; *Superba fl. pl.*, very double, flowers rich orange.

# Calliopsis, or Coreopsis.

Nat. Ord.—Compositæ. (Tick Seed.)

One of the freest flowering and most showy of the hardy annuals, of which the beautiful illustration gives a very fair idea. Some growers recommend sowing in pots or boxes and transplanting into the beds, but I prefer sowing where they are intended to flower and thinning out if too thick. The thinnings can be planted in other parts of the garden, where they will come into flower a little later than the plants in the original bed. Sow in October on the Plains and March to May on the Hills, i fairly rich soil. Do not allow the plants to seed and they will remain in flower for a very long season The various varieties mostly bear flowers in shades of yellow, but there are some with blood red flowers, which, if a mixture is sown, gives a very fine contrast in colouring. Amongst the best varieties are :—*Grandiflora*, flowers very large, bright yellow ; *Bicolor* or *Tinctoria*, bright yellow with crimson centre ; *Coronata*, large yellow spotted flowers ; *Drummondii*, very free flowering, yellow; *Hybrida Atrosanguinea*, blood red ; *Hybrida flore pleno*, a variety with very pretty, semi-double flowers ; *Marmorata*, a rather tall growing variety with curiously marbled and striped flowers ; *Cardaminifolia Hybrida*, flowers yellow, the lower portion of the florets being a brownish purple.

# CAMELLIA.

Nat. Ord —Ternstræmiaceæ. (Japan Rose).

Those who have seen the magnificent specimens of Camellias, in greenhouses at home, long to grow them with equal success in India but I am afraid this is practically impossible, except on the Hills. The Japanese Camellia can be grown quite easily from seed, but whenever possible, I advise readers to get plants from China or Japan. The plants soon deteriorate on the Plains and even when they do not die off, produce only very inferior flowers. Even at home the Camellia has to be well protected from direct sunlight, so readers will hardly have to be told that this is even more essential out here. Although one of the varieties of the Camellia,—Tea—which is one of the leading products of the country, of course luxuriates in most parts of India, yet the Japanese variety can only be grown with very moderate success, except on the Hills. Seed should be sown in October both on the Plains and Hills. Personally I prefer a compost composed almost entirely of peat, although I believe they are grown in Japan in a soil which is practically clay. Keep the plants in small tubs, which can be easily shifted from one position to another as required. Give a fairly liberal supply of water and syringe the leaves frequently. An occasional soaking with weak liquid manure will ensure healthy, vigorous growth and consequent free flowering. On the Hills keep in a glass house or warm verandah, more particularly during the winter.

## CAMPANULA.

Nat. Ord.—Campanulaceæ. (The Bell Flower).

Very beautiful both as pot plants and for planting out in the open garden. Are of very easy culture and should be much more grown than they now are. On the Plains sow in September, on the Hills, September or October and also in March and April. I advise sowing on the Plains in September, as there is then a good chance of getting the plants to flower during the cold weather, before they are cut down by the hot winds. The kinds most suitable for growing on the Plains, are *Calycanthema*, and the single and double *Medium*. On the Hills all the varieties do well, in fact several sorts are indigenous to the Himalayas. The best known sorts are :—*Calycanthema* which is a comparatively new race of the old "Canterbury Bells," in which the flowers are very large, resembling somewhat a cup and saucer, as shown in the illustration I give; *Medium* Single and Double, are the old Canterbury

Campanula, Medium Double.

Bells of the home gardens; *Speculum* (Venus' Looking glass), a very pretty variety bearing blue and white flowers, which keeps in flower for a very long period. This variety is more correctly a *Specularia*, but is now commonly classed with the other Campanulas. Several growers have specialised in the Campanula and some fine classes are now offered by many Seedsmen, for instance *Benary's Prize*, which comprises a great number of the most beautiful hybrid varieties.

CAMPANULA, CALYCANTHEMA.

# CANDYTUFT (Iberis.)

### Nat. Ord.—Cruciferæ.

One of the most easily grown of the hardy annuals, and consequently one of the most popular. On the Plains sow in September or October, March or April in the Hills, in light rich soil. This is one of the plants that transplants badly, and the seed should be sown where the plants are to remain. To increase the vigour of the plants give an occasional watering with weak liquid manure. A small sowing may be put down on the Hills in the Autumn to get plants for early flowering. The best kinds in cultivation are :—*Albida*, creamy white; *Carmine*, dense trusses of bright carmine flowers ; *Dobbie's New Spiral*, pure white, extra fine spikes ; *Dunnett's Crimson*, deep crimson ; *Dwarf Hybrids*, a very fine strain of dwarf habit and great diversity of colouring ; *Empress*, bears a series of candelabra-shaped branches, each producing a large truss of pure white flowers ; *Lilacina*, bright lilac ; *Nigricans*, in this variety the flowers are borne on compact well shaped plants, and on first opening are a delicate rose colour, but as they fully mature, change to a rich dark purple ; *Tom Thumb*, grows to a height of about 5 or 6 inches, with pure white flowers ; *White Rocket*, with long spikes of pure white flowers.

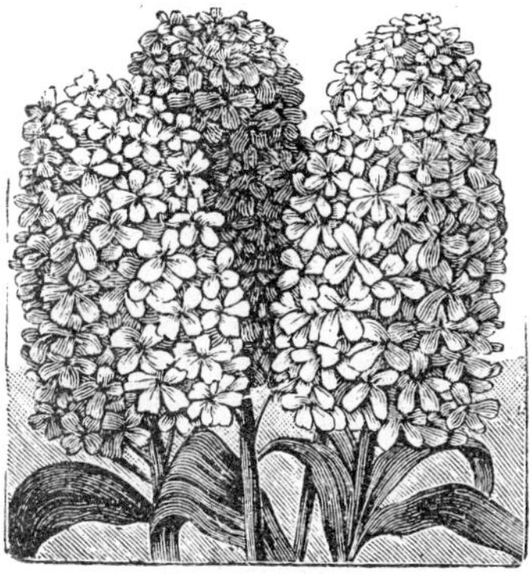

CANDYTUFT.

# CANNA

### . Nat. Ord. Scitamineæ.

### (Indian Shot.—Vern. Surooehjeea, Ukulbar.)

The beautiful illustration which I give of a group of Cannas, with a single flower enlarged, wi'l give readers a better idea of the beauty of the Canna, than I could give in reams of description, but it is really impossible in plain black and white, to give any real idea of the rare beauty and rich colouring of this most popular of flowers. The seeds can be sown both on the Plains and Hills practically all the year round. Plant in rich, well manured soil and give plenty of water. A light shade during the hottest part of the day will prevent the flowers from bleaching, and keep the plants in flower for a long season. Give an occasional drenching with liquid manure or top dress with "Ichthemic" Guano, which has been found particularly beneficial for this plant. The varieties of Canna are legion, but as plants of most of the varieties can be obtained from Nurserymen all over the country, the seed that is

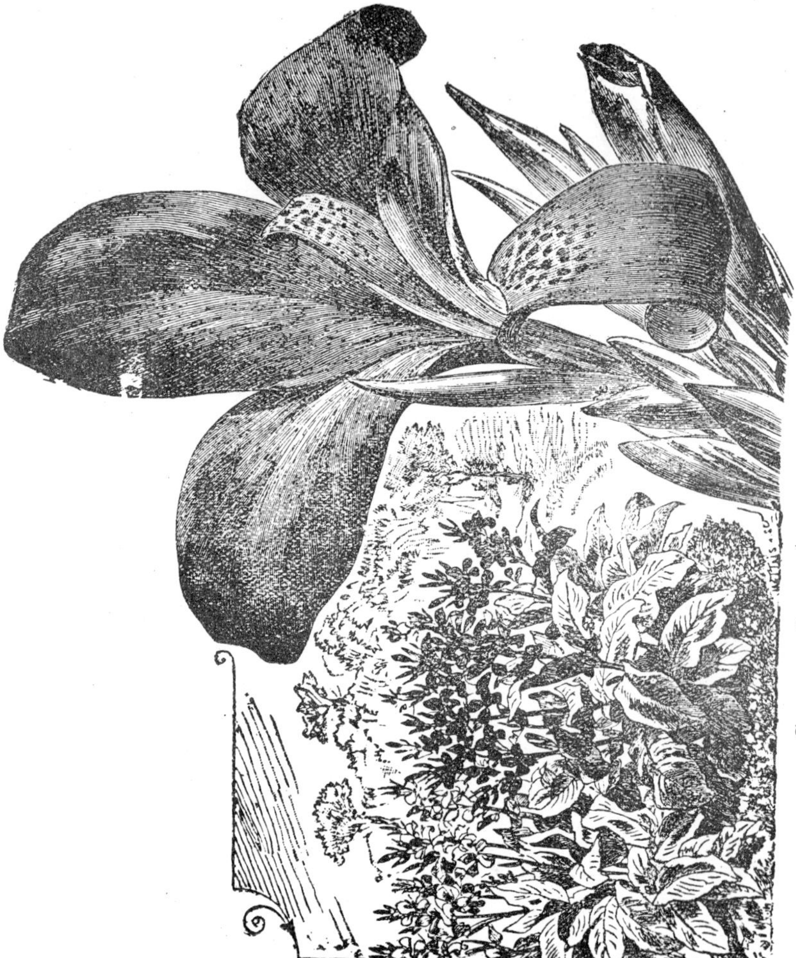

GROUP OF CANNAS.

usually sown is a mixture of the best kinds, and this can be obtained at small cost from all Seedsmen. A fine strain introduced by the famous hybridiser Crozy, is called *Crozy's Dwarf*, and in this strain will be found many sterling novelties. The foliage is luxuriant and very varied in colouring, while the plants are of very dwarf habit, seldom exceeding 3 or 4 feet. The flowers are large and of grand colours. They will come into flower in 4 or 5 months from time of sowing.

## CARNATIONS.

### Nat. Ord.—Caryophyllaceæ.
### (Dianthus Caryophyllus.)

The beautiful Carnation, which can be grown so easily on the Hills, where it flowers quite as well as I have ever seen it at Home, does not, as a rule, do well on the Plains. The plant is a perennial. and unless sown early, can seldom be induced to flower the first year, and it is almost an impossibility to preserve it through the hot weather. A new strain, known as the *Marguerite* or *Margarita* Carnation, has lately been introduced, from Italy I think, and as this variety will flower in January if sown in September, it will be found a great acquisition by lovers of the flower. The seed of Carnations should be sown on the Plains as early as possible in September, on the Hills from June, which is the best month for sowing,

THE CARNATION AS A POT PLANT.

right on to August. Sow in pans or boxes, and when the plants have made five or six leaves, transplant into 3 inch pots and shift on into larger ones as required. Use for potting, a compost composed of equal parts of good fibrous loam, leaf mould and well rotted manure, with a little sand. Give an occasional watering with liquid manure while the plants are in bud. In mentioning varieties usually grown, I will put *Margarita* first, as it is one which will be grown greatly in future by gardeners on the Plains This sort comes very true from seed, and will yield quite 75 per cent. of plants with double flowers. On the Hills, seed of this variety should be sown in March, and the plants will be in full flower by the end of June. Although the ordinary *Margarita* is of dwarf habit, a new variety called *Margarita Tom Thumb* has since been introduced, which is a great improvement on the older introduction. I give illustrations of the two which show the form of both. The flowers are very sweet scented, reminding me very much of the old English Clove Carnation. In Carnation *Germania* we have a pure yellow self with large, well formed flowers. *Malmaison* (C. Caryophyllus

CARNATION, MARGARITA.

CARNATION, MARGARITA, TOM THUMB.

Maximus *fl. pl.*) is perhaps the grandest of the ordinary kind of Carnations which has ever been introduced. The flowers are very large and of perfect form. *Mrs. Reynolds Hole*, named after the wife of the famous Rosarian, Dean Hole, is another grand sort, of a beautiful terra-cotta colour, and is very popular as a button-hole flower at Home. *Grenadin*, very dwarf and early, with double brilliant scarlet flowers. A number of mixed strains are offered by the leading Seedsmen, such as :—Bizarres, Flakes, Fancies, Selfs, Perpetual or Tree &c.

## CELOSIA.—(Cockscomb)

### Nat. Ord.--Amaranthaceæ.

CELOSIA CRISTATA.

The Cockscomb does well on the Plains, where it is usually sown in July and August On the Hills it grows practically wild and is sown in June Sow in pots and when the plants are large enough, transplant into beds of rich soil. Do not give too much water, but occasionally give a watering with weak liquid manure. If grown in pots should be repotted frequently to bring them to the fullest perfection. There are two distinct classes of Celosia, the Cockscomb proper, with large combs flower and the Plumed or Feathered varieties in which the flowers form large feathery plumes. I give illustrations of both kinds to show their distinctiveness. The following are varieties much grown :—

1. *Cristata or Crested* (the true Cockscomb) (Vern. Moorgha Gool-Kesh). *Glasgow Prize*, also known as *President Thiers* or *Tom Thumb*. A very fine variety with dark leaves and crimson combs. *Japanese* (Japonica variegata), the combs are cut most delicately, just like ruffled lace. *Sanguinea*, deep blood red. *Giant Empress*, dark bronze foliage, with enormous bright purple combs. Most Seedsmen stock mixed seed of the Dwarf and Tall varieties, and these will be found best by growers who want a variety of plants.

CELOSIA, PLUMOSA.

2. *Plumosa* (Feathered Cockscomb). In *Reid's Perfection* we have a very fine strain of this beautiful plant. The colours of the plumes are varied, and this will be found extremely useful as a pot plant.

# CENTAUREA.

## Nat. Ord.—Compositæ.

Under this heading I will describe the Cornflower (Centaurea Cyanus), Sweet Sultan (Centaurea Moschata) and the Silver Leaved Centaurea (Centaurea Candidissima). The Cornflower or old Blue bottle of the Home fields, is almost too well known to need any description, and this applies equally to the Sweet Sultan.

CORNFLOWER, NEW DOUBLE.

Sow the seeds of all the varieties early in October on the Plains, March to May on the Hills. The seed can either be sown in pots or boxes, and transplanted when large enough to handle, or sown in the border where they are to flower. They like a light rich soil, but will do very well in any ordinary garden soil. I illustrate a comparatively new form of the Cornflower, which differs from the old single variety and much resembles, in form, a double Gaillardia. *Emperor William* is a beautiful single variety of the true cornflower-blue colour. Of the *Sweet Sultans* there are a number of very distinct colours such as, *Alba*, white; *Cœrulea*, bright blue; *Purpurea*, purple; *Yellow* (Suaveolens), clear yellow. In *Centaurea Candidissima* we have a beautiful silver foliaged variety, which is very useful for bedding, particularly as a contrast to any highly coloured flowering or foliaged lants.

CENTAUREA, CANDIDISSIMA.

# CHAMÆPEUCE.

### Nat. Ord.—Compositæ.—(The Fish-bone Thistle.)

Very ornamental thistle-like plants, growing to a height of 2 to 3 feet. Make very fine specimens when grown singly. Sow on the Plains in October; Hills, October and April to June. The two varieties usually grown are, *Cassabonnæ* and *Diacantha.* The former bears flower heads of a beautiful pale purple, the spiny deep green leaves being veined with white. In the latter the flower heads are purplish and borne in dense spike-like clusters. The shining green leaves are marked with silvery lines, while the spines on the margins are ivory white.

# CHENOPODIUM ATRIPLICIS.

### Nat. Ord.—Chenopodiaceæ.

A novel and very showy plant, known as the 'GOOD KING HENRY,' which is a fine ornamental foliage plant. The different colours of the leaves resemble Amaranthus and Coleus, and vary from pale yellow to deep crimson, violet pink, brilliant red, partially striped and shaded with light and dark green, the younger shoots and leaves being covered with a fine violet powder. The plants grow from 3½ to 4½ feet high, forming beautiful pyramidal bushes. Grown as specimens or groups, it produces a striking effect, which increases under the influence of the heating sun. The stems are sometimes used as a substitute for Asparagus, while the leaves are used, while young, instead of Spinach. Sow on the plains in October; March to October on the Hills. Sow in rich soil, but in a fairly shady situation, and give plenty of water.

# CHRYSANTHEMUMS.

### Nat. Ord.—Compositæ.

There are few denizens of the garden that have received so much attention of late years by the hybridiser as the Chrysanthemum, and there are now a host of most magnificent varieties, such as our forefathers never even dreamed of. Chrysanthemums divide naturally into two classes—the annual and perennial. I will give a few hints on the cultivation of the annual varieties, but would refer readers to 'Chrysanthemums' by Mrs. Temple Wright, for full particulars regarding the perennial sorts, as the subject would, if treated properly, occupy too much space in a small booklet. The book costs only 8 annas, and can be obtained from most booksellers.

CHRYSANTHEMUM, TRICOLOR,

*Chrysanthemum Carinatum, or Tricolor*, with its numerous varieties, are exceedingly pretty annuals, but they are not so well known or so generally grown as they deserve to be. All of them are most easy of cultivation in this country, and should certainly find a place in every garden. Plants may be raised from seed sown early in October on the Plains, and from end of February to middle of May on the Hills, and if liberally treated, will commence flowering in three to four months, and keep up a constant succession of bloom. The flowers have a great range of colour, are of fine shape and substance, and with good cultivation measure 2 to 2½ inches in diameter. They are very effective grown in pots, and invaluable for cutting. The following are the varieties most grown :—

*Album*—pure white, with yellow centre ; *Atrococcineum*—scarlet ; *Burridgeanum*—white, crimson and yellow ; *Carinatum*—white and yellow ; *Eclipse*—Its large single flowers, 2 and 2½ inches across, are pure golden-yellow with a bright purplish-scarlet ring on the ray floret, the disk being dark brown ; *Golden Feather*—This new variety is almost identical with the well known *C. Burridgeanum*, both in habit of plant and colour of flower, while the foliage is of a pleasing shade of yellow, rendering it very effective in lines or masses ; *Lord Beaconsfield*—crimson with yellow centre ; *Luteum*—yellow ; *Purple Queen* (atropurpureum)—the darkest of all ; *The Sultan*—velvety crimson or maroon ; *W. E. Gladstone*—rich crimson.

There are also a number of double flowering varieties of which the best strain is one lately introduced under the name of *Double Annual*

*Hybrids.* This valuable and most unique novelty has resulted from carefully hybridizing and selecting for several years, the semi-double varieties already existing of this useful annual, until a high degree of doubleness has been attained. They are extremely variable, and it is impossible to describe the beautiful forms which have been produced. Some are pure white, yellow, or crimson, but the prevailing types are bronzy yellow, the florets tinged with red or lilac rose, the imbricated ray florets beautifully pencilled ; others have rich crimson centres with clear yellow guard petals. Although mostly very double, there will still be an occasional semi-double or even single, these being almost equally charming. The Horticultural Press has given most favourable comments respecting this novelty. The following distinct colours of this beautiful novelty can be obtained :—Golden Bronze, Delicate Lilac Rose, Purple Prince, Picotee edged, Crimson Queen, Snowflake (pure white.)

Other double sorts are :—*Coronarium*, in various colours such as sulphur yellow, pure white and bright yellow. *Dunnettii* in golden yellow, white &c.

There are many classes of the Perennial Chrysanthemums such as :—*Indicum fl. pl.*, commonly known as the Florist's Chrysanthemum, and known to the native as Gul Cheenee or Daoodee. This class bears fine double flowers. *Japonicum fl. pl.* The beautiful loose flowered Japanese Chrysanthemums are very popular and extremely beautiful. *Pompone Double*, is a class with very double flowers.

CHRYSANTHEMUMS, PERENNIAL VARIETIES.

CHRYSANTHEMUM FRUTESCENS, the French Marguerite or Paris Daisy, is always a favourite, as it looks very handsome when in flower, while the cut flowers last for a very long time in water, and are consequently most useful for decorative purposes. The variety now grown is known as *Comtesse de Chambord* and is a great improvement in size on the old Paris Daisy. A Yellow Chrysanthemum which is often called the Yellow Paris Daisy, is *C. Sibthorpi*.

# CINERARIA.

## Nat. Ord.—Compositæ,

Unfortunately this beautiful perennial can only be treated as an annual in most places on the Plains. In order to get the plants to flower, sow immediately the rains have ended. Sow in pots or pans of light, rich soil, and as soon as the seedlings are large enough to handle, prick out into pans, or singly into small pots, and repot into 6 or 8 inch ones as soon as the plants have made sufficient growth. The best soil for the Cineraria is one composed of equal parts of fibrous loam, leaf mould and well rotted manure, together with a good proportion of coarse sand. Charcoal dust may also be used with advantage in making the compost. Feed the plants well with liquid manure or "Ichthemic" Guano, in order to encourage vigorous growth, and so induce the plants to flower by the beginning of February. On the Hills, sowings should be made both in October and March to May. There are many fine strains of this beautiful plant, as many of the leading growers at home have made a specialty of it. *James' Strain* has flowers of extraordinary size, shape and substance, while the habit of the plant is extremely compact and robust. I give illustrations of two splendid hybrids, *Grandiflora* and *Grandiflora Nana*, both of which are excellent strains. Another good strain is *Hayes' Prize*, which has flowers of most brilliant colours,

CINERARIA, HYBRIDA GRANDIFLORA.

CINERARIA, HYBRIDA GRANDIFLORA NANA.

grand size and substance. The double Cineraria is not, in my opinion, equal to the single flowering sorts, but one of the best kinds is *Hybrida Grandiflora Plenissima*, in which the flowers are very double and comprise a great number of colours. There is also a white foliaged Cineraria which is useful for bedding. There are several varieties differing little but in name, such as *Acanthifolia, Maritima* or *Candidissima*.

## CLARKIA.

### Nat, Ord.—Onagraceæ.

The Clarkia is a very pretty free flowering annual and should be grown much more extensively. Sow on the Plains in October and on the Hills from March to May. It is much the best to sow where the plants are to remain, as they do not stand transplanting well. Sow in a light, rich soil and give an abundance of moisture.

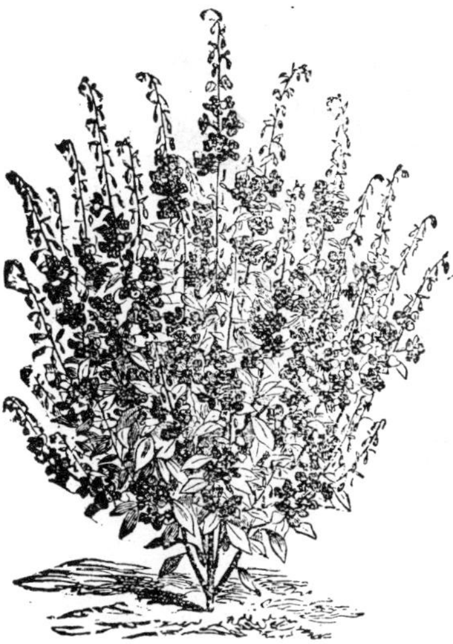

CLARKIA.

The following are the best varieties :—

*Elegans Carminea.*—A double variety with brilliant carmine flowers ; *Integripetala*—A very handsome free flowering variety ; *Mrs. Langtry*—Very free flowering and beautiful; flowers pure white with brilliant carmine centre ; *Pulchella*, Beautiful rose coloured flowers with narrow petals ; *Purple King*—Extra fine new double variety; *Salmon Queen*—Double salmon, a grand novelty.

## CLIANTHUS

### Nat. Ord.—Leguminosæ.
### (The Desert Pea or Glory Pea of Australia.)

One of the most beautiful plants in cultivation. The illustration on next page gives a good idea of the appearance of the flowers, which are of a rich shining scarlet, with large black blotches in front. On the Plains should be treated as an annual, and the seeds should be put in by the end of September or beginning of October. I advise the sowing of the seed in the pots in which the plants are to flower, as they do not stand re-potting well, the roots being extremely delicate. Grow in light, rich soil. On the Hills should be sown in March or April. The two varieties usually grown, are *Dampieri* in which the flowers are pear shaped, rich scarlet with conspicuous black blotch, and *Magnificus* which is a comparatively new introduction, with magnificent bright scarlet flowers.

CLIANTHUS. (See page 141.)

# CLINTONIA

**Nat. Ord.--Liliaceæ.**

Some Botanists place the Clintonia in the Natural Order Lobeliaceæ, but that Clintonia--Clintonia (Douglas)—is more properly named *Downingia.* A very beautiful little annual of extremely easy culture. Sow on the Plains in October; March or April in the Hills. Does best in a rather sandy soil. As the seeds are very tiny they should be very lightly covered with earth, or, better still, thinly scattered over the surface of the soil, which press down lightly after sowing; cover the pots with glass, and place in a shady situation, till the seed germinates. The soil for the Clintonia can hardly be too rich, and it requires any amount of moisture. If grown in pots, stand them in water. In order to get good flowers, keep the plants dwarf by pinching the tips of the leading shoots. *Elegans* has beautiful bright blue flowers, while *Pulchella* has blue flowers with yellow and white eye. There is also a very pretty pure white variety of the latter called *Pulchella Alba*.

## COBÆA.

### Nat. Ord.—Polemoniaceæ. (Mexican Ivy Plant.)

A Perennial on the Hills, where it grows splendidly, but can rarely be grown, except as an Annual, on the Plains. A very ornamental and free growing climber, as is shown in the illustration I give. Sow on the Plains in September or October; on the Hills sowings may be made both in October and in April and May. Plant out in well drained and moderately rich soil. Varieties grown are :—*Scandens*, large bell-shaped purple flowers; *Scandens Alba*, pure white, and *Macrostemma* (the "San Salvador." Cobæa) In this variety the foliage is of a bright vivid green, and the flowers are most strikingly effective, with their long stamens, as shown in the illustration which I give on next page.

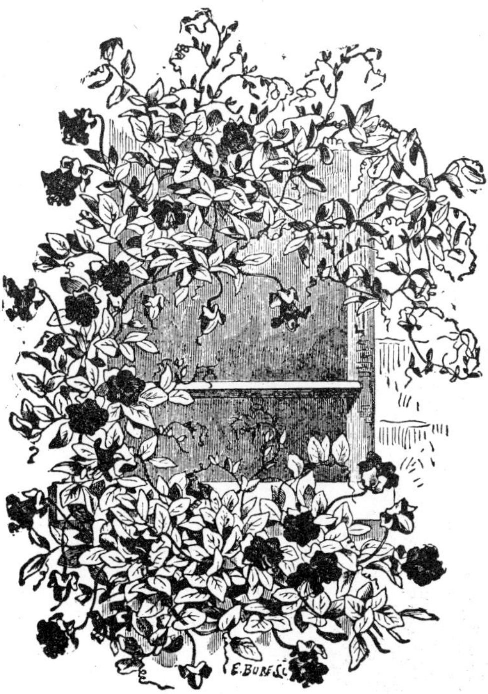

COBÆA SCANDENS.

## COLEUS.

### Nat. Ord.—Labiateæ (Flame Nettle.)

One of the best known plants in India, where it grows magnificently. The Coleus requires a light, rich soil to bring it to perfection.

On the Plains sow in July, also in October, while on the Hills I prefer sowing in October, under glass, as nice young plants are then ready for potting off in the early Spring. The Coleus is difficult to keep alive during the Winter on the Hills, and requires the protection of a glass frame, or sunny glazed verandah. I remember some few years ago losing a splendid collection of some 40 distinct varieties, although the plants were kept in a greenhouse exposed to the full sun, but this was in Landour, at an altitude of close on 7000 feet. The Coleus succeeds best in a compost composed of one-half fibrous loam, one fourth thoroughly rotted manure, and the remaining quarter made up of equal parts of coarse sand and well rotted leaf mould. A new strain lately introduced is *Hybridus Macrophyllus* in which the leaves are very large, and most magnificently coloured. Most Seedsmen stock the seed of Coleus in mixed strains only, and if the seed is obtained from a reliable firm, many fine sorts can be raised from such seed.

COBÆA, MACROSTEMMA. (See page 143.)

HYDRID COLEUS.

# COLLINSIA.

**Nat. Ord.**—Scrophulariaceæ. (Collin's Flower.)

A well-known old annual which grows easily, and requires but little care. Is very useful for beds or borders and well worth growing. Sow on the Plains in October, March to May on the Hills. The best sorts are, *Bicolor*, white and rosy-purple, height 1 foot. *Candidissima*, pure white, and *Grandiflora* a variety with large, dark blue flowers. For all practical purposes, most readers will find a packet or so of mixed seed ample.

COLLINSIA.

# Convolvulus Minor.

**Nat. Ord.—Convolvulaceæ.**

**(Morning Glory.)**

These only grow about 1 foot high; the flowers are freely borne, and remain open all day, if pleasant; splendid for bedding and for hanging baskets. Sow in October on the Plains; March in the Hills. Requires a light, rich soil.

Does not succeed very well in some places on the Plains, but does admirably on the Hills.

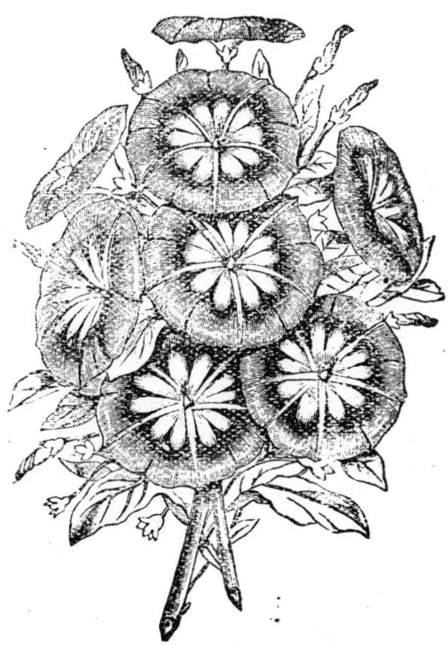

CONVOLVULUS MINOR.

# CONVOLVULUS MAJOR,

## Or Ipomœa Purpurea.

### Nat. Ord.—Convolvulaceæ. (Morning Glory.)

This is one of the most free flowering and beautiful of all the annual climbers. Is of very rapid growth and succeeds admirably on the Plains, where the seed should be sown at any time from June to August, also in October. On the Hills sow from April to July. There are many beautiful colours in this annual, such as, Crimson, Carmine, Dark Purple, Lilac, Rose, Striped, White &c.

CONVOLVULUS MAJOR.

In Convolvulus Major New Double (Ipomœa Purpurea fl. pl.) has been introduced a really first class novelty, which, as the number of hardy annual climbers is not very great, will be greeted as a welcome addition to this class of plants. It is of rapid growth and produces its double flowers very freely, resembling in form those of the Calystegia pubescens fl. pl. They are white with a slight spot of red or of blue at the base of the larger petal. About 80 per cent. of the seedlings will reproduce themselves true from seed, the remainder will flower semi-double or single. Other colours are also being introduced, so we may soon expect to see all the popular colours of the single kind.

In *Convolvulus Mauritanicus,* we have a very pretty little twining perennial, bearing flowers of a beautiful blue, with white throat and yellow anthers, about 1 inch across. Is excellent for hanging baskets.

Under the heading of IPOMŒA will be found a number of other very fine Convolvuli.

CONVOLVULUS MAJOR NEW DOUBLE.

# COSMEA (Cosmos.)

**Nat. Ord.**—Compositæ. (The Mexican Aster.)

An annual which is becoming extremely popular in India, where it grows very well. The illustration gives some idea of the appearance of the plant, but it has to be grown in order to fully see its beauties. The flowers resemble a single Dahlia, in fact the Cosmea is a first cousin to that plant Sow in October on the Plains, April or May, and October on the Hills. Generally grows to a height of about 2 feet, but in rich soil will often reach 4 feet. The variety mostly grown is *Bipinnata*, of which there is an early flowering form known as *Earliest Flowering*.

COSMEA, (COSMOS.)

# CYCLAMEN PERSICUM.

**Nat. Ord.--Primulaceæ.—(Sow bread, Apple of the Earth or Mitre Flower )**

A most beautiful, free flowering bulbous plant, which grows well in most places on the Plains and comes to great perfection on the Hills. Sow in September or October, both on the Plains and Hills, in a compost composed of equal parts of gar'en loam, leaf mould and river sand, with a small proportion of thoroughly rotted manure. Requires very thorough drainage, otherwise the bulbs will rot off. When the young plants are large enough, pot off into 3 or 4 inch pots, in which they can be left to flower the first season. After flowering, gradually withold water till the plants die down. As soon as the tubers again begin to grow, repot into 5 or 6 inch pots in fresh compost, taking care not to disturb the roots too much. In potting, leave the tops of the bulbs above the soil. Place the pots in a slightly shaded position, as the Cyclamen is not fond of too much sun. The variety usually grown is *Persicum*, of which there is also an improved large flowering strain, known as *Giganteum* or *grandiflorum*, of which the flowers often

CYCLAMEN PERSICUM.

measure from 2 to 2½ inches in length, are of fine form, with broad massive petals. Colours vary from pure white, through shades of rose to dark red. Many of the flowers are marked with deep purple spots.

## DAHLIA.

### Nat. Ord.—Compositæ.

Not so very many years ago, the Dahlia was almost invariably grown by division of the fleshy roots, but nowadays the veriest amateur grows his plants from seed. It is very easy to do so, as seedlings will flower in three or four months from time of sowing, and will

Dahlia, Single Striped.

Dahlia, New Single Cactus.

give an enormous variety of colours and forms. For many years hybridisers did all they could to raise plants giving flowers as double as possible, but within the last few years public opinion has begun to favour the single varieties, of which there are now a very great number of forms. I illustrate two, which show two very distinct forms of flowers ; while in a third illustration of a single variety, I show the free flowering and robust growing habit of another single sort. On the Plains the seed should be sown in September or October in pans or boxes ; March to May in the Hills. The soil used should be light and sandy; a mixture of equal parts of fibrous loam, leaf mould and coarse sand will be found the best. When the seedlings have made their second pair of leaves, transplant into small pots and shift on as they require it. Water freely, and give a good soaking with weak liquid manure once or twice a week When the plants have finished flowering let them die down, and when dry, knock them out of the pots and store in dry sand. I advise growers to plant out their tubers the second year in the open garden, or

DAHLIA, WHITE QUEEN.

if pot plants are wanted, pot in as large pots as possible, 12 inch at least. Tubers of both Double and Single Dahlias are procurable from gardens on the Hills, and these should be put down as soon as possible after the middle of October. On the Hills the tubers should be lifted at least every third year, otherwise they will deteriorate. I always lift my tubers every second year and store in a cool godown. There are numerous forms and varieties innumerable. A very useful strain known as *Cheal's Tom Thumb* has lately been introduced, and as these only grow to a height of about twelve inches, they will be found very useful for bedding or for edgings to beds, borders or shrubberies. In the *New Single Cactus* we have a new type which is becoming very popular. The petals are twisted or fluted in

DAHLIA, DOUBLE CACTUS-FLOWERED.

the same way as the Double Cactus-Flowered, and as the colours are very various and beautiful, they are well worth growing. *Dwarf White Queen* is a very compact, free flowering variety, as shown in the illustration I give. The flowers are perfect in shape, pure white with yellow centre. *Single Striped* is a comparatively new class in which the flowers are beautifully striped, mottled and blotched. *Double Liliput* is a variety with miniature pompone-like flowers. *Juarezii* is one of the double Cactus flowering strains, in which the flowers resemble those of the Cereus Cactus, as shown in the illustration. The colours are very beautiful, being pure white, rich scarlet, crimson and various shades of reds.

# DATURA.

Nat. Ord.—Solanaceæ.

(*Jamestown Weed, or Thorn Apple.*)

(Vern.—Dhootura, or Jooz Masul.)

The Datura does not require much description, as it is well known all over India, many varieties growing wild in various parts of the country. Many of the cultivated sorts are very beautiful, and as they are of easy culture, should be widely grown. They will grow anywhere but do best in a light, rich soil. Sow on the Plains in July; June on the Hills. The variety I illustrate is a most magnificent one. As many as 200 to 300 flowers have been counted in a season on a single plant. The stems are dark purplish maroon, while the flowers, which are nearly 8 inches long by 5 inches across, are a beautiful glistening French White inside with purple exteriors. To add to their beauty, they are delightfully fragrant. In the *Fastuosa* varieties we have large flowering sorts. *Fastuosa Alba fl. pl*, being pure white, edged with purple, and *Fastuosa Purpurea fl. pl.* bright purple with yellow base. The *Huberiana fl. pl.* varieties are hybrids of Fastuosa and are very double, in many fine colours.

## DELPHINIUM.

Nat. Ord.—Ranunculaceæ (Dolphin Flower, or Larkspur.)

DELPHINIUM, HYBRIDUM.

The Perennial Larkspur is difficult to grow on the Plains, where it should be grown as an Annual. Sow about the middle of November. On the Hills sow in April, and they will flower in the following Spring. Should be grown in a fairly deep soil, which should be very liberally manured.

## Dianthus or Pinks.

Nat. Ord.—Caryophyllaceæ.

There are few more beautiful annuals than the various kinds of Dianthus, and as they grow freely in practically any kind of soil, should be grown in every garden. On the Plains sow in October; March to May on the Hills. Plant out in light rich soil as soon as they have made six or eight

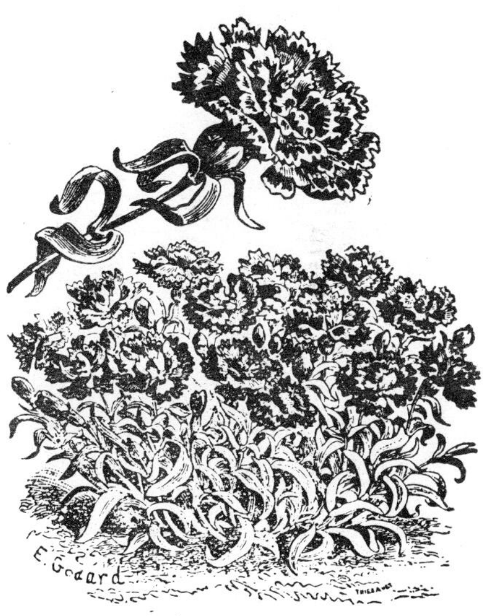


DIANTHUS, CHINENSIS NANUS, FL. PL.

DWARF DIADEM PINK.

leaves. There are a great number of varieties of this useful plant, many of them being particularly beautiful. One of the best sorts is the *Dwarf Diadem Pink.* (Dianthus Diadematus Nanus fl. pl.). The plants grow to a height of about 7 to 9 inches, and the flowers are of good form and very large. The illustration given shows the form of this sterling sort. One of the best of the single flowering varieties, is a new one called *Cyclops,* in which the flowers are quite six inches in circumference, are borne in great profusion and are very fragrant. A variety which has always been a great favourite is *Laciniatus fl. pl.,* in which the large double white flowers are striped with various shades of red, from the most delicate rose to the deepest shades. Two fine self coloured varieties of Laciniatus have been introduced under the names of *Snowflake and Crimson King,* the flowers being of enormous size, very fragrant and delicately fringed at the edges of the petals. *The Bride,* one of the single Japanese Pinks, is a novelty of great beauty. The large, perfectly formed flowers are snowy white with conspicuous centres of velvety dark purple. One great want in the annual Dianthus has been the want of yellows, but this has been removed by the introduction of the *Guillaud.* The flowers are very large, fragrant and last a

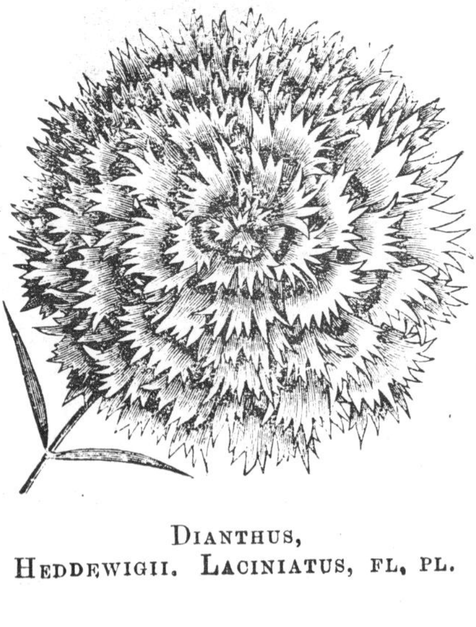

DIANTHUS,
HEDDEWIGII. LACINIATUS, FL, PL.

long time, either cut or on the plants. The strain contains flowers of pure yellow and others with yellow stripes. Another shade which has hitherto been wanting is salmon, but in *Salmon Queen* we have a beautiful double variety with flowers of the most brilliant salmon. The plants grow to a height of some 10 to 12 inches. *Mourning Cloak*, as its name implies, is a very dark coloured sort, of which the illustration given gives a very good idea. The flowers are of a rich black purple with white edges. The double Imperial Pinks (*Imperialis* fl. pl.) have very large double flowers, of a great variety of colours. *Eastern Queen*, single, with large bright rose flowers. *Crimson Belle*, a variety similar to *Eastern Queen* in form, but bearing flowers of a deep glowing crimson. In *Chinensis fl. pl.* we have the old fashioned double Indian Pink, the flowers are very double and of every shade from pure white to deepest purple, many being peculiarly blotched and marbled. A new dwarf growing form has been introduced under the name of *Chinensis Nanus fl. pl.*, in which the plants seldom grow higher than 6 or 8 inches. A good sort for bedding. Other good kinds which are much grown are :—*Heddewigi*, single flowering blooms 3 to 4 inches in diameter ; *Heddewigi Albus fl. pl.*, pure white, large extra double flowers. *Hybridus fl. pl.*, very large flowering, intensely double.

DIANTHUS, MOURNING CLOAK.

# DIGITALIS.

### Nat. Ord.—Scrophulariceæ.—(Fox Glove, Dead Men's Bells, Fairy Fingers, Finger Flower or Flap Dock.)

The Fox Glove is known by many names, but by whatever name it be called it still remains the old favourite of the home hedgerow. Unfortunately it is difficult to grow on the Plains, where seed should be sow

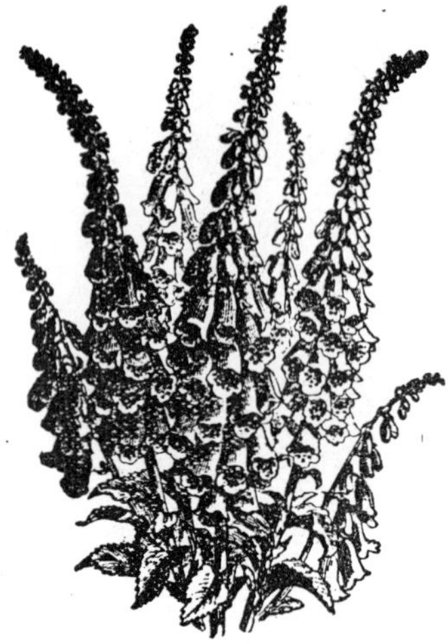

DIGITALIS.

at the end of September or beginning of October. Lovers of the old home flowers, who are resident on the Hills, can get the Fox Glove in great perfection by sowing the seed in March. Any ordinary garden soil will do. *Alba* is a very fine strain with beautiful white flowers, many being prettily spotted. *Gloxinoides* is a fine strain with Gloxinia-like flowers, beautifully spotted in many pretty colours. *Purpurea* is the common Fox Glove which is known by the many names I give at the heading. Grows to a height of 3 to 5 feet. Colour purple, marked on the inside with dark spots, edged with white.

---

## DODECATHEON, MEADIA.

### Nat. Ord.—Primulaceæ.—(American Cowslip.)

This is a most beautiful plant. The flowers are various, rosy purple, white or lilac, with yellow anthers; grows to a height of 10 to 16 inches. In America known as "Shooting Star." I doubt very much whether this could be induced to flower on the Plains, but if the plants can be grown in a very shady, moist situation, they are well worth trying, as the flowers are very pretty. Sow on the Plains at the end of September; Hills October and in March. Does best in a compost composed of equal parts of leaf mould and fibrous loam.

---

## ERYTHRINA.

### Nat. Ord.—Leguminosæ. (Coral Tree.)

A very beautiful member of the Pea family, which is worthy of much more extensive cultivation. Sow during the rains, both on the Plains and Hills. The plants grow to a height of some 6 to 8 feet and bear beautiful bright scarlet flowers. Plant in a soil made up of about equal parts of loam, leaf mould and sand, and in a position well exposed to bright sunshine.

# ERYTHROLÆNA, CONSPICUA.

## Nat. Ord.—Compositæ. (Mexican Thistle.)

Also known as Cnicus Conspicuus. The plants form densely leaved bushes, and, when in full flower, attain a height of about 4 to 6 feet ; the flower stems are blackish brown, erect and many branched ; the leaves dark green with brownish red ribs, 2½ to 3 feet in length, by 15 to 18 inches in breadth. Flower heads conical, 3 and 4 at the top of each branch, resembling in form and in their lovely bright orange-carmine colour, the buds of a Phyllocactus. The flowers, which do not spread like most of the other Thistles, are also conical, and present with their stamens of a beautiful pink, tipped carmine, a splendid aspect, showing three distinct bright colours. A really fine ornamental foliaged, as well as an ornamental flowering plant, which will prove of great effect either for large groups or as single specimens. As cut flowers they retain their unique colour for a long time. It will be sure to be a fashionable cut-flower in the future. Sow on the Plains in October Spring on the Hills. Grows well in any ordinary garden soil.

ERYTHROLÆNA, CONSPICUA.

---

# ESCHSCHOLTZIA.

## Nat. Ord.—Papaveraceæ—(The Californian Poppy.)

A very handsome, free flowering, hardy Annual. As it does not stand transplanting should be sown where it is to flower, in October on the Plains ; on the Hills, March to May, also in October. Succeeds in any ordinary garden soil. The varieties most grown are :—

*Californica*—A handsome variety with hoary green, much divided foliage ; bears a profusion of large, expanded, bright yellow flowers, height of plants 1½ feet ; *Carminea Grandiflora*—A charming variety

ESCHSCHOLTZIA.

of this deservedly popular section, with large flowers of intense carmine rose. It is perfectly distinct and much superior in every respect to the well known *E. Rosea*. In habit of growth, foliage and size of flower, this novelty is the counterpart of *E. Mandarin*, and like it, blooms freely until late in the season. *Crocea Flore Pleno.*—Fine orange colour, producing a large proportion of double flowers, height 1 foot. *Mandarin*—A new, distinct variety; the outer side of the petals of a most brilliant orange crimson, the inner side rich orange; very showy. Most Seedsmen offer a mixture of the best varieties, and this will be found best for most gardens, where separate colours are not specially required.

# EUCALYPTUS.

## Nat. Ord.—Myrtaceæ. (Gum Tree.)

The Eucalyptus, when well grown, is one of the most beautiful of trees, and is said to make feverish places healthy. The variety *Globulus* has been known to attain a height of 300 feet, so cannot be recommended for the *flower garden*. They make very fine avenues and the timber is very durable. Sow both on the Plains and Hills in October, in pots or pans of light, sandy soil. When large enough pot off singly in 5 or 6 inch pots, and when thoroughly established, plant out in rich soil. A mixture of fibrous loam, leaf mould and well rotted manure suits them admirably. There are a very great number of more or less distinct varieties, but the two most grown in India are the old *Globulus* and the sweet scented *Citriodora.* I have found the scent of the leaves of the former, if crushed between the fingers, very beneficial in headaches. The leaves of *Citriodora* are even more highly scented than those of the Lemon scented Verbena.

---

# EUPHORBIA, HETEROPHYLLA.

## Nat Ord. Euphorbiaceæ.--(Annual Pointsettia or Mexican Fire Plant.)

This rare and beautiful *hardy annual* is a native of Mexico and Southern Texas; with its brilliant colour and leafy habit it resembles *Pointsettia Pulcherrima.* The plants grow two to three feet high, of decidedly branching, bush like form, with smooth, glossy, fiddle-shaped leaves. The leaves are first entirely green, but about mid-summer, at the end of each branch appear greenish white flowers, enveloped in *beautiful orange-scarlet bracts* and the surrounding leaves are either *blotched with vivid carmine* or are *carmine, with green tips.* Whether grown as specimen plants or in masses, the effect of this combination of brilliant colouring is very striking. The earlier the plants are started, the sooner

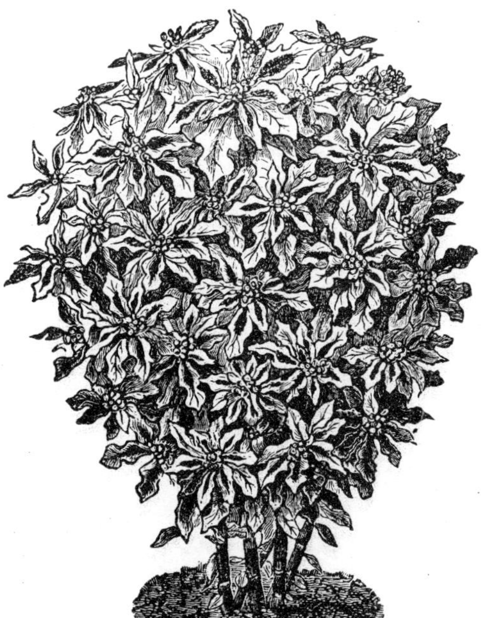

EUPHORBIA, HETEROPHYLLA.

will they develop their fine brilliant colours. Give them a sunny situation and water in very hot weather. They are also fine plants for house culture, seed sown early, producing plants that will bear their snowy bracts and carmine-blotched leaves throughout the cold weather, making elegant house plants. The compost best suited for this beautiful plant, is one composed of two parts fibrous loam, and one part each of dried cowdung and leaf mould. If grown as pot plants, should be grown in 7 or 8 inch pots. Sow both on the Plains and Hills in October.

# EUTOCA.

### Nat. Ord.—Hydrophyllaceæ.

Perhaps more commonly known as PHACELIA. Thrive in any ordinary garden soil. Very pretty, free flowering plants. Do not transplant, but sow where they are to remain, in October on the Plains and March to May on the Hills. There are a goodly number of varieties, among the best being:—*Multiflora* with pale blue flowers; *Viscida*, purplish blue, height 1 foot; *Wrangleana*, light violet.

# FERNS.

### Nat. Ord.—Filices.

The raising of ferns from spores or seed, is one of the most interesting operations in a garden, and, with ordinary care, cannot fail to produce a successful result. As the spores are very minute, great care should be used in sowing. Scatter thinly on the surface of fairly open soil, and cover the pots with a sheet of paper and a piece of glass, until the spores germinate. The tiny seedlings should be pricked out in little clumps, into other pots, and when large enough to handle, should be transplanted into small pots and potted on as required Ferns require very light, well drained soil. Spores may be put

FERN.

down at any time of the year, but I would recommend during the Rains, both on the Plains and Hills. The varieties of Ferns are legion, and when separate varieties are wanted, it is best to get them out from Europe. Indian Seedsmen seldom stock spores in separate varieties, usually contenting themselves with a mixture of the various kind of *Adiantums* (Maidenhair Ferns) and a mixture of the other varieties such as, *Asplenium*, *Davallia*, *Lastrea*, *Osmunda*, *Pteris*, *Onychium*, *&c.*, *&c.*

## FICUS.

### Nat. Ord.—Urticaceæ (Fig. Vern. Unjeer)

Very handsome foliage plants or trees. There are few plants more grown as pot plants for room decoration than *Ficus Elastica*, the Flower Markets at home often being literally glutted with them. Grow well in sandy loam mixed with a little leaf mould. The leaves should be frequently sponged and water should be given liberally. Sow in September or October both on the Plains and Hills. The varieties usually grown are *Cooperii* and *Elastica*. In the former the leaves are dark green, 1 foot long by 3 or 4 inches wide. *Elastica* is the Indiarubber plant. The leaves vary from 6 to 18 inches in length by 3 to 6 in width; upper portion dark, shining green, yellowish green underneath.

## FUCHSIA.

### Nat. Ord.—Onagraceæ. (Ear-ring Flower.)

I do not recommend readers to grow Fuchsias from seed on the Plains as it is most difficult, if not impossible, to keep the plants alive during the hot weather. Plants can usually be obtained from Hill gardens at the beginning of the cold weather, and these should be obtained and after growing till the beginning of the hot weather, either thrown away or sent up to the Hills again. On the Hills plants can be raised from seed fairly easily, and it is most interesting to watch the plants in the various stages of their growth, with the

FUCHSIA.

chance of raising some new variety to add interest to the operation. Sow the seed in October under cover of a glass frame or warm sheltered verandah, or in the Spring. The Fuchsia likes an open soil made up of fibrous loam, leaf mould and sand in about equal parts. When the seedlings are large enough to handle, pot off into small pots and shift on as required. The Fuchsia can be propogated very easily from cuttings put down any time from March to the beginning of September.

---

# GAILLARDIA.

### Nat. Ord.—Compositæ. (Blanket Flower.)

Many of the Gaillardias are hardy perennials, but it is almost useless trying to grow them as such on the Plains. Sow in October and treat as annuals, transplanting as soon as large enough to handle, into light, rich soil. On the Hills sow in October and in the Spring. The Gaillardia is most useful for cutting, as it stands a long time in water. It is one of the most easily grown plants we have, as neither heat, damp or drought seem to affect it. There are many fine varieties, of which the following are perhaps the best :—

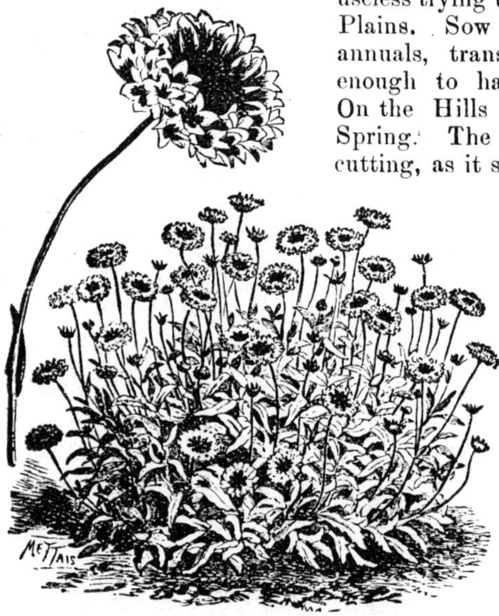

GAILLARDIA.

*Amblyodon*—Flowers bright crimson with black crimson centre, very showy ; *Hybrida Grandiflora*—Flowers bright crimson and yellow ; very showy and free flowering ; *Picta or Drummondi*—A very fine variety of compact habit. The flowers, which are of large size, are of a reddish crimson colour, bordered with yellow ; *Picta Lorenziana*—A variety of recent introduction, producing large heads of double flowers in various brilliant colours. In the new *Perennial Hybrids*, has been introduced a strain unrivalled for brilliancy, rich blendings of colours, magnificent size and profusion of bloom. If grown in masses in a fairly shady situation, are very effective, but should be plentifully supplied with water during

HYBRID GAILLARDIA

hot weather. The plants grow to a height of about 18 inches and flower the first season from seed.

## GERANIUMS.

### Nat. Ord.—Geraniaceæ. (Crane's Bill).

I do not advise readers to attempt the growing of Geraniums from seed on the Plains. It is much more satisfactory to get plants or cuttings from the Hills at the beginning of the cold weather. However, if readers want to try the experiment, they should sow the seed in October. Sow in very light soil composed principally of sand and leaf mould, with a small proportion of fibrous loam added The feathery portion of the

GERANIUM, DOUBLE ZONALE.

seed should not be covered with soil. Plants grown from seed seldom, if ever, show any of their distinctive features during their first year, but improve immensely during the second and third years. When your young seedlings are large enough to handle, prick out into pans or boxes, and when established, pot singly in 3 inch pots, shifting on as required. For potting use a fairly rich soil composed of equal parts of loam, leaf mould and thoroughly rotted manure. On the Hills sow in spring under cover. The Geranium is much improved by an occasional watering with weak liquid manure; a liquid made with "Ichthemic" Guano will be found very beneficial. There are many classes of Geraniums and Pelargoniums, the latter being merely a class of the former, but the following list comprises most of the classes of Geraniums usually grown: —*Odoratissimum* (Apple Scented), the leaves of which are very strongly scented; *Ivy Leaved*, very useful for hanging baskets or for training over trellises; *Tricolor*, of various colours, in which the leaves are beautifully banded or blotched in various colourings, as golden, golden and bronze, silver &c. *Zonal* e Single and Double, which bear grand flowers of many colours.

GERANIUM TRICOLOR.

# GESNERA.

## Nat. Ord.—Gesneraceæ.

A very pretty member of the tuberous rooted family of plants. Do not do particularly well in most parts of the Plains, but, if sheltered from direct sunlight, are well worth growing. Succeed admirably on the Hills. Sow on the Plains in September or October; March in the Hills. Require a very light sandy soil and plenty of moisture, with thorough drainage. There are several distinct sorts, but a few seeds of mixed hybrids will be found sufficient for most gardens.

# GILIA.

## Nat. Ord.—Polemoniaceæ.

A genus closely resembling the Phlox and requiring much the same treatment. On the Plains sow in October and plant out when about 2 inches high. Sow on the Hills in March. Require a rather light soil. A mixture of colours makes a very pretty edging to beds. The colours are very various including red, pink, white, violet, lilac, &c. The plants grow to a height of only about 6 to 9 inches.

# GLADIOLUS.

## Nat. Ord.—Iridaceæ (Sword Lily.)

Beautiful bulbous plants, very free flowering and grow well on the Plains. Are easily raised from seed. On the Plains sow in September and October, and at the same time on the Hills, where sowings should also be made in February and March. The Gladiolus likes a light, rich, well drained soil, which should be deeply dug before planting. Sow the seed in pans or boxes, transplant the young plants into small pots when large enough, and plant out in the open garden in November on the Plains and in the Spring on the Hills. Look best when planted in rows or clumps, and particularly well when planted in front of a row of shrubs. The colours are very varied and the plant is one of the most beautiful in cultivation. What adds to its value, is the fact that the flowers last a very long time in water, for if cut when the bottom flowers of the spike have opened, the remainder of the flowers will open in succession.

GLADIOLUS.

The *Gandavensis* varieties are very large flowering, with strong, well formed spikes. A comparatively new race has been introduced by the famous hybridiser M. Lemoine, which is known as *Lemoine's Hybrids.* The spikes are smaller than in the Gandavensis strain, but are most magnificently coloured.

---

# GLOXINIA.

## Nat. Ord.—Gesneraceæ.

The Gloxinia is undoubtedly one of the most beautiful flowering plants in cultivation, and has been immensely improved during the past few years. The seeds are very small, and when sown, require very little soil for covering; in fact I prefer to dispense with it entirely, giving them the same treatment as recommended for Tuberous Begonias. There are very many distinct classes and sorts, some with upright flowers, others with horizontal ones, and others again with drooping flowers. All are beautiful in their own way, and the plant is one worthy of the widest cultivation. One of the best strains in cultivation is known as *Hetherset Hybrids.* The flowers are all erect, very large, 3 to 4 inches across, with large open throats, displaying to the fullest perfection their gorgeous colourings, which are of every conceivable shade from pure white, pink, clear rose, lilac, scarlet, crimson, maroon, and purple, to rich purplish black, most profusely spotted in the throat, some having the limb heavily marked with colour, without spots. Various selections of *Crassifolia grandiflora* such as *Erecta* (Erect flowering), Horizontalis (semi-erect flowering) and *Pendula* (drooping flowering), are much grown. The French tigered and spotted hybrids known as *Hybrida Punctata,* contain many very beautiful varieties. Those who prefer separate colours will find them in such sorts as :—*Emperor Frederick,* the flowers of which are enormous in size, and of a fiery scarlet colour to nearly the base of the throat, and encircled at the edge by a clearly defined, broad, pure white band ; *Princess Maud,* another of the large flowering section. The throat is a light, shining, crimson red, shading to the top a rich dark carmine, followed by a beautiful edging of pure violet, while a broad band of white spotted violet surrounds the whole of the fine waved bloom. *Scarlet Defiance,* of intense glowing crimson-scarlet colour. The flowers are large and the edges of the petals delicately frilled.

GLOXINIA.

# GODETIA.

### Nat. Ord.—Onagraceæ.

Closely allied to the Evening Primrose (Œnothera), and a very beautiful free flowering hardy annual. Sow early in October on the Plains ; Hills, March to May. Should be transplanted into a light, very rich soil, and given plenty of water, with an occasional drenching with weak liquid manure, which will greatly increase the size of the flowers. Besides being very beautiful plants for the open border, make splendid pot plants, if liberally treated and well grown. There are very many varieties all of them very pretty. The following list comprises most of the best. *Duke of York*, the individual blooms are of very large size, and of the most intense satiny scarlet carmine colour, with lighter centre; *Fairy Queen*, flowers white, passing into blush with large carmine spots at the base of each petal; *Pumila Hybrida*, a very fine strain of dwarf compact habit, with flowers of most brilliant and varied coloursa ranging from pure white to rich crimson; *White Pearl*, pure white variety of very dwarf, compact habit, peculiarly fitting, it for dwarf beds or ribboning; *Bijou.*—The dwarfest variety, very bushy plants, covered with pure white flowers, marked with a dark rose spot; *Bridesmaid.*—A splendid variety, flowers in shape and size resembling "Lady Albemarle," but of a very delicate shade of pink; *Duchess of Albany*—Flowers of a beautiful satiny white, each when fully expanded, measuring about 4 inches across; *Lady Albemarle*—Flowers of an intense carmine crimson, shaded towards the edge of petals with a delicate lilac tint; *Lady Satin Rose*, (Lady Albemarle Compact.)—A lovely variety, the flowers being of a beautiful deep rose pink, the surface shining like satin. One of the most beautiful varieties yet raised; *Princess of Wales*—Ruby crimson, pencilled with pale rose and silver grey; *Rubicunda Flore Pleno*—A fine double variety, with deep crimson flowers; *The Bride*—Pearly white flowers with carmine margin; *Whitneyi Brilliant Compacta*—A highly effective variety with brilliant carmine flowers; *Whitneyi Flammea*—Carmine and rose coloured flowers, very bright and attractive.

GODETIA.

## GOMPHRENA GLOBOSA.

### Nat. Ord.—Amaranthaceæ.

### (Globe Amaranth—Vern. Gulmukhmul.)

One of the Everlastings which, when grown in large masses, is very effective. Sow, both on the Plains and Hills, in June and July in pots or pans, and transplant when large enough to handle. If the flowers are wanted for drying for decoration, they should be cut just before

GLOBE AMARANTH.

coming to maturity. The ordinary variety is *Globosa*, which has flowers of a great variety of colours. From the original sort, distinct varieties have been selected, such as *Nana Compacta*, a dwarf growing species which rarely exceeds 6 inches in height, but with flowers quite as large as the parent variety. In *Globosa Variegata* we have a very pretty sort with distinct variegated foliage.

---

# GOURDS, ORNAMENTAL.

## Nat. Ord.—Cucurbitaceæ.

A large and interesting class, producing a great variety of curiously shaped fruits, many of which are peculiarly marked; most of the fruits, when fully ripe, are hard shelled and may be kept for years, forming objects that will excite much attention. On the Plains sow from

May to October; Hills, middle of April to middle of June. Require a rich, heavily manured soil, with plenty of water. Give the support

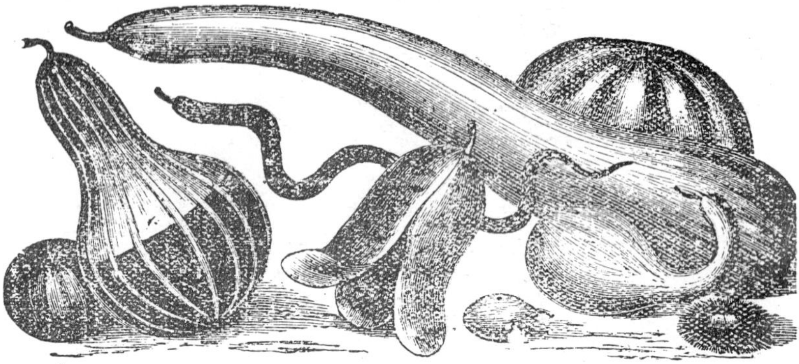

GOURDS, ORNAMENTAL,

of a stout trellis. The dried fruits make a very unique and striking collection.

## Grasses, Ornamental.

Nat. Ord.—Gramineæ.

These certainly deserve a place in every garden. Not only are they exceedingly beautiful in growth, but many of them, for mixing with cut flowers, are certainly worthy rivals of the popular Maidenhair Fern. Sow in October on the Plains; March to May on the Hills. Sowings may also be made during the rains.

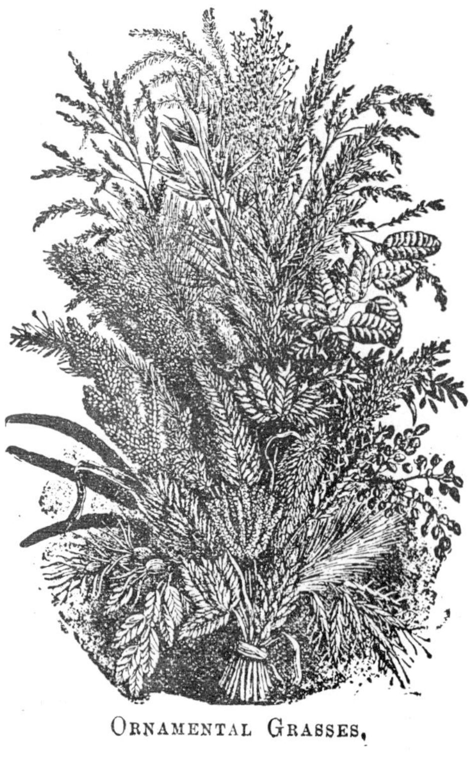

ORNAMENTAL GRASSES.

The most ornamental sorts are :—

*Arundo Donax* (Distaff Cane); *Avena Sterilis* (Animated Oat); *Briza Maxima* (Pearl or Quaking Grass); *Bromus Brizæformis*; *Coix Lachrymæ* (Job's Tears, *Vern.* Gurgur); *Eulalia Japonica*;

*Festuca Rigida*; *Gynerium Argenteum* (Pampas Grass); *Hordeum Jubatum* (Squirrel tail Grass); *Stipa Pinnata* (Feather Grass); *Zea Gracillima Variegata* (Miniature Maize); *Zea Japonica Variegata* (Stiiped Leaved Maize.)

## GREVILLEA.

### Nat. Ord.—Proteaceæ.

An ornamental tree which grows readily in India. Makes a very pretty pot plant, as shown in the illustration. *Robusta* is the variety usually grown. The soil most suitable is composed of fibrous loam, a small proportion of peat, if obtainabie, or leaf mould, with some coarse sand added. The plants will be benefitted by doses of weak liquid manure, which should be given once a week. On the Plains sow in October, while on the Hills sowings may be made both in October and in the early Spring, under cover. Sow in pans or boxes, transplanting into small pots and shifting on as required. When too large for pot culture, plant out in the open garden. In order to have well shaped trees, take care not to break the leading shoot.

GREVILLEA ROBUSTA.

## GYPSOPHILA.

### Nat. Ord.—Caryophyllaceæ. (The Chalk Plant.)

The Gypsophila, as its common name of Chalk plant implies, is fond of a chalky soil, and to grow it successfully, a good amount of old lime or brick rubbish should be used in the compost in which it is grown. I doubt very much whether this plant could be grown on the Plains, but on the Hills it grows well. Sow the seed in Spring, Some of the best varieties are :—*Elegans*, rosy white, a very beautiful variety which grows to a height of 1½ feet ; *Paniculata*, grows to a height of some 2 to 3 feet, and bears numerous whitish flowers. A very elegant and graceful perennial, the flowers of which are very useful for table decoration ; *Muralis*, a very dwarf growing sort, bearing rose coloured flowers. Useful for rockwork or edgings..

## HABROTHAMNUS.

### Nat. Ord.—Solanaceæ.—(Syn. Cestrum.)

A very pretty genus, most of them of climbing habit. To grow successfully should be planted in a compost composed of fibrous loam, leaf mould and a small proportion of sand. Thorough drainage is an absolute necessity and the plants should be given plenty of root room. The flowers are something like the Erica (Heath) and are borne in dense bunches. Is not quite hardy, so should be given the protection of a glass house or warm verandah during the winter. Seed should be sown in October, both on the Plains and Hills. *Elegans*, the variety usually grown in India, bears purplish-red flowers, in large flattened panicles. The branches and under sides of the leaves are downy.

## HEDYSARUM.

### Nat. Ord.—Leguminosæ. (French Honeysuckle, Maltese Clover or Red Satin Flower.)

A plant of very easy culture in any ordinary garden soil, but a deeply dug soil, in a fairly sunny situation, suits it best. Sow in October on the Plains ; March or April on the Hills. Sow in pots or pans and transplant into the garden when large enough. The variety usually grown is *H. Coronarium*, of which there are two colours, red and white. Grows to a height of some 3 to 4 feet.

HEDYSARUM, CORONARIUM.

## HELENIUM BIGELOWI.

### Nat. Ord.—Compositæ. (The Helen flower or Sneeze wort.)

One of the most useful plants for cut flowers. The flowers are borne on long stalks, are most elegantly shaped, and are of a vivid golden yellow, with black centre. The plants grow to a height of nearly 3 feet, and produce their flowers in great abundance. Sow both on the Plains and Hills in October, while a sowing may also be put in on the Hills in the Spring

HELENIUM BIGELOWI.

# HELIANTHUS.

## Nat. Ord.—Compositæ. (Sunflower).

(Vern. Sooruj Mukhee.)

One of the most popular of the æsthetic flowers, and many of the varieties are well worth a place in every garden A number of new sorts have been introduced of late years, many of which are really beautiful. Sow both on the Plains and Hills in July, but put in small sowings in October on the Plains and March to May on the Hills, for successional flowering. Plant out when the seeedlings are about six inches high, or sow where the plants are to flower. As most of the tall growing sorts are rampant growers, they should be given plenty of room to allow them to develope properly. The following are amongst the best sorts :—

HELIANTHUS, TALL SINGLE.

### Single Varieties.

*Nanus Folsis Variegatis*—Green and variegated foliage ; very ornamental ; *New Miniature*—A grand dwarf, small flowering variety. The flowers, which are borne in great luxuriance, are of a pale yellow, with dark centre. A very valuable variety for cutting ; *Oscar Wilde or Golden Nigger*—A new single variety ; flowers medium size, with bright yellow petals changing to brown at the base ; *Primrose Yellow*—A variety of *Helianthus Annuus* with blush and primrose coloured flowers, which cannot but prove a very striking and

SUNFLOWER, DOUBLE MULTIFLOR.

desirable acquisition ; *Russian Giant*--Flowers 18 to 20 inches in diameter, grown principally for the seed, of which it is very prolific.

## Double Varieties.

*Californicus Flore Pleno*--Extra double, bright golden yellow ; *Double Multiflor*--Found amongst Helianthus Globosus ; it differs from it by a new and most distinct feature. Instead of being branchy and bearing the flowers at the ends of the shoots, this plant is pyramidal in shape, and the flowers are produced in immense numbers at the base of each leaf, which gives it a most picturesque and highly ornamental aspect. The illustration shows the form of this beautiful novelty; *Globosus Fistulosus*--Flowers of a globular outline, 12 to 18 inches in diameter, of a rich saffron yellow ; one of the best of the doubles ; *Nanus Flore Pleno*—Fine dwarf variety.

## HELICHRYSUM MONSTROSUM.

### Nat. Ord.--Compositæ (The "Immortelle" or Golden Moth-Wort.)

One of the finest of the Everlastings, and grows well in India. If the flowers are cut as the buds commence to open, and dried in a cool, airy place, they will keep their colour for years. On the Plains sowings should be made in October ; March and April on the Hills. Require a good rich soil. When the seedlings are about 3 inches high, they should either be potted off singly in 5 or 6 inch pots, or planted out in the open border. The variety commonly grown is *Monstrosum Double Mixed*, a selection in which there is a great variety of colours. A very pretty pure white selection has been made from *Monstrosum* which can be obtained from Seedsmen under the name of *Silver Ball*. The plants grow to a height of about 2½ feet, with luxuriant bright green foliage, and produce, in great abundance, large beautifully

HELICHRYSUM MONSTROSUM.

formed double flowers of the purest possible white. Another fine selection known as *Tom Thumb*, is well worth growing, as the plants seldom grow more than a foot high, and, when in full flower, are almost entirely covered with flowers of every shade of colour.

---

# HELIOTROPE.

### Nat. Ord.—Boraginaceæ. (Cherry Pie or Turnsole.)

On the Plains it is essential that seed should be sown as soon as possible after the rains, to enable the plants to mature sufficiently to flower before the hot weather sets in. The soil should be light, but well manured with thoroughly rotted cow manure and leaf mould. When the seedlings are about 2 inches high, they should be potted off into 10 or 12 inch pots. Give plenty of water and a good drenching with weak liquid manure every few days. The plants should then bloom freely in February or March. On the Hills sow from March to May. Amongst the best sorts are :—

HELIOTROPE.

*Madame de Blonay*—Nearly white; good for bouquets; *Peruvianum*—Bright lavender, very free flowering; *Queen of the Violets*—Bright violet; *Roi des Noirs*—Very dark blue, almost black; *Triomphe de Liege*—Beautiful bright purple; *Voltaireanum*—Splendid dark variety; *White Lady*—Pure white, large truss.

---

# HEUCHERA, SANGUINEA.

### Nat. Ord. Saxifragaceæ (The Alum root.)

Is of easy culture, growing well in any ordinary garden soil. This variety bears spikes of brilliant crimson flowers, and grows to a height of 9 inches to 18 inches. A sterling novelty, well worth a place in every garden. On the Plains sow in October and on the Hills at the same time, where a sowing should also be made in March or April.

# HIBISCUS.

Nat. Ord—Malvaceæ. (Marsh Mallow).

The Hibiscus is one of the most beautiful plants to be found in Indian gardens, and, when well grown, makes a most magnificent addition to any garden. The best compost for it is largely composed of peat, but as this is not readily obtainable in India, I advise a mixture of well rotted leaf mould and fibrous loam in about equal parts, together with a little coarse sand and charcoal dust. Do not break up the compost too fine, but leave it rather lumpy. The African Ketmia (*H. Africanus* or *Trionum*) is a very pretty annual, bearing in great abundance, large yellow flowers with purple centres. The seed should be sown on the Plains in October; March on the Hills. This plant grows to a height of 2 feet. The many varieties of *Hibiscus Rosa Sinensis* are extremly popular and do well in India. The flowers are of very varied colours and are both single and double. Its common name is the Chinese Rose or the Chinese Shoe Plant, and it is known to the native mali by several names, such as, Jasoon, Joona and Jupa. This is a Perennial and seed should be sown in October, both on the Plains and Hills. The plants vary in height from 10 to 15 feet. In addition to being very beautiful when allowed to attain its full height in the open garden, it makes a very pretty pot plant when comparatively small, as shown in the illustration I give.

# HOLLYHOCK.

## Nat. Ord.—Malvaceæ. (The Holy Hoke. Vern. Gul Kheera.)

Although the Hollyhock (Althæa Rosea) is, properly speaking, a biennial, it can only be grown as an annual on the Plains, where the seed should be sown as soon as possible after the rains. The Hollyhock will grow in any ordinary garden soil, but it well repays feeding, so I advise readers before planting out, to have the ground well trenched and liberally manured; a good top dressing with well rotted manure when the flower buds are forming, will greatly improve the plants, and consequently the flowers. The Hollyhock is, unfortunately, very liable to be attacked by a certain fungus (Puccinia Malvacearum) and care must be taken not to allow this to spread if once it starts. The fungus shows on the under side of the leaves in small spots of a reddish brown colour. The only thing to be done when plants are attacked, is to destroy all the attacked leaves as the fungus appears. On the Hills the seed should be sown from the beginning of March to about the middle of April. Personally I prefer to sow my Hollyhock seed in pots or pans and transplant when large enough, but this has to be done carefully, as the plant does not bear transplanting well. The seed can be sown where the plants are wanted to flower, and thinned out to a distance of 3 to 4 feet between the plants. The flower stems will require to be staked, as they are apt to become top-heavy. An occasional drenching with weak liquid manure will be found very beneficial. Mr. Chater is perhaps the most famous hybridiser of the Hollyhock, and his strain will be found extra fine.

HOLLYHOCK.

# HONESTY.

## (Lunaria Biennis.)

### Nat. Ord.—Cruciferæ.

The old fashioned Honesty is but little grown now, although I can remember some 25 years or so ago, when it was to be found in every cottager's garden at home. I used to be very much interested in the peculiar flat, parchment-like, transparent seed pods, which were much used for mixing with dried grasses and everlastings for winter decorations. They succeed in any ordinary garden soil, but thrive best in a rather sandy compost. The variety usually grown is *Biennis*, which grows to a height of about 2 to 3 feet and bears pretty lilac coloured flowers. The seed should be sown on the Plains in October, and March to May on the Hills.

---

# HUMULUS.

### Nat. Ord.—Urticaceæ—[Hop].

The illustration hardly gives a fair idea of the beauty of this plant, which is one of the most useful climbers now in cultivation for covering verandahs, trellises, fences, arches, &c. It is one of the quickest growing Climbers known, and heat, drought and insects do not trouble it. The plants will grow in any ordinary garden soil, but to do really well, require a deep, loamy soil. There are two garden varieties in cultivation, and the common Hop (Humulus Lupulus) also makes a very useful climber. The garden varieties are introductions from China and Japan and are known as *Japonicus* and *Japonicus Variegatus*. Sow the seed in October on the Plains; on the Hills in October and again in the Spring. The commoner sort—Japonicus—has most luxuriant green foliage, but in the variegated variety we have a sterling novelty, in which the leaves are most beautifully marked with silvery-white, yellowish-white, yellowish-green or dark-green, sometimes in stripes, while other leaves will be marbled or blotched, and in some cases practically pure white leaves will be borne. It is no uncommon thing for the plants to attain to a height of 15 to 20 feet within four months from the sowing of the seed. The plants should be well watered at all stages of their growth.

HUMULUS, JAPONICUS.

# ILEX.

Nat. Ord.--Aquifoliaceæ or Ilicineæ.—[Christmas, or common Holly.]

Unfortunately the old English Holly cannot be grown on the Plains, but it succeeds admirably on the Hills, where it can be grown either from cuttings or seeds. The seed should be sown under cover in October and planted out in the Spring in a good, dry, loamy soil. The common green leaved Holly has given way, to a very great extent, to the silver and golden variegated varieties—*folio argentea* and *folio aurea*, both of which are very beautiful.

---

# IMPATIENS SULTANI

Nat. Ord.--Geraniaceæ. (Touch-me-not, or Zanzibar Balsam.)

This most distinct and beautiful plant is of a compact, neat habit of growth, with good constitution, and almost a perpetual bloomer. The flowers are of a brilliant rosy scarlet colour, and are produced so freely that a well grown specimen appears to be quite a ball of flowers, and continues in full beauty during several successive months. Sow in October both on the Plains and Hills. A sowing might also be made on the Hills in the Spring. Pot off singly in small thumb pots, when large enough and, when well established, transfer into 5 or 6 inch pots, which will be quite large enough for them to flower in. Require a rich, open soil.

IMPATIENS, SULTANI,

# IPOMŒA.

Nat. Ord.—Convolvulaceæ. (American Bind-weed or Morning Glory.)

Many of the varieties of Ipomœas are most beautiful, and, which adds much to their beauty, are very sweet scented. On the Plains sow in July; March to May on the Hills. To do well, the Ipomœa requires plenty of root room, so should be sown in a deeply dug, well manured border. The best soil for the Ipomœa is composed of fibrous loam, thoroughly rotted manure and leaf mould. The soil should not be made too fine, but used fairly lumpy Are very useful for covering trellises or arches. Amongst the best varieties are :– *Bona Nox* (the Moon Creeper or Good-night flower) which bears large pure white, sweet scented flowers which open in the evening, The plants grow to a height of about 10 feet. *Grandiflora Alba* is a very large flowered form of the preceding, with pure white flowers the size of a small plate. *Hederacea Grandiflora*, a fine variety with pale blue, fragrant flowers. The leaves of this variety resemble the Ivy (Hedera) and the plants grow to a height of 10 feet. *Learii*, very free flowering variety, with intensely bright blue flowers. Commonly known as the Blue Dawn Flower. *Roxburghii* is a very early flowering variety, as plants will come into flower in six weeks from time of sowing. The flowers are borne in bunches and are pure white. *Rubro-cærulea* is one of the best known of the family and succeeds particularly well on the Plains. The flowers on first opening are pure white, but when fully developed change to a rich purplish-blue.

THE MOON FLOWER
(IPOMEA GRANDIFLORA).

KALMIA LATIFOLIA.

# KALMIA.

### Nat. Ord.—Ericaceæ.

### [American mountain Laurel, Calico Bush, or Spoonwood tree.]

The Calico Bush is the common Laurel of the United States, and is certainly one of the most beautiful of evergreens, both on account of its beautiful foliage and the abundance of its elegant, delicate pink, rose, or nearly white flowers. Is of easy culture; the compost should be to a great extent composed of leaf soil. I do not think there is much use in attempting to grow the Kalmia on the Plains, but it does well on the Hills, where it will grow to a height of from 10 to 20 feet. The most popular variety is *Latifolia*, which bears beautiful, almost pure white flowers, which are borne in large bunches, as shown in the illustration I give. On the Hills sow in October under cover, in pans filled with sandy peat; when large enough to handle, pot off into small pots and plant out in the Spring.

# KENNEDYA.

### Nat. Ord.—Leguminosæ. (The Native Bean-flower of Australia).

A very free flowering, evergreen climber, bearing beautiful spikes of pea-shaped flowers. Are very ornamental and useful for cutting. Sow during the rains, both on the Plains and Hills, while a sowing should also be made on the Hills in the Spring. Make very fine pot plants if trained over wire balloons or trellises, but do best if planted out in the open ground in a compost composed of fibrous loam and leaf mould. Require plenty of water. The two varieties in general cultivation are *Ovata Alba* and *Rubicunda*. The former is perhaps better known as *Hardenbergia Monophylla*, of which it is a white flowering form. *Rubicunda*, which is also known as *Glycine rubicunda*, bears dark red flowers.

# LARKSPUR.

### Nat. Ord.—Ranunculaceæ.

A most popular flower, and one that, with a little care, can be brought to great perfection on the Plains, where it should never be sown before the middle of November or beginning of December. Sow in seed pans or pots and, when large enough to handle, prick out in beds of light, rich soil, or the seed can be sown thinly where the plants are wanted to flower. If a good strain of acclimatised seed can be obtained, it can be sown with other annuals in October, and the plants will flower much earlier than the imported seed sown at the end of November or beginning of December. On the Hills sow at any time from the middle of March to the end of May. See also DELPHINIUM.

LARKSPUR, HYACINTH FLOWERED.

There are many classes of this most free flowering and useful plant, and the following are amongst the best. *Candelabra-Formed*—The best of the many new forms of this useful family; plants about a foot in height and the same in diameter; flowers very large and perfectly double. *Dwarf German Rocket*—Of very dwarf habit, flowers very large, extra double. *Dwarf Ranunculus Flowered Rocket*—A beautiful class with globular flowers spirally arranged on long elegant spikes. *Emperor (Syn. Delphinium Imperiale)*—A magnificent class of symmetrical bushy habit; single plants frequently producing upwards of 50 spikes. *Hyacinth Flowered Improved*—A splendid new strain; flowers large and brilliant in colour, borne on immense trusses [see illustration]. *Tall Double Rocket*—Plants attain a height of two feet; flowers very double and brilliant in colour.

## LATHYRUS LATIFOLIUS.

Nat. Ord.—Leguminosæ —(Everlasting Pea)

A very free flowering, easily growing Perennial creeper. Is also known as L. *Sylvestris Platyphyllus*. Unfortunately does not succeed in Lower Bengal, but it flowers most luxuriantly further up country and on the Hills. I have seen plants in England, trained on walls, literally covered with bunches of beautiful flowers, and always have a few plants growing in my own garden in Mussoorie Sow in October on the Plains and on the Hills in March and April. also in October: the Autumn sowing should be under cover of a glass frame or a warm glazed verandah. Should be sheltered from excessive rain and also from the great heat of the warmer months. The flowers are borne in flat bunches, are rose coloured and about the size of a Sweet Pea flower, See also SWEET PEA (Lathyrus Odoratus).

## LAVATERA.

Nat. Ord—Malvaceæ. (Tree Mallow.)

A beautiful foliage plant, growing to a height of some 6 to 10 feet. On the Hills sow in October, also in March and April; Plains, in October. A splendid variegated form—L, *Arborea variegata*—is now much grown.

## LEPTOSIPHON.

Nat Ord.—Polemoniaceæ.

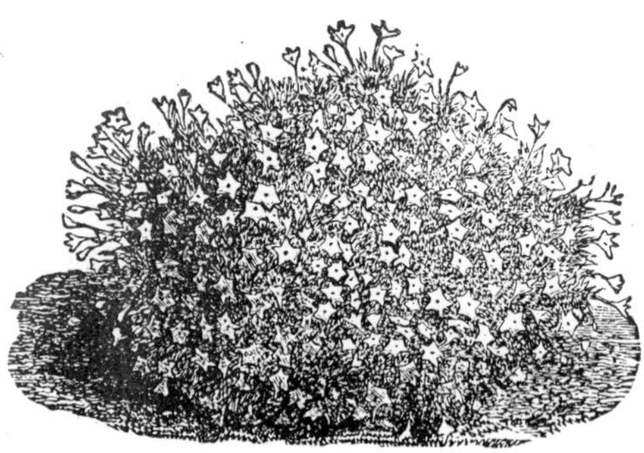

LEPTOSIPHON.

Very free flowering, dwarf growing annual, which looks well when grown in masses. Sow in pots, or in the open garden, in October on the Plains, March to May and also in October, on the Hills The colours are very varied, including whites, yellows, roses &c. As the plants do not bear transplanting well, it is best to sow where they are to flower. Require a light, rich soil.

# LEUCANTHEMUM.

**Nat. Ord.**—Compositæ. (Ox-eye Daisy.)

This is a Perennial Chryanthemum which is very useful for cutting. The plants grow to a height of 2 feet. Sow on the Plains in October, and at the same time on the Hills, where a sowing should also be made in Spring. Any ordinary garden soil suits the Leucanthemum, but it repays feeding by its much improved flowers. There are two varieties in general cultivation, *Grandiflorum*, a very free flowering variety, with large white flowers and *Uliginosum*, which is said to be an improvement on the other.

# LIMNANTHES.

Nat. Ord.—Geraniaceæ.

A low growing, trailing annual, bearing sweet scented flowers, which on opening are yellow, but fade off into white, streaked with grey. Is very useful for dwarf beds or rockeries. The plants of *Douglasii Grandiflora* grow to a height of about 8 inches only. Will succeed in any ordinary soil. Sow on the Plains in October; March to May on the Hills.

# LINUM.

Nat. Ord.—Linaceæ. [Flax.]

The Scarlet Flax is one of the most popular annuals in cultivation, and one of the most brilliant in colouring. The plants grow to a height of some 8 to 12 inches and bear their flowers in the greatest profusion. I do not advise transplanting, but prefer to sow the seed where the plants are to remain. On the Plains sow in October and November, and on the Hills from March to May, in beds of light, well manured soil. They may be grown in pots, but come to much greater perfection when grown in the open garden. The variety *Grandiflorum Rubrum* has brilliant scarlet flowers, while *Grandiflorum Roseum* has bright rose coloured ones, which form a splendid contrast to the scarlet sort.

LINUM GRANDIFLORUM.

# LISIANTHUS RUSSELLIANUS.

**Nat. Ord.—Gentianaceæ. (Syn. Eustoma Russellianum.)**

This most elegant and showy plant needs only to be grown and seen to become an universal favourite for pot culture. It belongs to the Gentian family. Flowers are large, Campanula-shaped, and borne in a cluster on the top of a stalk about 18 inches in height. Colour rich deep lilac, with black centre and bright yellow stamens. Both on the Plains and Hills sow in October in seed pans or pots, and when large enough to handle, pot off singly in small thumb pots in a compost composed of equal parts of fibrous loam and well rotted leaf mould, to which should be added a fair proportion of coarse sand and charcoal dust. When the plants are well established in the thumb pots, they should be transferred into 8 inch ones, which will be quite large enough for them to flower in. The plants are tender, so will require the protection of a warm verandah or glass house, during the winter on the Hills.

# LOBELIA.

**Nat. Ord.—Campanulaceæ.**

The Lobelia is one of the prettiest border plants we have, and is grown in large quantities both on the Plains and Hills. Some of the varieties bears flowers of a shade of blue seldom, if ever, found in any other plant. The seeds of the Lobelia are very tiny and should be mixed with dry sand before sowing, in order to ensure the seed being sown evenly. Cover the pots with a sheet of glass till the seed germinates. Sow on the Plains early in October; March to May on the Hills, where, if required for early planting, a sowing may also be made in October. The Lobelia is a gross feeder and the soil in which it is planted can hardly be too rich. An excellent compost is made up of equal parts of leaf mould and well rotted manure. Grow in a fairly shady situation and give plenty of water. I have

LOBELIA, IN THE OPEN GROUND.

always found that in order to get bushy, free flowering plants, the best plan is to cut the plants down to about an inch from the ground, when they are showing their first buds.

LOBELIA, AS A POT PLANT.

There are very many distinct varieties and the following list comprises most of the best sorts in cultivation.

*Barnard's Perpetual.* The flowers are of the most brilliant ultramarine blue, strikingly ornamented with a pure white marking at the base of each of the two lower petals. It is of compact habit and alike useful for bedding and growing in pots, while the bright and effective colouring of its flowers, combined with its perpetual blooming character, ensures it the premier position in parterres and ribbon borders. *Crystal Palace Compact.*—This beautiful variety unites the deep blue colour of the true Crystal Palace sort, with the compact habit of the *erecta* section, being of great value in ribbon bedding and for cultivation in pots. *Erinus Compacta, Golden Queen.*—A golden foliaged form of this very popular and useful dwarf section ; it is quite a contrast to the dark-leaved varieties and exceedingly attractive. Similar in growth to the well-known *Lobelia Emperor William.* Neat and compact in habit ; the flowers are of good size, and of a beautiful dark blue colour A most valuable vaiiety for bedding purposes, as well as for edgings or for cultivating in pots, coming quite true from seed. *Erinus Speciosa.*—A really fine strain very compact, producing in great profusion, large blue flowers with white centre. *Erinus Paxtoniana.*—Beautiful dark blue with clear white centre. *Emperor William.*—Beautiful light blue, of very compact habit ; splendid variety for bedding. *Fulgens Nanseniana.* By this splendid novelty, the Lobelia fulgens group has been enriched with an excellent variety. It is distinguished by an increased profusion of flowers of a brilliant purple-crimson colour, contrasting beautifully with the foliage, which is very dark. This variety comes absolutely true from seed. *Hybrida Grandiflora*—A very robust variety, with brilliant large flowers. *Prima Donna*—A very distinct colour, the flowers being of a deep purple red. *Royal Purple*—In colour this fine Lobelia is quite different from any other variety in

LOBELIA, NANSENIANA.

commerce, the flower, which is of a very rich shade of violet purple, without any trace of blue, as in all other sorts, is very striking and effective, thus showing off its large and clear white eye; the habit is semi compact, not quite so compact as the "*Pumila*" varieties, but not at all straggling.

## LOPHOSPERMUM.

LOPHOSPERMUM, SCANDENS.

Nat. Ord.—Scrophulariaceæ.

A very beautiful Perennial climber. The plants require a fair amount of root room, should be planted in a rich sandy soil and given plenty of water. Sow in pots or pans and transplant into the open ground when large enough. The kind usually grown is the one I illustrate—*L. Scandens*. In this variety the flowers are large in size, resemble the Digitalis in shape and are of a rich purplish-violet colour. Is also known as Maurandya Scandens.

## LUPINS, (Lupinus.)

Nat Ord.—Leguminosæ.

Although many of the Lupins are Perennials, it is only possible to grow them as annuals on the Plains. The seed should be sown in October on the Plains, March to June on the Hills. The seeds of most of the varieties are very hard, so before sowing, soak for some hours in almost boiling water. Do not attempt to transplant, but sow where the plants are to remain. Should be grown in light, rich soil and fully exposed to the sun. The following are excellent varieties.

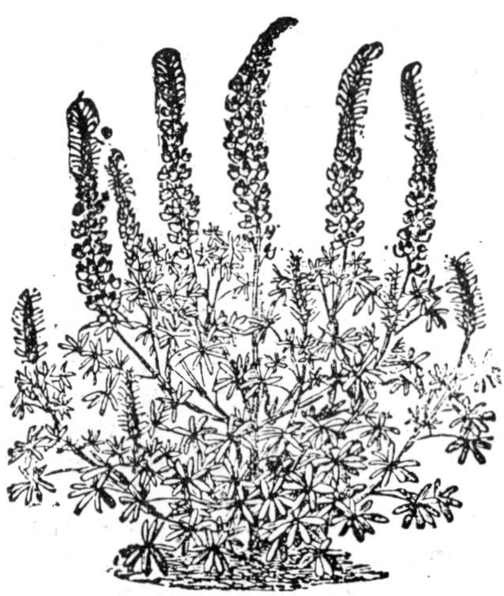

LUPINUS.

*Affinis.*—Bright blue very dwarf, height only 9 inches. This is a Perennial. *Cruikshanki* —Splendid blue and white flowers with a large yellow mark in centre. Grows to a height of 5 feet and is a really beautiful variety. *Dutch Blue*—Very fine light blue *Menziesi*—A splendid new variety of dwarf habit, bearing large spikes of bright yellow flowers. *Nanus*—A dwarf growing variety which seldom attains a height of more than 1 foot. The flowers are blue and lilac as a rule, but other colours will sometimes be found. *President Cleveland* [*Syn.* Hybridus Duplex.]--A fine double flowering variety, very distinct.

---

# MAGNOLIA.

## Nat. Ord.—Magnoliaceæ. (Laurel-leaved Tulip-tree.)

*Magnolia Grandiflora* is a magnificent free flowering tree. In a suitable situation, will grow to an enormous height, trees having been seen as much as 70 to 80 feet high The tree is a most handsome one, is evergreen, and bears, in great abundance, enormous, pure white, sweet scented flowers, which are often as much as 8 inches in diameter. The leaves are very large, of a beautiful shining green on the upper surface, while the under surface is a rusty brown. On the Hills, and in fact from an altitude of about 2000 feet up to 6000 feet, the Magnolia does magnificently and flowers freely. About the best situation to give it is a large wall, which it will soon cover Grows well in a fairly rich soil. On the Plains does not do at all well and is seldom found more than a few feet high. . Sow both on the Plains and Hills in October and pot off into small pots, potting on into larger ones as required. Plants will flower well in 12 inch pots. Take care when potting not to disturb the roots. On the Hills I prefer to plant out in the open garden, where the plants soon become very ornamental, particularly when in flower.

# MALLOTUS.

## Nat. Ord.—Euphorbiaceæ.

The Mallotus is perhaps more commonly known under the name of TREWIA and ROTTLERA, but the variety I now treat of was introduced from Japan under the first name I give–Mallotus–and so I will call it. The Trewia is a native of the East Indies and so the variety now mentioned should do well here. *Mallotus Japonicus* does well in a compost made up of sandy loam and well rotted leaf mould in equal parts. The seed should be sown in October, both on the Plains and Hills.

# MARIGOLD (Tagetes.)

## Nat. Ord.--Compositæ.

The Marigold, or "Ghenda" of the native, is too well known to need any description, but in the following notes I will describe some of the newer sorts, which are great improvements on the varieties usually found in Indian gardens I need hardly say that the Marigold will grow anywhere, both in the poorest and the richest of soils, but perhaps the soil best suited to them is a moderately rich one Sow on the Plains at any time from June to October; on the Hills March to May and also in the autumn. The Marigold is usually classed under two distinct headings--AFRICAN (Tagetes Erecta) and FRENCH (Tagetes Patula) In the Africans, shades of lemon and orange predominate, while in the French, a much greater diversity of colouring is found, while the plants are much more dwarf and compact. The following are all good sorts that I can recommend

AFRICAN. *Eldorado*, a variety with enormous double quilled flowers, which are often as much as 14 inches in circumference. *Lemon*, flowers of a beautiful pale lemon yellow. *Prince of Orange*, very large, double quilled flowers of a deep orange colour.

FRENCH. *Brunea*, a very dwarf growing variety; flowers maroon striped yellow. *Cloth of Gold*, deep golden yellow. *Gold Striped*, bright yellow, striped brown. *Pulchra fl pl.*, golden yellow spotted crimson. *Queen of the Dwarfs* is a very dwarf growing strain in a great variety of colours. *Sulphurea*, pale sulphur-yellow.

MARIGOLD, AFRICAN.

MARIGOLD, FRENCH STRIPED.

In addition to the separate varieties I have mentioned, most Seedsmen stock seed of Tall and Dwarf varieties in mixture, and most readers will find a packet or so of these, ample for an ordinary garden.

## MATHIOLA, BICORNIS.

Nat. Ord. Cruciferæ. (Night Scented Stock.)

See STOCKS for culture. A very fragrant Annual, with pink and lilac flowers.

## MAURANDYA.

Nat. Ord.-Scrophulariaceæ.

The illustration I give shows the form of this most charming climber. Is splendidly suited for hanging baskets, on account of its graceful, slender growth, and elegant flowers and foliage. The seed may be sown on the Plains at any time from June to October, and from March to May on the Hills. Is a very free flowerer

MAURANDYA, BARCLAYANA.

and seems to be in flower practically all the year round. Grow in a fairly rich, sandy loam. The colours of *Maurandya Barclayana* are very varied, as there will be found in a mixture, plants with white, mauve, blue, rose, violet and lilac coloured flowers.

## Mesembryanthemum, Crystallinum.

### Nat. Ord. Ficoideæ. (The Ice plant)

A very interesting hardy annual The plants are covered with large glittering papulæ (superficial glands); which give them the appearance of being covered with ice. The leaves are sometimes used for garnishing. Make beautiful plants for rockeries, and are also very pretty as pot plants. On the Plains sow in October; March to May on the Hills. Does well in a moderately rich soil, and should be grown in a sunny situation.

## MIGNONETTE

### [RESEDA ODORATA.]

### Nat. Ord.—Resedaceæ.

The old Mignonette is perhaps *par excellence the* favourite of the garden, both at home and abroad. Most of the varieties are very sweet scented, and perhaps nothing is sweeter than a bed of it in the garden. There are very many varieties now in cultivation and one would hardly recognise *Ma Mignonette* who had been accustomed to the modest little flower as was known to our forefathers. The Mignonette does not stand transplanting, so the seed must be sown where the plants are to remain, unless they are to be grown in pots, for which purpose I will give separate directions. For the open garden sow on the Plains at any time from the middle of September to the middle of December, on the Hills at any time from March to September. The

MIGNONETTE.

soil in which it is grown can hardly be too rich, but it must be light. Give liquid manure occasionally, and plenty of water at all times. The bed chosen for the Mignonette should be in a position fully exposed to the sun-light. Do not leave your plants too thick in the bed, otherwise they will be lank and weedy, and the flowers will be poor. Now for a few hints for growing in pots. The pots in which they will flower best are 7 or 8 in. ones. First get your pots ready by putting a good covering of crocks (broken pots) or gravel, at the bottoms, then fill up to about half an inch from the top with rich, light soil. In each pot sow about 8 or 10 seeds, covering with a light covering of soil. When the seedlings have thrown out their second pair of leaves, remove all the plants with the exception of the healthiest and strongest looking. Foster these plants as much as possible, by feeding well, in order to induce them to make vigorous growth. For about a month after the plants begin to show buds, remove them as they form and give a good soaking of liquid manure every second or third day. If these hints are carried out, readers can depend on having strong, vigorous, free blooming plants in three months from time of sowing.

The varieties of Mignonette in cultivation are almost legion, but the following list comprises all the best :—

*Crimson Giant*—This new variety is one of the finest and most desirable for pot culture. It is of dwarf, vigorous, pyramidal, short branched habit, with very thick, dark green leaves, and throws up numerous stout flower-stalks terminated by extremely broad spikes of delightfully scented bright flowers ; *Diamond*—A beautiful new variety, flowers creamy white, spikes large and well shaped, a valuable novelty ; *Dwarf Compact*—This dwarf branching variety is exceedingly neat in habit and of robust growth ; very valuable for pot culture. The fine stout spikes are densely set with red coloured flowers ; *Garraway's Improved Double White*—This is one of the grandest Mignonettes ever introduced. The spikes are very large and dense, many of them being very double, while even the single flowered plants are well worth growing, as they are so much finer than the majority of Mignonettes ; *Giant Red*—The illustration gives a good idea of the form of this beautiful novelty, which is a much improved form of the popular "Machet." The spikes are large, dense, and of a bright red colour ; the plants being of a very dwarf pyramidal habit ; *Golden Queen*—A fine new variety, with flowers of a decided golden hue, wonderfully free flowering and fragrant ; *Grandiflora* [Large Flowered]—Sweet scented ; *Imperialis or Gabriele*—A new variety strongly recommended for pot culture ; *Machet* [New]—The best for pots ; one of the finest of recent introductions ; *Miles Hybrid Spiral*—Much admired variety ; habit dwarf and branching, spikes often attaining a length of 8 or 10 inches ; powerfully scented ; *Parson's White Tree*—The nearest approach to pure white of all varieties ; *Tall Pyramidal Compact*—A very strong-growing variety with very dark red flowers, forming long thick spikes ; *Victoria or Prizetaker*—A very handsome variety with immensely large flowers and of deeper red colour than those of any other variety ; the plants are of a free branching, compact habit.

## MIMOSA.

### Nat. Ord.—Leguminosæ.

### (The Sensitive or Humble Plant. Vern. Chooee-mooee.)

The soil in which the Sensitive Plant succeeds best, is a mixture of equal parts of loam and peat, or failing peat, leaf mould, to which should be added a small quantity of sharp sand. Sow on the Plains in October ; on the Hills in October and in April or May. The variety usually grown is *Pudica*, which bears small, round, reddish coloured flowers. The plants only grow about a foot high.

## MIMULUS.

### *(Monkey Flower.)*

### Nat. Ord —Scrophulariaceæ.

This is one of the most beautiful annuals in cultivation and should be much more extensively grown than it is in India. Sow on the Plains in September or October ; on the Hills, March to May and also in the Autumn. Sow in pans in a light soil composed of one part fibrous loam, one part leaf mould and two parts sharp sand. As the seed is very tiny, it is best to mix it with sand, to ensure an equal sowing. Place the pans in a shady situation till the seeds

MIMULUS AS A POT PLANT.

germinate. As soon as the seedlings are large enough, transplant singly into 3 inch pots, and when well established, shift on into larger ones. The leaves are very sensitive to damp, so the plants should always be watered by placing the pans or pots in a tub of water until the soil has become thoroughly saturated. It is well to give frequent transplanting, so shift on gradually into the larger sized pots in which the plants are to flower.

There are a number of very good varieties and strains, of which the following will be found amongst the best :—

*Cardinalis*—A tall variety producing flowers of the most brilliant colours, height 1 to 3 feet ; *Clapham's Superb Strain*—Remarkable for the great size and superb colouring of the flowers ; *Duplex*—Beautiful double hose-in-hose flowers of various colours ; *Emperor*—This new variety was raised by crossing the well-known old " *Mimulus*

*Duplex*" with flowers of the large flowering strain, and after very careful selection and hybridising of the finest and largest flowers for several years, this grand novelty has been obtained. The calyx is of very great size and of the same rich and wonderful colouring as the flower itself, It will be found a charming plant for borders or small beds, also admirably adapted for pot culture. *Fire King*—A very beautiful addition to the large flowering varieties of Mimulus. The flowers are of immense size, of a deep golden yellow, with a broad margin of fiery scarlet, the throat being profusely spotted with the same colour. *Hybridus Grandiflorus*—Superb strain, containing the most brilliant colours and the largest flowering varieties only; *Queen's Prize*—A splendid new class with very large flowers, most fantastically marked; *Tigrinus, Finest Spotted*—A splendid strain of this beautiful and profuse blooming plant, producing very large flowers of finest quality and form, elegantly spotted, and richly marked, the colours being brilliant.

## Mimulus Moschatus.—(Musk).

The old fashioned Musk is quite distinct from the large flowering varieties of Mimulus, and so requires a section to itself. Few plants are better known at Home, where every cottager is practically certain to have a few pots on the window-sill. The plant is a perennial, but I am afraid can only be grown as such on the Hills, where it comes to great perfection. The musk requires the same treatment as the other varieties of Mimulus. The old variety *Moschatus*, bears small yellow flowers, while the leaves have a peculiar, healthy, musk like perfume, which is very pleasing. It is apt to grow rather straggly, but this fault has been remedied in a new introduction which is known as *Moschatus Compactus*. The branches of this variety are short and more vigorous than in the old Musk, and the plants thus form compact bushes of erect habit. The plants are just as floriferous as the old sort, and emit the same delightful fragrance.

## MINA, LOBATA.

Nat. Ord.—Convolvulaceæ.

This is a perennial, but can only be grown as an annual on the Plains, where the seed should be sown in October. On the Hills will grow on year after year, but as it is very tender, requires protection to prevent it being harmed by the frost. Sow on the Hills in March.

MINA LOBATA.

The illustration I give shows the form of the flowers, which are borne about 20 to a spike and are of a bright red colour, changing to orange and cream. As the plant is a very vigorous grower, it should be supported on a strong trellis. On the Plains the plants will come into flower in about four months from time of sowing.

---

# MIRABILIS.

## Nat. Ord.—Nyctaginaceæ.

### (Marvel of Peru or Four o'clock. Vern-Gul Abas-Krushna Kelee.)

One of the commonest plants in this country, and one of the most beautiful. Should be planted in large beds or masses, when their rich, glossy leaves, together with their profusion and diversity of bloom, present a most gorgeous sight during the late afternoon and early morning. The seed can be sown practically at any time during the year, but the best time is from May to July and again in September and October on the Plains, and April and May on the Hills. The colours are very various and beautiful In the ordinary varieties the plants grow rather tall, but a dwarf growing strain, known as *Tom Thumb*, has been introduced, in which the plants only grow about 10 inches high. Another very pretty introduction is a variety known as *Variegated*, in which the foliage is prettily striped with golden bands, which contrasts beautifully with the brilliant colours of the flowers.

---

# MUSA.

### Nat. Ord.--Scitamineæ.—[The Banana or Plaintain.]

The *Musa Ensete* forms one of the most effective foliage plants imaginable, and as plants will grow to a height of 10 to 15 feet the first year from seed, they are well worth growing. The illustration gives a fair idea of what the plants look like, when grown as single specimens. Perhaps the ornamental Musas should more properly be classed as *Heliconias*, but I have no intention of going into Botanical differences in this book, so will leave *Ensete* under the heading I have given it. The seed should be sown as early as possible on the Plains, say by the end of August. On the Hills I generally sow about the beginning of October. The seeds are very hard and it is best to drop them into a basin of *boiling* water and allow them to soak for some hours before sowing. Sow in pans or boxes of rich soil and give plenty of water. When the plants are well up, pot off singly in small pots and shift on, and when about a couple of feet high, plant out in beds of very rich, well manured soil. I have found them useful for growing in large tubs, as they are very ornamental and most effective for decorative purposes. On the Hills should be protected during the winter, or will be killed by the frost.

MUSA ENSETE.

# MYOSOTIS.

### Nat. Ord.—Boraginaceæ. (Forget-Me-Not, or Scorpion Grass.)

The old Forget-me-not can rarely be grown except as an annual on the Plains, as it is difficult to keep the plants alive during

MYOSOTIS [FORGET-ME-NOT.]

the hot weather. As the plants are semi-aquatic, they require any amount of water, in fact, it is best to put the pots in which they are grown into fairly deep pans filled with water, so that they stand to about half their depth in water. On the Plains sow in October and November; on the Hills, September and October and also March to May. As soon as the plants are large enough to handle, pot off into thumb pots, and repot as required. The plants should be grown in a fairly shady situation and one as moist as possible.

The following are some of the best varieties :—

*Alpestris Robusta Grandiflora* [*Elisa Fonrobert*]—The flowers of this new and distinct variety are considerably larger than those of any other Forget-me-not, and of a beautiful sky-blue colour, with clearly defined yellow eye. The plant resembles, in habit, the form of a candelabrum, a peculiarity which distinguishes it from any other sort. As it comes perfectly true from seed, this fine Myosotis cannot fail to become a general favourite. *Alpestris Robusta Grandiflora Alba*—A splendid new white variety of the preceding. *Alpestris Palustris Semperflorens.* [The true Forget-me-not.]—Beautiful transparent azure—blue flowers. *Alpestris Victoria*—This new Forget-me-not is of extremely robust habit, growing only 5 to 7 inches in height with a diameter of 8 to 10 inches, and when fully grown, is quite globular in shape and perfectly covered with flowers. A very useful plant for beds, edgings, &c. *Sylvatica* [*Alpestris Improved*]—Alpine Forget-me-not. Beautiful pale blue. *Sylvatica Alba*—Same as the preceding, but with beautiful pure white flowers.

# MYRSIPHYLLUM, ASPARAGOIDES.

( *Syn.* Smilax. )

### Nat. Ord.—Liliaceæ. (The Wreath Lily.)

One of the most useful Florist's plants in cultivation. Is also known as *Medeola Asparagoides.* On the Plains sow in August or

September, in boxes of light rich soil. As soon as the plants are three inches high, prick them out into shallow boxes, and then, when established, into thumb pots. When required, shift into three inch pots, and grow on, till ready to plant out; plant 6 inches apart and twelve inches between the rows. While growing, should be liberally supplied with liquid manure. Should be grown in a partially shaded situation. On the Hills should be sown in October under cover, also in April and May.

# NASTURTIUMS.

## Nat. Ord.—Tropœolaceæ. (Indian Cress.)

There are, as everyone knows, two distinct classes of Nasturtium, the *Tall* and the *Tom Thumb* or *Dwarf*. I will first of all give a few hints on the cultivation of the Dwarf or Tom Thumb Varieties.

NASTURTIUM, TOM THUMB.

It is a great mistake to grow the Tom Thumb Nasturtiums in rich soil, as they will make any amount of growth, so far as leaves are concerned, but what flowers are produced will be comparatively small, and quite hidden by the superabundance of foliage. A good mixture of ordinary garden soil and broken brick rubbish is about the best compost in which they can be grown. The seed should be sown where the plants are to remain, as they will not stand transplanting. Sow on the Plains as soon as possible after the close of the rains, and right on into November. On the Hills sow at any time from March to June. In order to get the seed to germinate freely, it should be soaked for some hours in hot, not boiling, water. Besides being splendid border plants, the Tom Thumb Nasturtiums make beautiful pot plants, when well grown. There are very many more or less distinct kinds, but the following will be found amongst the best. Where special colours are not particularly required, a good m'xture, such as is sold by most Seedsmen, will be found excellent.

*Beauty*--Yellow and scarlet. *Cœruleum Roseum*--Beautiful peach colour. *Crimson*--Dark crimson. *Crystal Palace Gem*--Sulphur coloured flowers blotched crimson. *Empress of India*--The leaves are of a very dark purplish blue colour, making a suitable background for the brilliant crimson—scarlet flowers, which stand out in bold relief. Its profusion of bloom and dazzling richness of colour are remarkable. *Golden King*--Golden yellow ; very fine. *H. M. Stanley*--A splendid new dark flowered variety entirely distinct from any other kinds. *King of Tom Thumbs*—Exceedingly deep scarlet flowers, rich dark coloured foliage. *King Theodore*—Brownish black flower, dark foliage. *Lady Bird or Spotted King*— Its striking flowers are produced in profusion throughout the season. The ground colour of the flower is rich golden yellow, each barred with a broad vein (starting from the base) of bright ruby crimson. *Pearl*-Creamy white ; the palest of all Nasturtiums, *Rose*--A delicate shade, very attactive. *Ruby King*-Crimson rose flowers ; foliage varying from green to purple. *Scarlet*-Deep, pure scarlet. *Spotted*-Rich orange, spotted with maroon. *Yellow*-Pure yellow; very effective.

# Nasturtium, Tall.

## (Tropæolum Majus).

The tall Nasturtiums require practically the same treatment as the Tom Thumb varieties, with two exceptions. While the soil for the Dwarf sorts can hardly be too poor, that required for the tall ones can hardly be too rich, and while the Tom Thumb require no support, the tall need a strong trellis on which to climb. The seeds should be sown about 6 inches apart. I might say here, that the green seed of the Nasturtium, when

NASTURTIUM, TALL, CHAMELEON.

pickled, makes an excellent substitute for Capers. The various varieties differ only in the colour of the flowers, with the exception of the one I illustrate, and which I will describe at some length.

*Chameleon.*—This highly interesting new variety presents a most unusual feature, which is, that the flowers are of different colors on the same plant, and that they are variously blotched, splashed, striped and bordered with several colors, On one and the same plant self-coloured flowers are found, others curiously stained or flushed on clear ground, while others are broadly edged with light shades or have dark margins. The illustration given shows the distinctiveness of this beautiful novelty. The marvellous contrast produced by the numerous blooms, each so conspicuously different in appearance from its neighbours, is of the most charming effect, and renders this variety unsurpassed for covering trellises, fences, embankments, etc. Other good sorts and colours are :—

*Crimson*—The darkest of all; *Dunnett's Orange*—Bright orange-red; *Regelianum*—Striped yellow and scarlet; *Scarlet*—Pure scarlet; *Yellow*—Bright yellow.

## NEMESIA, STRUMOSA SUTTONI.

### Nat. Ord.—Scrophulariaceæ.

I quote the following from the description given by the introducers :—

"This charming plant is undoubtedly one of the most beautiful "annuals that has been introduced into cultivation for some years past. "The colour of the flowers is exceedingly variable, being white, ochreous, "pale yellow, deep yellow, orange, orange-scarlet, magenta, carmine, "light rosy purple, orange stippled with orange-brown and shaded with "mauve &c., the throat being dotted with black on a yellow ground. and "the outside is often veined and marked with purple. The variation "in the colour of the flowers is one of the most interesting features "of this plant."

Sow the seed where the plants are to remain, in October on the Plains, and March to May on the Hills. Succeeds in any ordinary garden soil. but the plants should not be crowded in the beds.

## NEMOPHILA.

### Nat Ord.—Hydrophyllaceæ.

### (Californian Blue Bell or Love Grove of North America).

Very pretty free flowering Annual. Like the Larkspur, should not be sown on the Plains till the cold weather has well set in. In most places on the Plains can be sown by the middle or end of November. On the Hills sow at any time from March to May.

As it does not stand transplanting, the seed should be sown where the plants are to remain. Sow in a light, rich soil, in a fairly shady situation Requires plenty of water, and is greatly improved by an occasional watering with weak liquid manure.

The following are the varieties mostly grown :—

*Atomaria*—A fine new variety. Flowers white to light blue with dark spots. Plants grow to a height of about 5 inches. *Discoidalis*—Flowers almost black, edged with white. *Insignis*—Sky blue flowers, light centre *Insignis Alba*—A pure white flowered variety of the preceding. *Insignis Purpurea Rubra*—Very pretty rosy purple flowers. *Maculata*—Fine spotted variety, the flowers being white with violet purple blotches. Grows about 6 inches high.

# NICOTIANA.

## Nat. Ord.—Solanaceæ. (Tobacco.)

*Nicotiana Affinis* is one is of the sweetest scented flowering plants in cultivation, and should be found in every garden. On the Plains sow in September or October, or at the beginning of the rains. Sow on the Hills in March to May. Should be grown in a light, rich soil. The seed should be sown in pans or boxes, and the seedlings transplanted when large enough to handle. *Affinis* is the variety usually grown in gardens and bears pretty pure white, deliciously scented flowers, about 3 inches long. The plants grow to a height of about 2 to 3 feet. The best situation for the Nicotiana is a moist one, and the soil should be deeply dug. In *Colossea* we have a splendid new ornamental foliaged plant. It is of very vigorous growth, attaining a height of 5 to 6 feet; the leaves, about 3 feet long by 18 inches wide and of a dark glossy green colour, contrast in a most pleasing manner with the reddish brown ribs.

NICOTIANA, COLOSSEA.

Many readers would doubtless like to grow some of the smoking Tobaccos, and seed is now obtainable from most Seedsmen, who generally stock seed of the best Continental and American varieties.

# ŒNOTHERA.

### Nat. Ord. Onagraceæ. (The Evening Primrose.)

Although many of the Evening Primroses are Perennials, all the varieties will have to be grown as Annuals on the Plains, where the seed should be sown by the end of September. On the Hills, where they grow most luxuriantly, and soon become quite naturalized, sow under cover in October, or from March to September. As the plants do not stand transplanting, the seed should be sown where the plants are wanted to flower. Grow in a light, rich soil, in a shady situation. A number of bright flowering varieties will be found under the heading GODETIA.

The best varieties of the ordinary Œnothera are :—*Acaulis* (or *Taraxacifolia Alba*, pure white ; hardy perennial ; height 6 inches. *Bistorta Veitchii*—Hardy annual, yellow with crimson spots. The fruits are about $1\frac{1}{2}$ to 2 inches long and are peculiarly twisted on attaining maturity ; height 1 foot. *Drummondii*—Hardy annual, bright yellow ; height 1 foot. *Lamarckiana*—Hardy biennial ; immense bright yellow flowers ; height 3 feet. *Suaveolens*—Very sweet scented.

# PÆONIA.

### Nat. Ord.—Ranunculacæ. (Pæony or Piony).

Unfortunately it is quite impossible to grow the lovely Pæony on the Plains, but the plant does extremely well on the Hills, and is more than worthy of the most extensive cultivation. On the Hills sow in October, under cover of a glass frame or warm glazed verandah. In the Spring pot off into 6 or 8 inch pots, and when large enough, transfer to 12 inch ones. They do best in a compost composed of fibrous loam and thoroughly rotted leaf mould. The soil should be very deeply trenched before planting, and a good amount of well rotted manure should be incorporated with it. When growth is being made, the soil should be top-dressed with manure and frequent drenchings with liquid manure given. *Pæonia Arborea* is a splendid selection of herbaceous varieties, and a good strain will contain a great number of colours, from pure white, through reds, to dark purple.

# PANSIES.

### Nat. Ord—Violaceæ.

### (Heartsease. Vern. Kheeroo, Rutun Puroos)

These charming and universal favorites have of late years been much improved in size, shape and colour, by Scotch, French and German specialists, who, by careful hybridising and selection, have brought

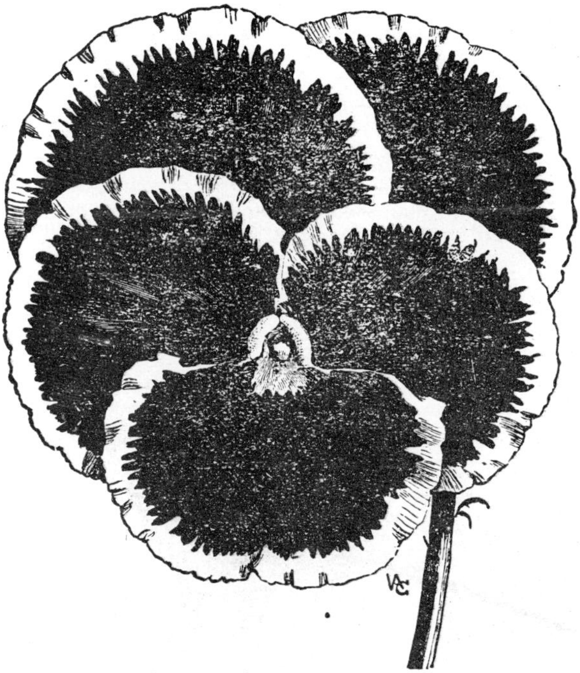

PANSY, CASSIER'S GIANT.

this ever popular flower to such perfection, that one can scarcely realize that the modest little Pansy of a few years back, could assume such grand proportions and such gaudy colours as the new sorts now offered.

On the Plains sow during September and October ; on the Hills, March to May and also in the Autumn. Seed should be sown in well drained pots or pans filled with a rich, light soil, covering the seed but very lightly. They should then be placed in a close, shady situation, under a glass frame if available ; or a very good substitute is, to cover the pot or pan with another one of the same size, which will induce the seed to germinate more freely. When once the plants are well above ground, the only real difficulty in the cultivation of the Pansy has been surmounted. As soon as the plants are strong enough to handle, they should be transplanted into three inch pots, one plant in each. When they have become well established and are growing freely, they should be watered every third or fourth day with weak liquid manure. What suits them best is guano, mixed at the rate of half an ounce to the gallon of water ; or, failing this, fresh cow dung answers very well. When the pots have become well filled with roots, the plants should be shifted into larger ones for flowering in. As a rule, six inch or eight inch pots will be found sufficiently large for this purpose. The compost used must be light, rich and open ; one compost of one-fourth each of good rich loam, leaf mould, very old cowdung and coarse sand, invariably suits them well. After being re-potted, they should again be treated as before with regular dressings of liquid manure, till they commence flowering, when it should be withheld and the plants supplied freely with water only.

The varieties of Pansies now in cultivation are legion and the list is being added to every year, as, with the single exception of the Sweet Pea, I do not think there is any other plant that has received so much attention from the hybridiser. Many growers have put all their energies into the raising of varieties with enormous flowers, while others have seen to shape and substance, and we now have the benefit of their efforts in some of the most magnificent varieties it is possible to conceive. A grand strain, raised by the famous German grower Roemer, is known as Roemer's "Giant Prize" and there are many very distinct colours and varieties in the strain, known as follows :—

*Adonis*—A beautiful light blue, marked with a yellowish-white face and large dark blotches. *Aurikel Colours.*—The flowers of this variety present the rarest shadings, being peculiarly marked after the manner of Auriculas *Bright Golden Yellow*—Very fine rich yellow. *Emperor William.*—The flowers are of a true, splendid ultramarine-

PANSY, "GIANT PRIZE" STRIPED.

blue, with well defined purple-violet eye. *Fancy, (Improved Cassier).*—Splendid rich colours mixed, very attractive. *Fire King.*—Brilliant red and yellow. *Five Spotted.*—The "Ne plus ultra" of all varieties. This grand strain is a great improvement on the well known Odier or Prize Blotched. *King of the Blacks.*—Flowers intensely dark, almost coal black. *Lord Beaconsfield.*—Deep purple violet, shading off in the petals to a white hue. *Show (Improved Strain of Trimardeau)*—Splendid mixed colours. *Striped.*—The perfection of all the striped varieties. *White.*—Flowers pure white with large deep violet spots on each of the lower petals.

For many years growers have tried to raise a real red Pansy, and perhaps the nearest approach to success is found in the variety known as *Cardinal.* The colour is a rich brownish-scarlet, the three lower petals being marbled with a large dark blotch. *Gipsy Queen* is a very beautiful variety of a most striking colour, a deep terra cotta or bronze, slightly tinged with purple. *The Peacock* (*Pavoninum*). The distinctive feature in this beautiful novelty consists in the two upper

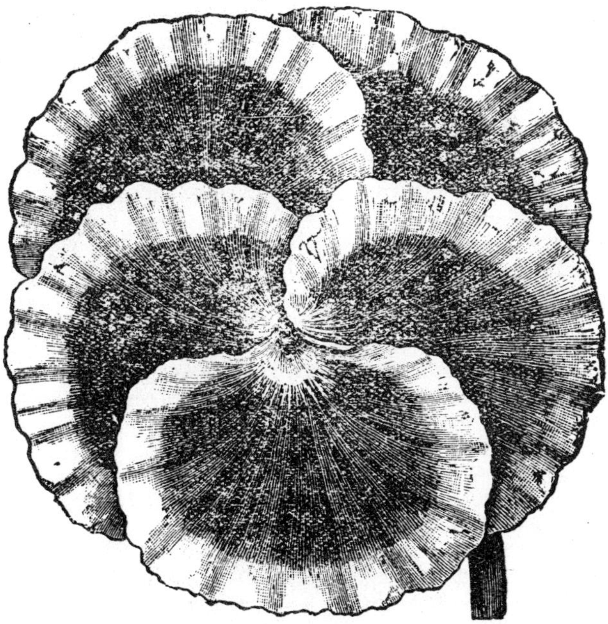

PANSY, "GIANT PRIZE" FIVE SPOTTED.

petals being marked with a central spot of pale violet blue, which deepens into intense violet near the margin and shades off into claret colour to the edge, which is white. The two lateral petals, as well as the lowest one, are of a deep claret, but the latter has a distinct blotch of rich violet, similar to those seen on the upper ones, but rather smaller. The effect of the conspicuous blue spots on the darker ground colour is very striking, and as the plant is faithfully reproduced by seed, and blooms throughout the season in good soil, it cannot fail to become a favourite One of the favourite strains for many years past, has been the well known *Mammoth Butterfly* in which the flowers are of enormous size, matchless form, colouring and markings. This is a strain which I can very strongly recommend,

Pansies have been favorites in the gardens of rich and poor for considerably over a hundred years, but their popularity has not been so great even as it might have been, on account of the lack of scent. This defect has been overcome, and in *Sweet Scented* Pansies we have a class combining the beauty of the Pansy and the perfume of the Violet. This new class is the result of crossing the Pansy (*Viola tricolor*) with the Sweet Violet (*Viola cornuta*): the resulting hybrids, in addition to retaining the delightful violet perfume, produce the most beautiful Pansy-like blossoms, 2 to 2½ inches across, of great substance and of an endless variety of colours. The selfs are of remarkable purity, and include white, lemon, orange, claret, crimson, maroon, lavender, purple, silver grey, rose, black, blue, etc., etc The fancy varieties are exquisitely tinted, striped, blotched, feathered, picotee-edged, etc. Their combinations and blendings of colour are more chaste and harmonious than ordinary Pansies, and more varied than the rainbow. The plants are of easy culture, and of hardy, vigorous growth, forming deep-rooting, compact, tufted clumps Planted in masses or lines, they form perfect mats covered with myriads of flowers. They are more perennial in character than ordinary Pansies, throwing out new roots annually, adapting them, where situation and soil are congenial, to permanents beds, edgings, etc., where they begin to make our gardens gay in spring almost when surrounded by snow, and continue to bloom with marvellous freedom until autumn The flowers are borne on long stems, which shoot up, like the Violet, directly from the roots, rendering the flowers of special value for cutting purposes. They are not all equally fragrant, though the majority are as highly scented as the sweetest Violet, and the other high merits of this new strain, aside from their perfume, destine them to wide popularity.

One of the finest of the French introductions is the well known *Giant Trimardeau*, and this is a strain which is hard to beat. The plants are of vigorous, though compact habit; the flowers are of extraordinary size, good shape and brilliant colour. Two other grand strains are *Bugnot's Giant Spotted* and *Cassier's Giant*, in both of which the flowers are very large and of magnificent colourings. Amongst other grand introductions of the famous Quedlinburgh hybridiser Roemer, is his *Exhibition Prize* strain of Pansies, which is a class deserving of the most extensive cultivation.

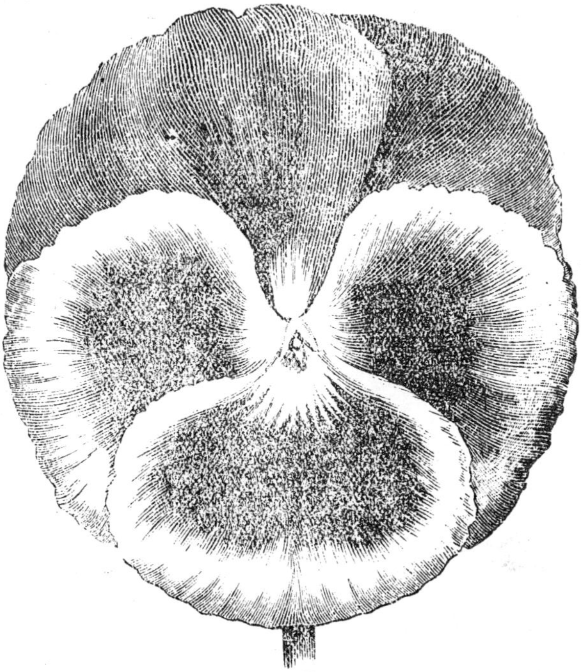

PANSY, GIANT TRIMARDEAU.

The following list contains most of the best of the ordinary varieties of Pansies and the separate colours will be found useful when colours are wanted for special situations. *Baron de Rothschild*—Fine fancy varieties. *Black Blue*—Very dark colour, striking and constant, most beautiful for bouquets. *Blackish Brown, shaded gold bronze*—Very rare and beautiful. *Bright Purple* (*Royal Purple*)—A very fine colour. *Bronze Coloured*—Various shades of brown; very distinct. *Brown Red* (*Meteor*).—Fine for bedding. *Canary Bird*—Very fine new variety with large golden yellow flowers, beautifully spotted with brown. *Candidissima* (*Syn.* Snow Queen, or Snowflake),—Flowers of a delicate pure satiny white; very pretty. *Emperor William*—Ultramarine blue; a very beautiful and popular variety. *Fire King*—Fiery orange with purple eye and yellowish edge; very fine. *Gold Margined*—A very distict class, flowers of various colours, with a distinct gold margin. *Golden Yellow*—The brightest of all the yellow varieties. *Improved Striped*—A fine new class producing large, beautifully formed flowers of the most brilliant and exquisite tints of colouring, the blooms being handsomely striped and mottled. *King of the Blacks* (*Roi des Noirs*)—This variety is also known as "*Dr. Faust*," "*Pluto*," "*Black Knight*," and "*Othello*." Flowers of good size and as black as jet. Very few persons have yet seen this dark variety, and scarcely anyone could imagine, without doing so, that there was such a dark colour in this family. *Pale Bright Blue*—Beautiful clear blue. *Lord Beaconsfield*—Purple violet, with the upper petals shading off to a light tint; flowers very large. *Mahogany Coloured*—Very distinct. *Odier's Spotted Varieties*—A magnificent strain of fine varieties, producing large handsome flowers of great substance and variety of colouring, the petals of which are beautifully marked. *Plum Velvet or Dark Purple*—An entirely new shade in this favourite flower; blooms of good size and shape, very free flowering; a beautiful novelty. *Purplsh Violet*—A distinct and beautiful colour. *Quadricolor or Rainbow*—A distinct and pretty variety.

In addition to stocking many of the varieties I mention, most Seedsmen offer various strains of mixed Pansies, which will be found useful by ordinary growers, who are not particular about having separate colours or strains.

# PAPAVER (Poppy)

Nat. Ord.—Papaveraceæ,

Poppy, Double Mixed.

The various kinds of Poppies are amongst the most gorgeous denizens of the gardens, and. fortunately, grow well all over India As the plants will not stand transplanting, the seed must be sown where the plants are to remain. Sow at any time from the middle of September to end of November on the Plains. On the Hills seed sown in October will provide fine, strong plants, which will flower in. Spring, but the main sowing should be made from March to May. The Poppy is a great self-sower, and when once established, plants will spring up year after year from the seed cast by the previous year's plants. I had a bed of most magnificent Poppies in my garden in

Mussoorie, which for years supplied beautiful flowers for the decoration of my own and friends' houses, the seed was sown years ago, but year after year the plants grew up without any trouble or care on the part of my gardeners.

The Poppy does not stand particularly well in vases, but if cut when they are opening, they will last for about 12 hours or so, and look very grand, if arranged in large masses in wide mouthed vases. The soil should be light and sandy, but at the same time fairly rich.

Amongst the many beautiful varieties now in cultivation, there are few to equal the exquisite *Iceland Poppies* (Papaver Nudicaule). These range in colour from the purest satiny white and yellow, to the deepest

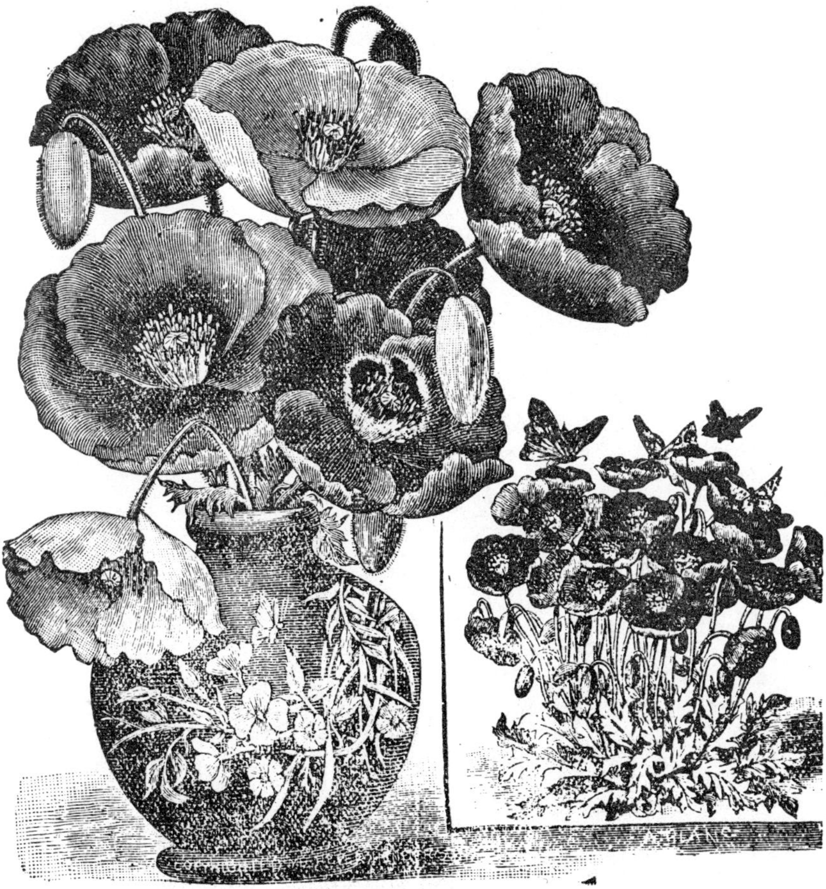

Ickland Poppies,

glowing orange-scarlet, and have a delicious lilac-like fragrance, the flowers being produced in the greatest abundance and for a very long season. Not only are they attractive in the garden, but for elegance in a cut state they are simply unsurpassed, lasting quite a week if cut directly they are opened. The plants grow to a height of some 9 to 12 inches, or even 18 inches in a rich soil.

Another most popular strain of Poppy has been introduced by the well known hybridiser, the Rev. Mr. Shirley, and is known as *The Shirley*, after the raiser. I take the following description of the beautiful strain, from an article which appeared some some years ago in "*Amateur Gardening.*"

"So much has been said already in praise of this charming section of the Poppy family, that any further comment in the same direction would appear unnecessary ; and yet it seems almost impossible to retire in our admiration, or stint our praise of anything so exquisitely fragile and beautiful. It is often remarked that Poppies are very lovely, but that the short lived beauty of the flowers is much against them. To my mind, with a plant so floriferous as the Shirley Poppy, this is a charm rather than an imperfection. The ever varying forms and constantly changing hues, which are daily displayed on good masses of them, bring more quickly the relief of novelty than is the case with more enduring flowers, and while we regret the shattering of to-day's perfection, the sight of the many flower buds which are straightening their slender necks in the evening sun, brings the assurance of still richer charms to-morrow. The brilliant flowers, craning their necks to catch the earliest sun-beams, and the well contented murmur of insect life, are charms which render a sowing of these poppies essential in any garden. All honour be to him, who by tireless patience and excellent judgment, gave to our gardens one of its greatest charms."

POPPY, THE SHIRLEY.

A very pretty variety is *Eider-Down* (Papaver somniferum album laciniatum fl. pl ) which is one of the most exquisite of recent introductions. The plants are of sturdy habit, growing about 1½ feet high, and bearing flowers like great round balls of eider-down, as white as snow, the edges of the petals being deeply pinked or slashed. It blooms the first season, remains in flower much longer than is usual with Poppies, and deserves a place in every garden. One of the prettiest of the Pæony-flowered varieties has been introduced under the name of *American Flag.* The flowers are extra large and very double ; colours pure white, the petals being margined with bright red. *The Mikado* (Papaver Marselli). One of the most charming sorts. The engraving

PAPAVER MARSELLI, OR MIKADO POPPY.

conveys a true idea of its quaint, yet artistic, beauty ; the petals at the edges are cut and fringed ; the colour is most attractive and pretty, being pure white at the back, while the fringed edges are of a brilliant crimson scarlet. *Nankeen Yellow* is another valuable addition to the Pæony Flowered varieties. The large globular flowers are perfectly double ; in colour a shining Nankeen Yellow, an entirely new colour in the genus. *The Tulip* (Papaver Glaucum) is quite a novelty. This interesting and beautiful Annual originated in Armenia. The plant rises to a height of

Poppy, Tulip.

from 12 to 14 inches and produces, well above the foliage, 50 to 60 large and splendid flowers of the most vivid scarlet imaginable, the colour being seen, even from a distance, of such glowing richness as to perfectly dazzle the eye. This Novelty will undoubtedly rank as one of the finest of our decorative Annuals, its brilliant and pleasing colour imparting brightness to plants and flowers of more sombre hues.

A very pretty single flowering variety is *The Bride*, in which the flowers are of large size and the purest snow-white colour. In *Danebrog* (Danish Flag) we have a very effective novelty. The flowers are of a brilliant scarlet colour, the base of each of the petals being blotched with silvery white, forming on the flowers a distinct white cross, as shown in the illustration I give. There are many strains of mixed Poppies offered by the various Seedsmen under such names as :—*Carnation Flowered*, *Peony Flowered*, *Double Pompone Japanese*, *French Dwarf*, *Double mixed* &c., all of which will be found useful by readers who do not particularly require separate colours for bedding &c.

The Danish Flag. (Poppy, Danebrog.)

Amongst the single red flowering Poppies the following four stand preeminent for form, beauty and brilliance of colouring. *Laevigatum*, *Orientale*, *Pavoninum* and *Umbrosum*. Laevigatum is an introduction from Persia and is a very showy annual. The plants grow to a height of some 2 to $2\frac{1}{2}$ feet, and bear, in great profusion, fine shaped flowers 4 inches in diameter. In colour a brilliant deep scarlet, with black spots surrounded with a white margin at the base of each petal. *Orientale* is one of the best known of the Perennial Poppies and was originally introduced from Armenia. The plant grows to a height of 2 to 3 feet. The flowers are deep scarlet with a dark purple spot at the base of each petal. *Pavoninum* (The "Peacock" Poppy) bears flowers nearly 4 inches across, which are of a vivid scarlet and cherry-crimson with a black zone near the centre. *Umbrosum* grows to a height of 2 feet and has flowers of a most dazzling scarlet with a jet-black blotch on the inner base of each petal, the blotch being occasionally margined with grey. This variety is commonly known as the Caucasian Scarlet Poppy.

# PASSIFLORA.

## Nat. Ord.—Passifloraceæ.—[The Passion flower.]

The Passion Flower is one of the most rampant growing creepers in cultivation, and one of the most beautiful. Up to an altitude of 5000 to 6,000 feet is quite hardy; I have had plants growing outside in my Mussoorie garden for years, and never remember losing a single plant during our more or less severe winters. Will grow well in practically any soil, but requires good drainage, while plenty of water should be given during the growing season. Perhaps the best compost for the Passiflora is composed of equal parts of turfy loam and leaf mould, with a fair proportion of sharp sand. It is not wise to plant in a too rich soil, as you will then have any amount of foliage but few flowers. Both on the Plains and Hills seed should be sown in October in seed pans or boxes. Pot out the seedlings when large enough to handle and pot on as required, or, better still, plant out in the open border. Should not be planted in a deep soil; the compost in which they are planted should not be more than about a foot deep. There are a great number of varieties, but

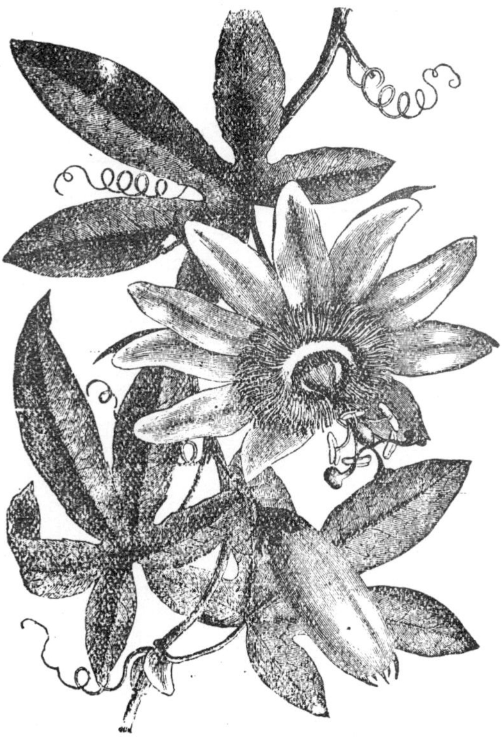

PASSIFLORA.

few growers will need more than three or four, which may be selected from the following :—

*Alba* or *Atomaria* is a pretty pure white variety and very free flowering. *Cærulea* is the best known variety. The flowers are slightly scented. There is also a large flowering variety of *Cærulea* known as *Cærulea Grandiflora*, which is a great improvement *Incarnata* is a sweet scented variety with flesh coloured flowers. In a good strain of mixed seed will be found a great number of more, or less beautiful varieties.

## PELARGONIUM.

Nat. Ord.—Geraniaceæ (Stork's Bill.)

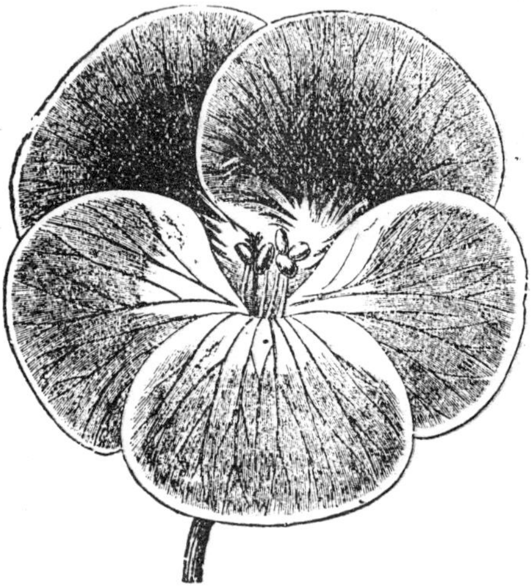

PELARGONIUM.

No plant is more popular than this, and, when well grown, its effect is matchless. The large bold flowers of the English, the beautifully spotted flowers of the French, and the elegant, delicate colours of the Fancy varieties, make them deservedly popular plants. For culture see GERANIUM. I advise readers resident on the Plains to get plants from Hill gardens at the beginning of the cold weather.

## PENSTEMON.

Nat. Ord.—Scrophulariaceæ.—(Beard Tongue.)

Flowers resemble Gloxinias in shape; mottled in crimson, pink, blue and white. Firminger says :—Plants raised from seed sown with the Annuals in October will continue in blossom during the hot and rainy seasons following." In the Hills sow March to May. My good friend "Landolicus" in his "Indian Amateur Gardener" says that the Penstemon flowers prettily if planted in open beds, but refuses to do so in pots. I differ from him, as I have at the time I write—August—a large number of plants in 8 inch pots, which have been in flower for weeks past, and are now making quite a grand show. There are a number of varieties, of which the various hybrids of *Hartwegi*, commonly known as *Gentianoides*, are amongst the best. The varieties

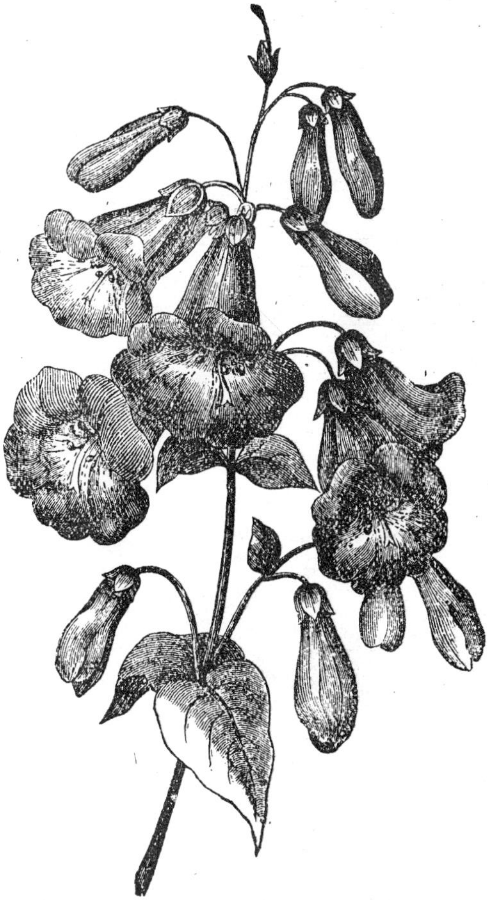

PENSTEMON.

differ in growth more than in flowers ; one of the best of the class, known as *Erectus* has beautiful flowers which are borne erect, unlike the other varieties, in which the flowers are more or less drooping, as shown in the illustration I give.

# PETUNIA.

Nat. Ord. Solanaceæ.

On the Plains sow from the middle of September to the end of November ; plants will then flower in March and will remain in flower until the commencement of the rains. Seed should be sown in pans of light, rich soil, which must be kept in a shady situation till they have germinated, when they must be allowed as much light and air as possible, only removing them under shelter during the continuance of heavy rains. To get such fine seed to do well, it is

PETUNIA, HYBRIDA INIMITABLE NANA COMPACTA MULTIFLORA.

important that the soil should be made perfectly smooth and level, and when this is done, watered through a fine rosed pot, so as to avoid having to wet the earth afterwards, till the young plants make their appearance By adopting this course and covering the pot or pan with a piece of glass, so as to maintain an equable temperature and prevent evaporation, success will be certain. Even the most minute seed may be induced to germinate in this way, but in all cases where it is so small that it has to be sown on the surface, it should have a sheet of paper laid over the glass to shut out the light for the first few days, after which it will require close watching, and must be uncovered immediately germination takes place In the Hills sow in February, March and April, when the plants will flower in the Autumn. A sowing may also be made in October, for plants to flower in the Spring.

There are very many varieties now in cultivation, as the plant has received much attention from hybridisers of late years. A very large flowering strain has lately been introduced under the name of ***Giants of California***." The strain is to be had both in singles and doubles. A beautiful double flowering variety is ***Fimbriata Venosa flore pleno.*** The deeply fringed flowers are of a light lilac colour, and almost entirely covered with reddish violet veins.

Amongst varieties useful for bedding I would mention the following :—

*Countess of Ellesmere*—Flowers deep rose; a good variety. *Hybrida Inimitable Nana Compacta. Multiflora.*—The plants are very compact, seldom growing more than 6 to 9 inches in height, with a diameter of 12 to 15 inches, profusely covered with brilliant cherry-red blooms, each of which is distinctly striped with white. The illustration gives a good idea of the habit of this excellent variety. *Inimitable*—A very distinct kind, flowers blotched and mottled in most fantastic forms.

PETUNIA, GRANDIFLORA.

Good mixtures of bedding varieties can be obtained from all Seedsmen for a few annas a packet, and these will be found ample for most growers.

A number of varieties of the *Hybrida grandiflora* strain have been introduced, of which the following are the pick :—

*Hender's Superb Strain*—Comprising the finest large flowered single varieties in cultivation. *Hybrida Grandiflora Fimbriata*—A splendid strain, surpassing anything hitherto offered. The flowers are very large and beautifully fringed. *Hybrida Grandiflora Intus Aurea*—A variety with bright yellow throats. *Hybrida Grandiflora Maculata*—Blotched and spotted varieties; very beautiful. *Hybrida Grandiflora Superbissima, Finest Mixed*—Splendid strain with enormous flowers of various colours, with broad white throats. *Hybrida Grandiflora Venosa*—Delicately veined varieties.

Double flowered Petunia seed does not always come true, in fact from the very finest strains, it is seldom that more than 25 to

30 per cent will produce plants with double flowers. The following are much grown sorts and I can strongly recommend them all. *Hybrida Grandiflora, Flore Pleno*—The finest double varieties hybridised with great care, and certain to yield the largest percentage of double flowering varieties; in every shade of colour. *Hybrida Grandiflora, Fimbriata Flore Pleno*—Large flowering double fringed; a very charming and distinct section with strikingly beautiful double flowers: highly recommended. *Hybrida Grandiflora, Robusta Flore Pleno*—A new and very handsome dwarf strain of great merit, includes both plain and fringed varieties.

PETUNIA, GRANDIFLORA FIMBRIATA, FL. PL.

## Phaseolus, Caracalla.

Nat. Ord.—**Leguminosæ.** [Greek Creeper or Snail Flower.]

This is a most beautiful Climber and is closely allied to the common Gram, the Kidney Bean, the Scarlet Runner, the Lima Bean and many others of the same family. The flowers resemble orchids in appearance, are sweet scented and of a peculiar purplish and yellow colour. Is a native of India and does well both on the Plains and Hills, but as it is not hardy, requires protection on the Hills during the cold weather. Sow during the rains.

## Physalis Franchetti.

Nat. Ord.—**Solanaceæ.** (The Chinese Lantern Plant.)

I have given full particulars re growing the Physalis under the heading of *Tiparee* on page 83. I consider this variety is only of use in the Flower Garden, as the fruits are very poor in flavor. The plants make very effective pot plants, and a few should be grown for decorative purposes.

PHYSALIS, FRANCHETII.

# Phlox Drummondii.

## Nat. Ord.—Polemoniaceæ

There is certainly hardly any other family of annuals that can compare with this in variety of colour and profuseness of bloom, or that retains its beauty for such a lengthened period. They require a good rich soil, liberally manured, and must be grown in a situation fully exposed to the sun. To render them effective, they should be grown in large masses.

On the Plains sow the seed for succession from September to November, in pans of light rich soil, which must be kept well shaded till the plants are up. When two inches high, transplant into the open ground, six inches apart, or, if grown in pots, three plants in a six inch pot. In the Hills sow March to May and treat as above.

The following are amongst the best of the ordinary *Drummondii* strain :—

*Alba*—Pure white. *Alba Oculata*—White with reddish purple eye. *Atropurpurea*—Deep blood purple. *Atrosanguinea*—Deep red with light edges *Coccinea*—Deep scarlet. *Hortensiflora*—Very deep rose. *Leopoldi*—Splendid red, white eye *Radowitzi*—Rose striped with white. *Violacea Alba Oculata*—Deep violet with white eye. *William I*—Crimson and white.

Of late years the ordinary *Drummondii* varieties have had to give way to the *Drummondii Grandiflora*, a strain in which the flowers are much larger, and of finer substance than in the older one. All the colours of the older strain are to be had and several others in addition. The following list will give readers a good selection to pick from :—

*Grandiflora Alba*—Pure white. *Grandiflora Atropurpurea*—Dark purple. *Grandiflora Atropurpurea Alba-Oculata*—Purple with white eye. *Grandiflora Chamois Rose*—With white eye. *Grandiflora Coccinea*—Deep scarlet. *Grandiflora Heynholdi*—The most brilliant colour yet introduced, the plants having been aptly likened to balls of fire. *Grandiflora Kermesina Alba Oculata*—Crimson with white eye,

THE STAR OF QUEDLINBURGH
[Phlox Drum. Cuspidata.]

PHLOX, FIMBRIATA.

*Grandiflora Leopoldi*—Bright rose with white eye. *Grandiflora Picta Atrorosea*—(Quadricolour). *Grandiflora Picta Atroviolacea*—(Quadricolour). *Grandiflora Rosea Alba-Oculata*—Rose with white eye. *Grandiflora Splendens*—Brilliant scarlet with white eye. *Grandiflora Striata Coccinea*—Scarlet striped. *Grandiflora Variabilis*—Dark violet; a very compact growing variety. *Grandiflora Violacea Alba Oculata*—Violet with white eye.

PHLOX, DRUMMONDII GRANDIFLORA.

In *Fimbriata and Cuspidata* we have two very pretty sorts, of which the illustrations I give, convey a very good idea. In the former the flowers are of medium size. The edges of the petals are prettily cut and are distinctly bordered with white. In *Cuspidata*, which is commonly known as *The Star of Quedlinburgh*, the centre teeth of the five petals are very much elongated, giving the flowers a pretty starlike appearance. Some of the double flowering sorts are very beautiful and perhaps the very finest is that splendid variety *Isabellina fl. pl.* or *Lutea fl. pl.*, which is an exquisite novelty in annual Phloxes. Plants of very bushy and branching habit, attaining a height of 15 to 18 inches, bearing in great profusion, large umbels of double flowers of charming yellow. Another very pretty variety is *Atropurpurea, flore semi-pleno*, which is a semi-double variety, bearing deep blood-red flowers. A very fine dwarf growing strain has been introduced under the name of *Dwarf Compact.* The habit of the plants is dwarf and compact, frequently measuring only 5 or 6 inches high, and forming a dense mass of flowers 9 or 10 inches across. The colours are very varied.

PHLOX DRUMONDII, DOUBLE.

# PHORMIUM (Chlamydia.)

### Nat. Ord.—Liliaceæ (Flax Lily, or New Zealand Flax.)

A very handsome plant, with stiff, sword shaped leaves, and orange coloured lily-like flowers. The foliage is beautifully variegated, which makes it a most ornamental plant for lawn decoration. Is of easy culture, requiring a light, rich soil. Sow on the Plains in October; Hills March and April. The variety commonly grown is *Tenax folium variegatum*, in which the leaves are dark green, beautifully striped with yellow and white, and are often 6 feet in length.

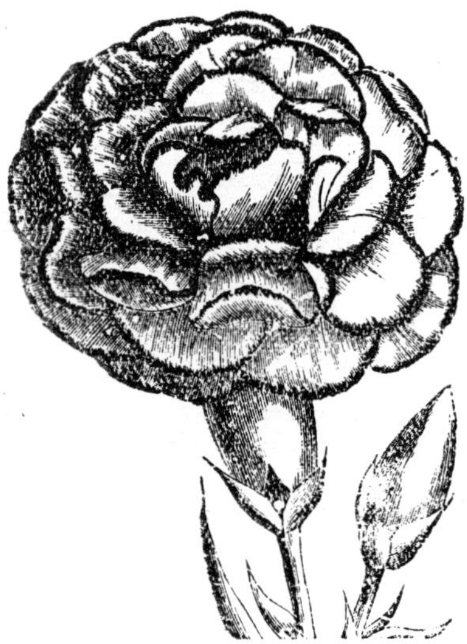

PICOTEE.

# PICOTEE.

### Nat. Ord.—Caryophyllaceæ.

The Picotee is a variety of Carnation in which the flowers are beautifully edged with a second colour, the main portion of the petals being white, yellow &c., with light or dark purple, rose or red edges. For culture see CARNATION.

# PLATYSTEMON, CALIFORNICUM.

### Nat. Ord.—Papaveraceæ.

A very pretty member of the Poppy family, and, like its cousins, of easy culture. As it will not stand transplanting, the seed should be sown where the plants are to remain, in October on the Plains; March to May on the Hills. The flowers are a pretty pale lemon yellow.

# POLYGONUM.

### Nat Ord.—Polygoniaceæ. (Knot-grass, Knot-weed, "Tear Thumb" of North America.)

This is a hardy herbaceous Perennial of very rapid growth and of easy culture, grows well in any ordinary garden soil, but well repay liberal treatment and a good position. Sow on the Plains in Oct. Hills in March and April, or in the Autumn under cover. There are

POLYGONUM.

a number of varieties in cultivation, such as :—*Lanigerum*, a variety with enormous silver-white foliage ; *Multiflorum*, a very free flowering sort and *Orientale foliis variegatis*, which is a most beautiful variegated-leaved variety of the old fashioned " Ragged Sailor " or " Prince's Feather," and also known as " The East Indian Knot Weed." The red flowers are borne in spikes 7 to 8 inches long. The leaves are variegated with white.

# PORTULACA.

## Nat. Ord.—Portulacaceæ--(Purslane.)

In brilliancy and beauty of colour the Portulaca surpasses all out-door plants. They delight in sunny situations and light soils, where they rapidly carpet the ground. On the Plains may be sown at any time from July to December ; it is advisable to mix the seed with sand before sowing, as it is very minute ; it may either be covered very lightly with soil, if in the open ground, or if in pots, a pane of glass laid over it will be sufficient. A mistake frequently made in the cultivation of this plant, is to allow them to become too crowded, as they thereby invariably produce very inferior flowers. If put out at a distance of six inches apart, they will quickly spread themselves and make strong bushy plants. They require good soil, will enriched with old manure, and should be kept liberally supplied with water. In the Hills sow from April to June.

PORTULACA, GRANDIFLORA PLENISSIMA.

There are a number of varieties of which the following *Grandiflora* single flowering sorts are amongst the best. *Alba Striata*—White striped crimson. *Aurea*—Bright golden yellow. *Splendens*—Vivid crimson. *Thelluseni*—Bright scarlet. *Thorburni*—Straw colour. *Plenissima, Double Mixed*—A very fine strain producing a large percentage of double flowers.

PRIMULA, SINENSIS FIMBRIATA

## Primulas.

Nat Ord —Primulaceæ.

(Primrose.)

In the Hills the Primula grows most luxuriantly, and fine specimens are easily grown with but little trouble. The best time to sow is August or September, when, if the plants can have the protection of a frame during winter, they will bloom freely by February or March. The Primula does not, as a rule, succeed well on the Plains. Firminger in his "*Manual of*

*Gardening* " says :—" I find it stated by Captain Hollings that they had "the English Primrose in magnificent blossoms at Lucknow on the "30th August 1844. On the Hills, however, it thrives and blossoms to perfection." The same treatment as recommended for CINERARIAS (see page 140) will do equally well for the Primula.

The following are all good sorts :—

*Sinensis Fimbriata, Alba Magnifica*—This splendid white Primula is of exquisite form and substance, and a great improvement on the old varieties. The habit of the plant is exceedingly compact, the flowers measure 2½ inches in diameter, are pure white, with large bright yellow eyes, and are borne in large trusses well above the foliage, each petal being deeply and beautifully fringed. *Sinensis Fimbriata Avalanche* (The Bride)—This is a robust grower, leaves of a beautiful dark green with red foot stalks The flowers are pure white, with yellow eye, very large, of good substance. and beautifully fringed. *Sinensis Fimbriata "Chiswick Red"*—This is best described as the most brilliant crimson-scarlet Primula yet sent out, with habit as robust as 'Alba Magnifica ;' the foliage very finely cut and deep green. *Sinensis Fimbriata Cœrulea*—Beautiful bright porcelain blue ; a very striking variety. *Sinensis Fimbriata Meteor*—The flowers of this magnificent strain are a purple-crimson. beautifully fringed, and of immense size and substance. *Japonica* (The Japanese Primrose)—This grand variety which has been termed "The Queen of Primroses," is undoubtedly the grandest member of this order, the flowers are of various colours, very large. and are produced in whorls or tiers on a long upright stem. *Obconica*—This plant possesses the useful power of flowering perpetually when grown in a pot and kept under glass. The flowers are produced on slender stems about 9 inches in height, white with a slight tinge of lilac, and in great profusion. It does best when allowed plenty of pot-room, and if in a 7-inch or 8-inch pot, all the better, giving good drainage, and using light loamy soil and sand mixed with some very old manure and leaf-mould. *Vulgaris*—The true common yellow Primrose, so popular in the old country. All lovers of the old fashioned Home flowers will welcome this.

A very fine hardy Primrose, has been introduced in *New Blue*, of which I give an illustration on next page. The most prominent feature of this variety and that which clearly distinguishes it from all others in cultivation, is its remarkable colour, which is developed into many shades of blue, from pale lavender to deep violet. The flowers are freely produced on footstalks rising well above the foliage, and are fully equal in size, shape and duration to the best of the older varieties. It has received six "Awards of Merit" from the Royal Horticultural Society, and a special "Award of Merit," Birmingham, April 24th, 1895,

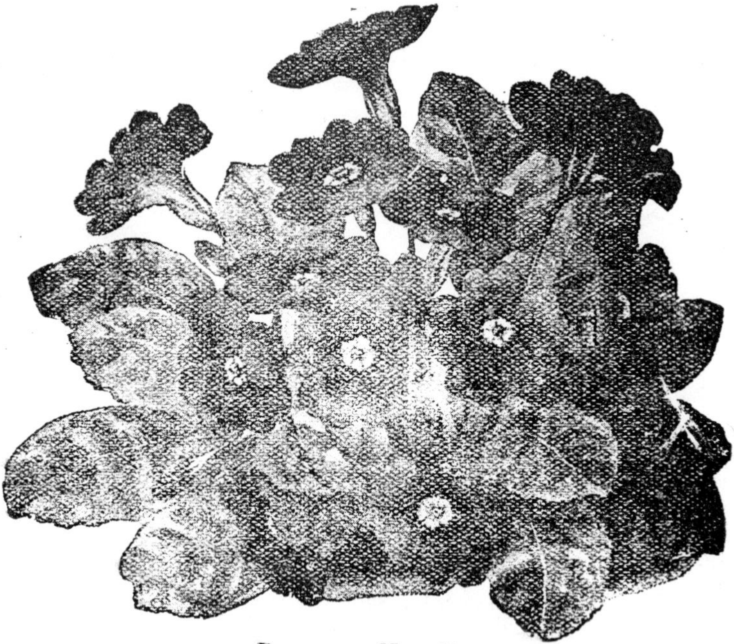

PRIMROSE, NEW BLUE.

# PYRETHRUM, AUREUM.

Nat. Ord.—Compositæ. (Golden Feather, or Feverfew.)

On the Plains do not sow the seed before the middle of October, as it will not germinate till the cold weather fairly sets in, and then only at very irregular intervals, some plants appearing within a week and others perhaps two months after seed is sown. Prick out the seedlings as soon they are large enough to handle; they require a moderately rich soil and a position fully exposed to the sun, to induce them to colour to the best advantage. Should be sown from March to May in the Hills.

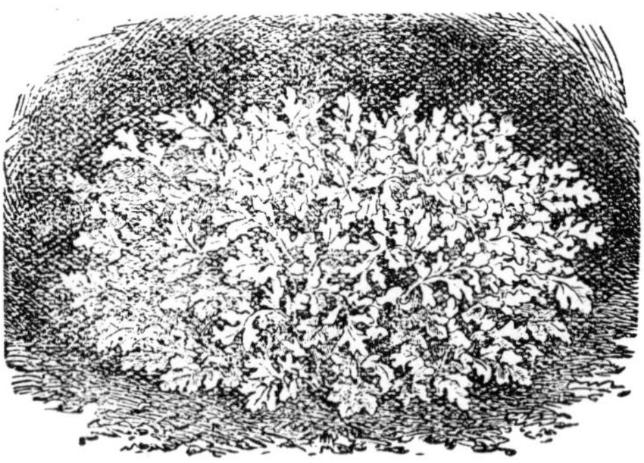

PYRETHRUM AUREUM, SELAGINOIDES.

The leaves of the Pyrethrum are very useful for driving away flies and insects.

The following are good sorts :—

*Golden Gem*—A very handsome variety with bright yellow foliage and double flowers. *Laciniatum*—A greatly improved variety with beautiful fern-like foliage. *Selaginoides*—A very distinct variety, of dwarf and compact habit, the flat leaves overlying each other, thus giving the plants a particularly fine level appearance. As the plant does not flower the first year, it does not require the constant pinching back which is so necessary with other varieties.

PYRETHRUM AUREUM, LACINIATUM.

## RHODANTHE.

**Nat. Ord.—Compositæ.**

A very beautiful "Everlasting," which is also known as *Helipterum*. Requires a light, rich, well-manured soil, and should be grown in a situation fully exposed to the sun. Seed must be sown on the Plains in October or November, in pans, and the plants pricked out as soon as they are large enough to handle. They are much benefitted by frequent transplanting. Sow on the Hills from March to May.

The following are sorts usually grown :—

*Maculata*—A very attractive variety with rose and yellow flowers. *Maculata Alba*—A pure white variety of the preceding. *Manglesi* (The Swan River Everlasting.)—A beautiful annual 10 to 12 inches high, of dwarf, erect branching habit ; flowers bright rose.

## RHODODENDRON.

**Nat. Ord.—Ericaceæ, (Rose Bay.)**

Unfortunately this is one of the plants which cannot be grown on the Plains, but which luxuriates on the Hills. Visitors to

Mussoorie and other. Hill stations cannot help being struck with the magnificent trees, 30 to 40 feet high, which about March and April are ablaze with colour On the Hills sow in October, keeping the seed pans in a greenhouse or warm, sunny verandah, or sow about March. The best soil for the Rhododendron is a sandy peat, and where this can be obtained it should be used in preference to any other compost. When the seedlings are large enough to handle, pot off singly in thumb pots and pot on as required Frequent shifts are advisable, but care should be taken when repotting, not to disturb the roots too much.

# RHYNCHOSPERMUM.

## Nat. Ord.—Apocynaceæ.—[Chinese Ivy, or Chinese Jessamine.]

### (Syn.- Trachelospermum.)

This is a very beautiful, sweet scented, free flowering climber, which is a native of India, China and Japan. In habit it much resembles the Jasmine, is a rapid grower and of extremely easy culture. Sow during the rains both on the Plains and Hills. The variety *Jasminoides fol. var.*, has pure white salver-shaped flowers nearly an inch across, and in the hot season on the Plains, flowers most profusely. Succeeds best in a compost composed of equal parts of fibrous loam and peat, but will grow well in any ordinary garden soil.

# RICINUS.

## Nat. Ord.—Euphorbiaceæ.

### (Castor Oil plant, Palma Christi.—Vern. Rendee.)

RICINUS.

The Castor Oil plants make very effective specimens when plenty of room can be given to them. Most of the varieties make very pretty pot plants, and as they possess the useful property of keeping flies out of a room, a few should always be kept for room decoration. The seed should be sown just about the end of the rains, and, if not required as pot plants, should be sown in the place where the plants are to remain. Give plenty of water during the early part of their growth. A new strain has lately been introduced under the name of *Zanzibariensis*, the leaves of which are very large and finely coloured. Other good sorts are :—*Cambogiensis*, a variety with large palm-like leaves of a bronzy red maroon colour, with large red veins ; the main stem or trunk being ebony black. *Gibsoni* or *Duchess* of *Edinburgh*—In this sort both the foliage and stems are of a dark purplish red. *Sanguineus* or *Obermannii*—Stalks and leaves of a bright metallic bronze colour, often almost as red as fire ; bunches of fruit brilliant crimson.

## ROMNEYA, COULTERI.

### Nat. Ord.—Papaveraceæ.—(The White Californian Perennial Poppy.)

A comparatively new plant, having only been introduced into Europe from California in 1875. Is a tall, showy, herbaceous Perennial. Does best in a rich sandy loam. Sow in October on the Plains ; March and April on the Hills. The seed often takes months to germinate, but I advise readers to try the plant, as it is extremely pretty. The plants grow to a height of 2 to 4 feet, and bear large, showy, pure white flowers.

## SAINTPAULIA, IONANTHA.

### Nat. Ord.—Violaceæ.

SAINTPAULIA, IONANTHA.

The leaves of this interesting novelty, which are dark green, of fleshy consistence and downy surface, spread themselves laterally just over the soil, and form as it were a rosette, in the centre of which springs up quite a bouquet of flowers violet like both in colour and shape, but 1¼ inches each in diameter, and gracefully borne on stalks 2 to 3 inches high. Has been awarded an "Award of Merit" from the Royal Horticultural Society of England. On the Plains sow in October ; March to May and also in the Autumn on the Hills.

# SALPIGLOSSIS.

## Nat Ord.—Scrophulariaceæ.—(The Tube Tongue.)

The beautiful Salpiglossis has been much improved during the past few years and well grown plants now form most handsome additions to the garden. On the Plains sow in October, and plant out the seedlings when they are about an inch high, in the place where they are to remain. They will commence flowering in March and flower on till the rains. On the Hills sowings should be made from March to May and also in October; plants from the latter sowing will flower the following spring. The Salpiglossis is closely allied to the Petunia, but I consider it a much more beautiful plant. The following are sorts usually grown :—

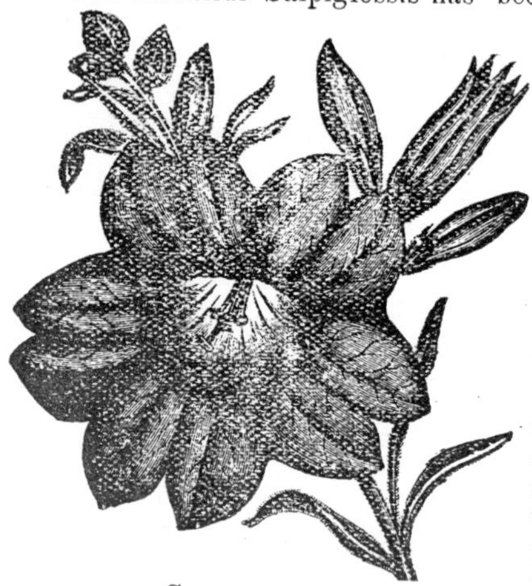

SALPIGLOSSIS.

*New Dwarf*—Flowers equally as large as in the grandiflora variety, the plants however, are very dwarf and compact, rarely attaining a height of over 12 to 15 inches. *Variabilis*—Has large funnel-shaped flowers, in various brilliant colours. *Variabilis Grandiflora*—A magnificent strain producing very large flowers, netted and veined in the most brilliant colours, from creamy white to black blue, and purple ; has a splendid effect.

# SALVIA.

## Nat. Ord.—Labiatæ.—(Flowering Sage).

The Salvias are all most beautiful plants and deserving of the most extensive cultivation. Perhaps a bed of the grand *Salvia Splendens*, when well grown, is one of the grandest sights imaginable. Unfortunately the plant does not grow well on the Plains, but if a little care is taken and protection given in a grass house during the hot weather, very fair specimens can be grown. Sow in October on the Plains ; March and April on the Hills. When about three inches high, transplant into light, rich soil. If you require the plants to grow bushy, peg the stems down, and as they throw up shoots, pinch them off. The Salvia makes a splendid pot plant, but if grown in pots, must have very rich soil

SALVIA, SPLENDENS,

and occasional waterings with liquid mauure. For pots a compost composed of equal parts of turfy loam and well rotted manure will not be a bit too rich There are hundreds of varieties, of which the following three are amongst the very best.

*Coccinea Grandiflora.* --A very fine scarlet flowering variety. The plants grow to a height of 2 to 3 feet. This is one of the oldest varieties, the original Coccinea having been introduced into Europe from Central or South America as long ago as 1772. *Patens.* One of most popular varieties on account of its fine habit and beautiful azure-blue flowers. The flowers are large and borne on plants about $2\frac{1}{2}$ feet high. *Splendens.* (The Scarlet Sage). The illustration gives some little idea of the beauty of this variety, but it must be seen to be fully appreciated. The flowers are of the most brilliant scarlet and are carried on spikes 10 to 12 inches in length, while there will often be a couple of hundred spikes on a well grown plant. They continue in flower for a very long season.

# SANVITALIA.

## Nat. Ord.—Compositæ. (Syn Lorentea.)

The variety *Procumbens fl..pl.* is a very beautiful dwarf creeping plant, which bears, in great profusion, bright yellow double flowers. Thrives in a light, sandy loam, to which has been added a small proportion of leaf mould. Sow in the open border at any time from August to October on the Plains ; March and April on the Hills.

# SAPONARIA.

## Nat. Ord.—Caryophyllaceæ.

## (The Calabrian Soap Wort or Bouncing Bet.)

*Saponaria Calabrica Pumila* is a most charming little Annual when covered with its beautiful star-like flowers, which are generally of a clear rose colour. The plants seldom grow higher than about 6 inches, and so are particularly well adapted for dwarf beds, edgings, rockeries etc. Sow in pans or boxes in October on the Plains and transplant into pots or beds in light, fairly rich soil. Sow from March to May on the Hills.

## SCABIOSA.

### Nat. Ord.--Dipsacaceæ.

**(The "Mourning Bride," Pincushion flower or Devil's Bit).**

The Scabious can only be grown as an Annual on the Plains as it will not live through the rains. The seed should be sown as early as possible on the Plains to ensure their flowering, so I advise sowing early in September. Sow in a compost of light, rich soil. Transplant when large enough. On the Hills sow in August or September under cover and transplant in the early Spring, when they will flower freely in April or May. A sowing may also be made on the Hills in March. There are several varieties commonly grown in gardens, such as :-- *Dwarf Double*, which is a mixed strain comprising plants growing only about one foot high. *Maxima Plena*, a large flowering strain, with double flowers borne on tall growing plants. *Victoria*, a new strain with intensely double flowers of a great diversity of colours.

SCABIOSA.

## SCHIZANTHUS.

### Nat. Ord.--Scrophulariaceæ.--(Butterfly-flower or Fringe-flower.)

A very pretty Annual, bearing in the greatest possible profusion, small flowers of a great variety of colours. On the Plains

SCHIZANTHUS.

should be sown as soon as possible after the rains, say by the middle or end of September. Sow from March to May on the Hills, while for spring flowering, a sowing should be made in October. Grow in a light, sandy but fairly rich soil. It is best to sow where the plants are to remain, as they do not stand transplanting very well; a few should be grown in pots, as they are particularly pretty when thus grown. If grown in pots should be transplanted into a rich compost in 7 or 8 inch pots. There are many varieties bearing flowers of different colours, such as :—White, lilac and yellow, rose and orange, rose and yellow, violet spotted purple, purple spotted red &c. The plants as a rule grow about 2 feet high.

# SHAMROCK.

"The dear little, sweet little, Shamrock of Ireland."

## TRIFOLIUM MINUS.

(TRUE)

"Thrives only on starvation."

"Good food, kindness or justice, kills us."

*Motto* :—THOROUGHLY IRISH.

The Rose, Thistle and Shamrock are dear to the English, Scotch and Irish all the world over, and it is now possible for the Irishman in a far off foreign land to have his little sprig of the Shamrock for St. Patrick's Day or any other National festival. Mr. Baylor Hartland of Cork sent some thousands of packets of the seed to the Duke of Connaught, for sowing on the graves of his compatriots, who had fallen in the late Boer War, and few gifts were more appreciated. For years past I have grown a few boxes of the plants for distribution amongst my Irish friends. Opinions differ very much as to what is the *true* Shamrock, some giving the palm to the Wood Sorrel, others to Trifolium Minus, but the consensus of opinion seems to be that the latter is the true National emblem of "*Ould Oirland.*" I take the following hints on the culture from the directions given by Mr. Baylor Hartland.

"Sow thinly in boxes of poor gravelly soil, well drained. If "some fine close grass seed be mixed with the seed all the better, and "when the tufts are strong, plant out before Winter. If grown as a "rock plant among rough stones, sand, gravel, &c., and some grass "seed sown also, the Shamrock will seed itself, and come up annually."

Sow on the Plains in September to November; March to May on the Hills. "May the Rose, Leek and Thistle long flourish, and twine round the sprig of Shillelagh and Shamrock so green."

## SILENE.

Nat. Ord.--Caryophyllaceæ (Campion or Catchfly.)

On the Plains sow as soon as possible after the end of the rains, in the place where the plants are to remain. On the Hills sow from March to June for Autumn flowering, or in October, under cover, for flowering in the Spring and early Summer. Succeed in any light, loamy soil. The varieties mostly grown are :—

SILENE PENDULA, DOUBLE.

*Pendula Compacta*—A very dwarf growing, compact variety. The individual plants form dense clumps some 2 to 3 inches in height by 9 to 12 inches in diameter, which are completely covered with bright pink flowers. *Pendula Compacta Ruberrima*—A crimson flowering variety of the preceding. There is also a very fine double flowering strain, of which I give an illustration. The flowers are of a number of colours.

## SOLANUM.

Nat. Ord.--Solanaceæ (Night shade.)

Many of the hybrid Solanums are most decorative objects, either from March to October; on the Hills, April and May. Require exactly the same treatment as the CAPSICUM (See page 18). If grown as pot plants, transplant from the seed pans when the plants are about two inches high. Pot in six or eight inch pots and treat liberally There are a number of fine strains, of which the following are the best. *Hayes' Covent Garden, Select Upright*—A splendid selection, bearing fruit of all shades, from pale yellow to deep crimson. *Hendersoni*—A handsome variety with bright orange coloured fruit. *Weatherill's Hybrids*—Easily grown decorative plants, producing their brilliantly coloured fruits in great profusion and of many shades of colour.

SOLANUM AS A POT PLANT.

## STATICE. (Syn. Taxanthema.)

### Nat. Ord.—Plumbaginaceæ—(Sea Lavender.)

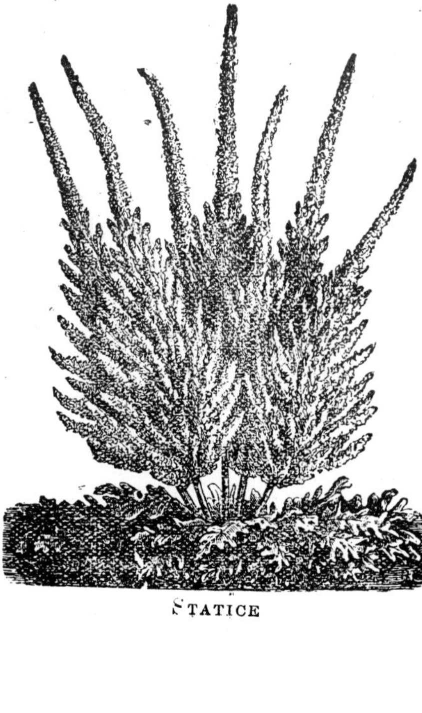

STATICE

A very striking looking plant and well worth cultivation. Sow in Sep ember and October on the Plains; March and April on the Hills Plant out when large enough, in beds of good turfy loam, with which a fair proportion of charcoal dust and sharp sand has been mixed. The two varieties I describe are the ones usually grown. *Superba*—This species is one of the most remarkable of this interesting genus. It differs conspicuously from the candelabra shaped *Suworowi*, by forming feathered or plumed flower spikes similar to the feathered Cockscombs. It grows to a height of from 18 to 24 inches, each plant producing a large number of beautiful spikes or plumes. The main flower stem rises 6 to 8 inches above the plume. When the plants begin to bloom they resemble closely a handsome flowering Heath (Erica.) The individual flowers vary in all shades of colours from pure white to deep rose. *Suwo owi*—Flowers of beautiful lilac colour, borne in dense branched spikes. A most strikingly b autiful hardy annual, Will remain in flower for two months

## STOCKS, TEN WEEK. (Mathiola)

Nat. Ord.--Cruciferæ. (Stock Gilli Flowers.)

There are few more beautiful flowers than the various varieties of Stocks. The plants grow well all over the Plains, but in some places it is difficult to get them to flower. Many of the best growers recommend growing in pots, without any transplanting, but I, in common with many others, advise the sowing of the seeds in the beds where the plants are to remain, as transplanting checks the growth of the plants so much, that they seldom recover fully from the effects. The Stock requires liberal treatment, so should be grown in a light well manured soil, with good drainage, while an occasional drenching with liquid manure during the time of growth, will greatly improve the vigour of the plants and, consequently, the size and form of the flower spikes. Sow on the Plains in October; March to June on the Hills.

STOCK, MAMMOTH WHITE COLUMN.

There are very many grand varieties now in cultivation, which are immense improvements on the sorts grown fifty years ago. I illustrate one of the finest introductions of late years—*Mammoth White Column.* The plant is of luxuriant growth, attaining in the open ground to a height of 3 feet, and producing only a single long, sturdy spike of bloom, closely furnished with enormous, faultlessly formed double flowers of the purest possible white. When grown in large groups is particularly beautiful. Another grand white variety is the Perpetual *Princess Alice*, which has been renamed *White Perfection, White Dresden* and *Cut and Come again.* The plant is of strong growth and fine branching habit: grows in the open ground to a height of 1½ feet. If sown early will produce uninterruptedly a great abundance of bloom. This variety does particularly well as a pot plant. Still another good white is the variety known as *White Queen*, which bears large double flowers of the purest snow-white. The plants are dwarf and bushy and come into bloom in about 3 months from the time of sowing. *Giant Tree* is a robust growing variety, the plants growing to a height of from 2 to 2½ feet by about the same in diameter, and are well covered with large double flowers in a great variety of colours. *Robust Rocket* forms a compact pyramid 2 feet in height and about 1 foot in diameter. The individual blooms are very large, being often 1½ inches across. One of the old favourite varieties is *Dwarf German*, a strain comprising a large variety of colours. An improved strain of the *Dwarf German* is now much grown under the name of *Improved Large Flowering Dwarf German.* In this new strain the plants are of strong, but dwarf growth, and fine branching habit, while the flowers are very double and deliciously scented.

## STOCK, VIRGINIAN.

### (Malcolmia Maritima).

Nat. Ord.—Cruciferæ.

This is a very pretty little Annual, which should be grown in fairly large masses to be really effective. Sow the seeds thinly in fairly rich soil, in October on the Plains, March to May on the Hills. The plants grow to a height of from 6 to 12 inches. There are a number of colours such as:—*white, yellow, Crimson*, of which there is an improved variety known as *Crimson King*, &c., but most Seedsmen stock the seed in mixture, as well as in the separate colours.

VIRGINIAN STOCK.

# STREPTOCARPUS

## Nat. Ord--Gesneraceæ.--(Cape Primrose).

These require exactly the same treatment as GLOXINIAS (see page 166).

The strain I illustrate—*New Hybrids*--originated at the Royal Gardens, Kew. These new hybrids are remarkable for their abundance of bloom, and the continuous succession in which the flowers are produced, as also for the long time the individual flowers last in perfection. The plant is a perennial, of dwarf, neat habit, growing about 9 inches high, with rather long, narrow, arched, and recurved stemless leaves, whilst the flowers, which are very graceful in form, are trumpet-shaped, and measure about $1\frac{3}{4}$ inches in length. I remember seeing a very fine collection of these hybrids at the Flower Show at the Temple Gardens, London, some years ago, which was very generally admired. The variation of colours in these new hybrids is very striking, scarcely two plants being exactly the same, and the colours range from pure white, through pale lavender, blue, lilac blue, light mauve, purple, violet, bright rose, and red, to rich rosy purple with all the intermediate tints. In all the flowers the throat and three lower segments are more or less marked or splashed with long blotches or spots of various shades of purple, generally shaded and relieved with white, which greatly enhance the effect and afford a pleasing contrast of colour.

STREPTOCARPUS, NEW HYBRIDS.

*Wendlandi*, also known as *Didymocarpus Rhexi*, is a grand variety with enormous leaves.

# SWEET PEAS.

Nat. Ord --Leguminosæ--(Lathyrus Cdoratus.)

Personally I do not think there is any flower in cultivation which can compare with the Sweet Pea, in delicacy of colouring, sweetness of perfume and abundance of flowers. As Keats says :—

Here are Sweet Peas on tiptoe for a flight,
With wings of gentle flush o'er delicate white,
And taper fingers catching at all things,
To bind them all about with tiny rings.

Had Keats lived in the days of Laxton, Eckford, Burpee and some of our other famous hybridisers of the present day, I can imagine how he would have rhapsodised over this queen of flowers. It is really marvellous how the simple little Lathyrus Odoratus which was known to our forefathers, has been improved out of all recognition during the past twenty years. and in these notes, which will have to be much shorter than I would have liked to have made them, I will try to describe some of the beautiful varieties which we now have in cultivation.

Fortunately the culture of the Sweet Pea is very simple. For the Plains it is best to get acclimatised seed if possible, as imported seed, although it will grow most luxuriantly, very often fails to flower. On the Hills and in many places on the Plains, the imported seed does admirably. Sow on the Plains in October in any moderately rich garden soil. On the Hills, I prefer to sow in October, covering over the seed with a fairly thick litter to protect from frost. October sown seed will be in full flower when the Spring sown seed is merely sprouting. It is advisable to sow on the Hills successionally from March to April, and these sowings will provide flowers when the Autumn sown seed is going out of flower. I am a great advocate for cutting flowers not only of the Sweet Pea, but of almost all plants, as doing so will greatly extend the flowering period. It is most essential in the case of the Sweet Pea, as the plants will stop flowering as soon as they are allowed to set their seed pods. Do not attempt to transplant, as, in common with other tap-rooted plants, it is almost impossible to do so. When I have wanted plants for special purposes and could not sow the seed where the plants were to flower, I have followed the plan I describe on page 96.

The varieties of Sweet Pea are literally legion, and it has been most difficult for me to select the very best from the enormous number I know of, but in the following lists I give first class sorts that are really worth growing.

First of all I will give the names and colours of 36 of the very finest varieties in cultivation :—

*Salopian*, scarlet ; *The Hon F. Bouverie*, pinkish salmon ; *Duke of Westminster*, rosy claret ; *Othello*, maroon ; *Mrs. Dugdale*, carmine rose, shaded with primrose ; *Venus*, salmon-buff, shaded rosy pink; *Captain of the Blues*, purplish mauve ; *Lovely*, pink ; *Lady Grisel Hamilton*, light lavender ; *Gorgeous*, orange salmon ; *Emily Henderson*, pure white ; *Miss Willmott*, orange pink, shaded rose ; *Chancellor*, rosy pink, shaded salmon orange ; *Blanche Burpee*, pure white ; *Lady Mary Currie*, salmon-pink, shaded carmine ; *Prince of Wales*, deep rose ; *Triumph*, creamy white, suffused with salmon-pink ; *Duchess of Westminster*, creamy white, shaded coppery rose ; *Prince Edward of York*, glowing scarlet, and deep rose ; *Colonist*, rosy pink ; *Royal Rose*, rosy pink ; *The Hon. Mrs. E. Kenyon*, primrose ; *Lady M. Ormsby-Gore*, primrose, shaded buff and fawn ; *Emily Eckford*, rosy purple and deep blue ; *Black Knight*, dark claret ; *Navy Blue*, almost a pure navy blue ; *Captivation* bright claret ; *Queen Victoria*, primrose yellow, slightly shaded faint purple ; *Aurora*, creamy white, flaked orange salmon ; *Countess of Lathom*, creamy white, shaded soft flesh pink ; *Lord Kenyon*, bright rose pink ; *Fascination*, rich mauve ; *Lady Nina Balfour*, delicate light lavender ; *Golden Rose*, primrose yellow, flushed rosy pink ; *Dainty*, white with pink edge, and *Majestic*, deep rose pink.

The following are all novelties introduced during the past few years and are most excellent sorts :—

*Aurora*. It is impossible to over praise the striking beauty of this gigantic flowered new Sweet Pea. The flowers are of fine substance, full expanded form (as shown in the illustration), and are *truly gigantic in size*. The immense flowers are borne three and four on a stem ; the stems are extra long and strong, the vines are vigorous in growth & bloom most profusely, the colour effect is gorgeous ; both standard and wings are flaked and striped, on a white ground, with *bright orange salmon*. For bunching alone or to brighten a bouquet of assorted colours, nothing could be more effective.

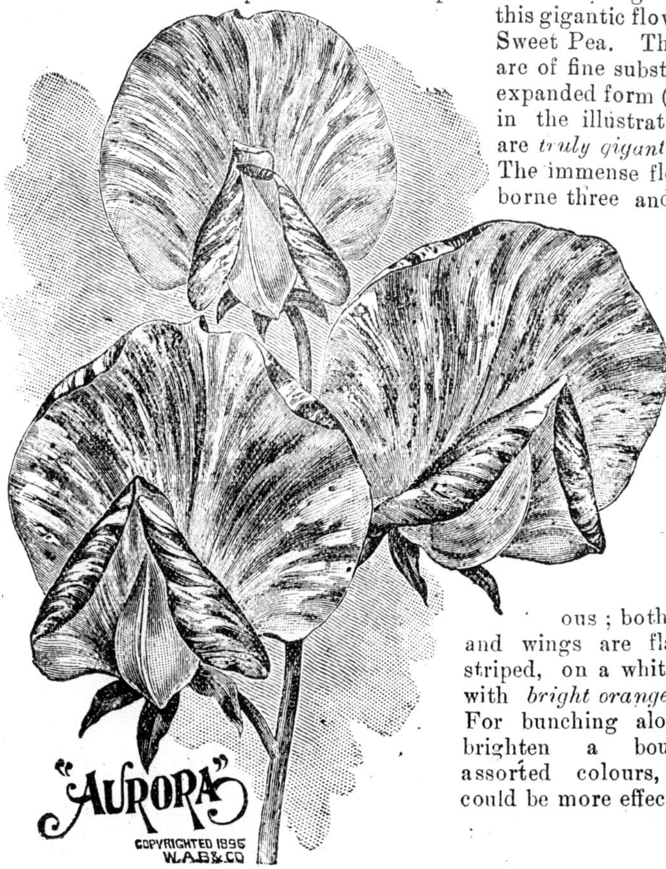

*Brilliant.* This will fill the need for a bright scarlet Sweet Pea of improved form. The flowers are of good substance; medium to large in size; the broad standard is inclined to hood, while the wings are well spread. The colour is of a rich, bright *crimson scarlet.* The wings nearly equal the standard in intense richness of colour. The flowers are borne *three on a stem.* A most important point is the fact that the flowers retain their full brilliancy of colour under the hottest sun—*never becoming marbled or burned.*

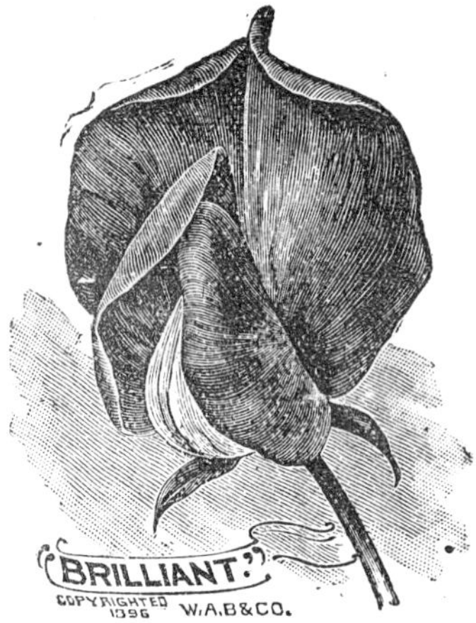

*Creole.* A chance seedling from *Lemon Queen.* The flowers are of the same open, expanded form, of good substance and large size, the vines average three flowers on a stem. The standard is light pinkish-lavender, while the wings are a pure lavender. The flowers are of a *most refined, delicate beauty.* and yet produced profusely. *Daybreak.* (*Raised by the Rev. W. T. Hutchins, the well-known specialist.*) "Daybreak" is the first novelty of his own that Mr. Hutchins has offered. In colour it has a white ground and on the reverse of the standard is a crimson-scarlet cloud, which shows through in the fine veins and network, giving to the centre of the front of the standard a fine crimson scarlet watered effect, the outer margins being white. The wings are slightly flaked with crimson.

*Emily Henderson.*—A gloriously beautiful acquisition has been obtained in this grand Sweet Pea, which has excited the hearty admiration of all who have seen it in flower. The "Emily Henderson" not only surpasses in every way, all other varieties of Sweet Peas, but it is the unanimous opinion of all who have seen it, that it is the most valuable addition made to our list of flower seeds in the last twenty years. In colour it is as pure as the driven snow; the flowers are large, equalling in size those of the "*Boreatton,*" the acknowledged Giant of the Eckfords. Its prodigal abundance of bloom is phenomenal, for where other varieties produce two flowers on a stem, the "Emily Henderson" bears never less than three or nearly as often four; it is even no uncommon thing to find stems bearing five or six flowers each. This variety has very strong stems which gives it an added value for cutting. In earliness of bloom the "Emily Henderson" out-rivals all competitors by nearly two weeks; the fragrance is most delicious, powerful, and distinct from any other varieties.

*Golden Gate.*—Its peculiar form, as shown in the illustration from a photograph, is *entirely unlike any other Sweet Pea known.* The flowers are of good substance and large size, with standard of fine hooded form. The novel feature is seen in the long, pointed wings, which stand upright (like the ears of a rabbit), nearly parallel with the standard. The wings never overlap or meet together, as in all other Sweet Peas. Their distinct, upright form, parallel with each other, suggested the name—*Gotden Gate.* The numerous strong stems bear three and four flowers each, while a remarkable feature is that two stems frequently grow together (united their entire length) bearing *six to eight flowers on one truss.* The standard is soft pinkish mauve, wings a lighter mauve and lavender.'

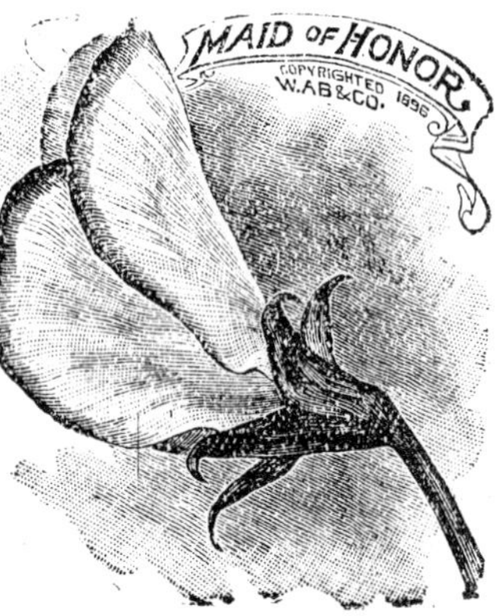


*Maid of Honor.*—This might be described as an *Improved Light Butterfly.* It has been developed from one plant selected some years ago, and is a decided improvement, both in size, form and color. The colouring is very beautiful—lighter than the original ***Butterfly.*** It is light blue on a white ground, shaded and edged. The flowers, borne three on a stem, are of the finest hooded form entirely free from the notches so conspicuous in the original *Butterfly*, while in size and substance they are fully equal to the *Lottie Eckford*. In the illustration of a single flower is shown a side view to illustrate the distinct *blue edge* and to show the entire freedom from the notches at side of standard, so conspicuous in *Butterfly* and *Indigo King*. *Oddity*,—A marked peculiarity is the irregularity of form in the flowers; the standards are inclined to curl considerably. Another distinct feature is that the stems are unusually heavy and strong; they generally bear four flowers on each. In colour the flowers are pale carmine edged with bright rose, giving it the appearance somewhat of a red-edged variety. It is a remarkably strong grower, and with its heavy stem, curly standard, and peculiar colouring, with a sort of netted surface, is certainly attractive, although not of a delicate, refined type.

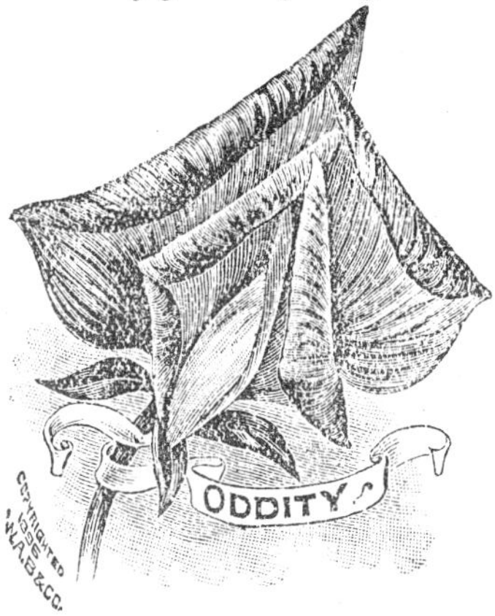


*Princess May*.—A most beautiful and distinct variety, of which the colouring is throughout of a delicate shade of pale heliotrope or lavender, appearing in the bud state of rather a darker tint than when fully expanded. The flowers are large, and of most pleasing colour, the wings and standard well expanded. The Gardening Press have unanimously spoken in high terms of this pretty and distinct novelty. *Ramona*.—Grand flowers of very large size

and improved hooded form, as shown in the illustration. It is a vigorous grower and bears three or four flowers to the stem. Its colouring is delicately beautiful ; a creamy white, daintily splashed with pale pink on standard and wings. The well known Sweet Pea Expert, Rev. W. T. Hutchins, writes :—Ramona is a favourite of mine. It has *the finest grandiflora form*, and is of excellent substance. The soft flesh-pink stripes on white ground are very dainty, and *its beauty is of the delicate order*. *Red Riding Hood*—A QUAINT VARIETY FROM CALIFORNIA. In this variety we have a fixed type, and an absolutely new departure in form. When fully developed, the standard and wings are a pleasing rosy pink, shading to blush white at the calyx ; the keel, which is almost completely enveloped, being nearly pure white. Although unusually robust in habit, it is early flowering. and in plentitude and continuity of bloom, excels all other existing varieties,

SWEET PEA
"RED RIDING HOOD"

The following are older sorts that I can very highly recommend:—

*Adonis*,—The standard is of a deep rose colour, while the wings are almost carmine. The difference in tints appreciable in a flower taken alone, disappears when one regards a tuft of this variety, the eye then only perceiving the lovely rose tint. *Apple Blossom*.—The standards are bright pinkish rose, the wings blush, a beautiful shade of apple blossom ; very pretty and distinct. A very fine large flowered variety. *Boreatton*,—A very fine dark Pea with bold, stout flowers, the standard being a rich, shining bronze, the wings of beautiful crimson purple. This is the Goliath among Sweet Peas. *Bronze King*,—The upper petals are of a rich shining bronzy-maroon, the lower a deep, rich purple. Very handsome. *Butterfly*,—A very beautiful variety; white suffused lavender, small dark blue edge. *Duchess of Edinburgh*,—(Autumn Tints.) Very beautiful ; standard light scarlet, slashed with crimson, slightly margined at the edge with cream-white; wings tipped with rose. *Indigo King,*—The standard of this charming variety is a dark maroon-purple with clear indigo-blue wings. *Isa Eckford,* A most charming variety ; the flowers being a beautiful creamy white, heavily suffused with rosy pink. *Invincible Carmine* [ "Cardinal" or "Beauty."]—A splendid, robust growing variety, producing a great profusion of bright glowing carmine flowers : the brightest coloured of all Sweet Peas. *Miss Blanche Ferry,*—Deep red with white. Very early and free flowering. An excellent variety. *Primrose.*—Quite novel and distinct in colour, the standards and wings pale primrose yellow. (First Class Certificate Royal Horticultural Society.) *Princess of Wales,*—A novelty, shaded and striped with mauve on a white ground, in a most pleasing manner ; flowers of great substance and perfect shape. It has been awarded a First Class Certificate by the Floral Committee of the Royal Horticultural Society. *Queen of England,*—A grand large variety of good substance *Queen of the Isles,*—Very distinct and handsome ; the large and stout standard being bright scarlet flushed and mottled with white, wings flaked and margined with rosy-purple. *Splendour.*—(*Awarded a First Class Certificate by the Royal Horticultural Society.*) Colour rich, bright pinkish rose, shaded with crimson, flowers large, and of the finest form. A most superb and distinct variety. *The Queen.*—A very beautiful and pleasing variety, the light rosy-pink standard being in charming contrast to the wings, which are light mauve.

During the past few years quite a new form of Sweet Pea has come to the front—the "Cupid" Dwarf. The plants grow to a height of only some 5 to 8 inches, with flowers quite as large as the tall growing sorts and most of the colours and varieties have been reproduced in the dwarf, till there are now some 50 or more distinct sorts.

I give an illustration showing "Cupid" growing in a field at Burpee's Farm in Philadelphia; another shows its beauty as a pot plant; while a third shows a single spike. It is almost impossible, even with the help of illustrations, to describe properly this floral wonder, and I advise readers to try it for themselves. There is one great thing about the novelty, and that is that it comes absolutely true from seed. The flower stems are rather short, but the individual flowers are very large—quite as large as some that are looked upon as giants among the taller growing sorts. The flower stems bear two or three and sometimes four flowers on each, and as all the flowers open at the same time, there is no need to pick stems with buds and open blossoms. The "Cupid" Sweet Pea makes a very pretty pot plant, and it may be of interest to readers to know how I grew mine. I filled a number of thumb pots with fairly rich

A Field of Cupid,—The Wonderful Dwarf Sweet Pea.

A Single Plant of "Cupid."

compost, and into the middle of each pot I pressed one seed, slightly covering it with the soil Every seed I potted germinated, and when the roots had reached the bottom I prepared 8 inch pots and carefully knocking out the plants from the thumb pots, crocks and soil being undisturbed, I placed them in the larger pots filling up with fresh soil. In a very short time the plants completely covered the surface of the pots, as shown in the illustration I give, and I soon had the pleasure of having a number of very pretty pots of Sweet Pea for the decoration of my rooms. The raiser recommends growing "Cupid" in 12 inch pots, but I find the 8 inch ones are quite large enough for decorative purposes.

For many years hybridisers tried unsuccessfully to raise a double flowered Sweet Pea, but now this is *au fait accómplit* and in *Sweet Pea Double* we have a welcome addition to this popular flower. The flowers are large, sweet scented, and can be obtained from Seedsmen in a variety of colours.

SINGLE SPIKE OF "CUPID" SWEET PEA.

SWEET WILLIAM, SINGLE.

## Sweet William.

Nat. Ord.—Caryophyllaceæ.

(Dianthus Barbatus).

On the Plains sow in October: March to May, and also in October, on the Hills. Firminger gives the following directions in his "Manual of Gardening":—

"The fine varieties of this plant, though they thrive well, rarely, if ever, open their beautiful trusses of bloom in the locality of Calcutta. The seed may be sown in October on the Plains, and in March on the Hills, and the young plants kept through the succeeding hot and rainy seasons, by sheltering them from the wet, without at the same time screening them too much from the light. In November, pot them singly in large pots with fr sh and rather rich soil. During the dry weather they will be benefitted by having their pots sunk in water to the rim, for an hour or two every four or five days."

An old writer says of this old inhabitant of the flower garden, that it was esteemed "for its beauty to deck up the bosoms of the beautiful, and garlands and crowns for pleasure '

There are several good strains of Sweet William ; in Singles, *Hunt's Perfection and New Dwarf Compact,* and in Doubles the *Extra Selected,* all contain varieties with fine flowers in a great variety of colours.

## SYRINGA.

### Nat. Ord—Oleaceæ (The Lilac, or Pipe Tree.)

Unfortunately it is quite impossible to grow the beautiful Lilac on the Plains, but the plant does quite as well on the Hills as it does at Home. It is rather strange that this plant will not grow on the Plains, as it is supposed to have been introduced into Europe from Persia, but the fact remains that many attempts to grow it have been made, but always without success. On the Hills I advise sowing in October and potting off the plants when large enough. Do not plant out till the plants are two or three years old, as, if planted sooner, they are almost certain to die off during the rains. Succeeds in any ordinary garden soil, but grows all the better if top-dressed occasionally with a good rich compost. *Syringa Vulgaris,* the common Lilac of the home gardens, is now found in a number of colours in shades of reds, purples, blues and white.

TECOMA, RADICANS.

## TECOMA.

### Nat. Ord.—Bignoniaceæ—(Trumpet Creeper or Trumpet Flower.)

Most of the varieties of Tecoma are Climbers, but a few are shrubs and amongst the best of these latter is the variety *Smithi,* which has lately been introduced, and which I illustrate and describe further on. Fortunately the various varieties of Tecoma succeed admirably on the Plains, and as they are really very beautiful plants, are well worth much more extensive cultivation. The creeper *Radicans* should be sown on the Plains in October or November in light, sandy soil. On the Hills sow in October, if protection can be given to the young seedlings during the winter months, and a sowing should also be made during the Spring. The plants will climb to a height of over 20 feet if trained, but training is essential as the plants are of rather a creeping character and the branches will root wherever they are allowed to touch the ground. The variety *Radicans* is a very free bloomer and, on the Plains, is in flower practically all the year round. The flowers are borne in corymbs, or bunches, as shown in the illustration, and are of a pretty orange-scarlet colour, the individual flowers being about 1½ inches long. Of quite a different style of growth is the novelty *Smithi*, which, instead

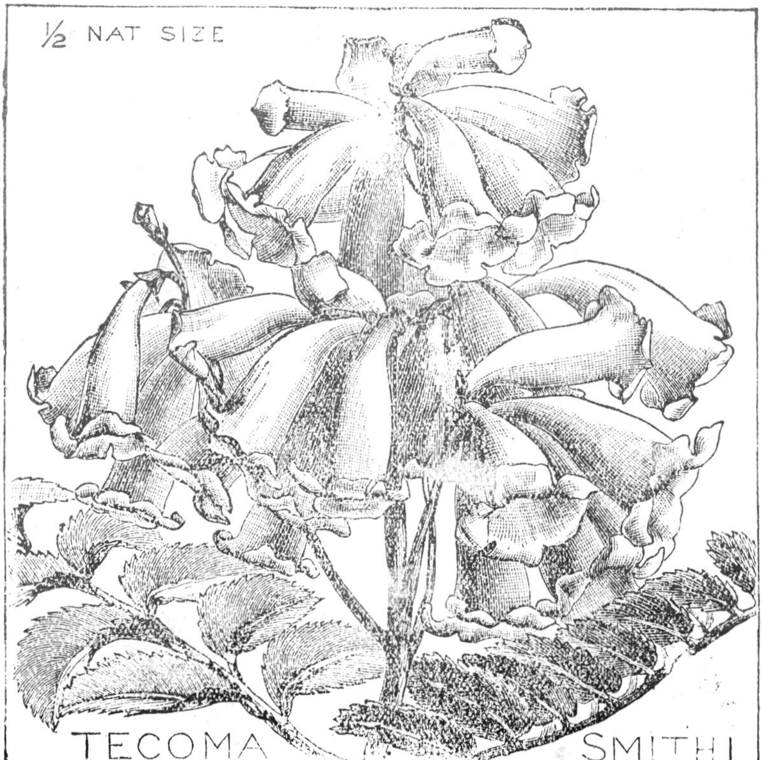


of climbing or creeping, grows as a small shrub. It is one of the finest seed novelties yet introduced, and an exceedingly beautiful addition to our flowering plants. The handsome pinnate leaves, surmounted by the large terminal corymbiform heads of orange-coloured blossoms, are most charming and effective. The seed may be sown at any time on the Hills, but I advise sowing in October on the Plains. It is as easily managed as a Chrysanthemum, the flowers lasting in perfection upwards of a month. As many as 100 flowers are sometimes produced from a single shoot, the total height of which is not more than 18 inches; the individual flowers are about 2 inches long, tubular, of a rich lemon and dark orange combined, the mouth of the tube being about 1 inch in diameter. First Class Certificate Royal Horticultural Society.

## THUNBERGIA, ALATA.

Nat. Ord.—Acanthaceæ.

A very pretty, hardy, Annual climber which succeeds well in all parts of India. Should be grown in a rather rich soil, a compost composed of equal parts of good loam, leaf mould and well rotted manure will be found best. Sow on the Plains in October or November; March to May on the Hills. When the seedlings are large enough to handle, pot off singly in pots or hanging baskets. The flowers are very pretty and of many colours, such as white, buff, orange yellow, and are about 1½ inches long. Many of the flowers are self coloured, while others have a dark purple eye.

## TORENIA

Nat. Ord.—Scrophulariaceæ.

The Torenia is one of the prettiest plants in cultivation for growing in pots or hanging baskets. They require any amount of moisture, so should be grown in a moist, shady situation, or with the pots standing in saucers of water; should be sown from March to July, both on the Plains and Hills; transplant as soon as large enough, placing 3 plants in a 5 inch, or 5 in an 8 inch pot.

TORENIA.

The soil most suitable is composed of equal parts of loam and leaf mould, with a small proportion of sharp sand and charcoal dust added. There are several varieties, but a small packet of mixed seed will be found ample by most growers. *Bailloni* (syn. Flava) has flowers of a bright golden yellow, spotted brown or purple; grows to a height of from 6 to 10 inches. *Fournieri* is a particularly pretty sort from Cochin-China. The tubes of the flowers are pale violet, with yellow backs while the base is relieved with a bright golden yellow blotch. The plants grow about 6 or 8 inches high. There is also a white flowering variety known as *Fournieri Alba* or *White Wings* and a large flowering one *Fournieri Grandiflora*.

TROPÆOLUM, LOBBIANUM.

# Tropæolum, Lobbianum.

(LOBB'S)

Nat. Ord.—Tropæolaceæ, or Geraniaceæ.

These are most beautiful plants for growing on trellises or arbours, or for hanging over vases, rockwork etc. The flowers are not so large as those of Tropæolum majus (Tall Nasturtium), but they are borne in much greater profusion. The plant does not succeed on the Plains, but grows with great luxuriance on the Hills. Sow where the plants are to remain, on the Plains in November; Hills March and April There are several distinct varieties of which the following are amongst the best.

*Brilliant.*—Rich scarlet; *Geant des Batailles*—Carmine; *Napoleon III.*—Yellow, striped rosy scarlet; *Roi des Noirs*—Black; *Spitfire*—Fiery red; *Triomphe de Gand*—Orange scarlet.

# TROPÆOLUM CANARIENSE.

Syn. Peregrinum.

Nat. Ord.—Tropæolaceæ or Geraniaceæ.—(Canary Creeper.)

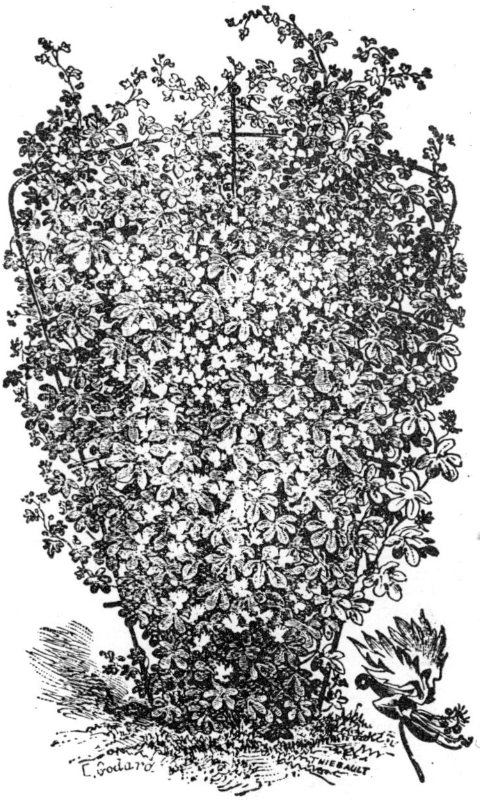

TROPÆOLUM CANARIENSE.

The well-known Canary Creeper is an universal favorite and is most useful for festooning trellises or arbours. On the Plains do not sow until the cold weather has set in, say about the middle of November. On the Hills sow at any time from March to June.

# TYDÆA.

Nat. Ord. GESNERACEÆ.

These are much like the Achimines, but the tubes of the flowers are not so flat, and the leaves are beautifully blotched and mottled. Require the same treatment as ACHIMINES (page 99). The flowers are very richly coloured.

TYDÆA, HYBRIDA GRANDIFLORA.

# VERBENA.

Nat. Ord.—Verbenaceæ,—(Vervain.)

There are few plants more useful for bedding than the Verbena, and few more easily grown. Although a Perennial, it can only be grown as an Annual on the Plains. Grows best in a compost largely composed of leaf mould. Sow on the Plains during the first week of October; March to May on the Hills. Grows well in pots, but does best if planted out in the open border. Prepare your soil by thoroughly working in a liberal supply of well rotted manure and leaf mould. A layer of the mixture about three or four inches deep should be spread over the soil, and then worked in with the spade to

VERBENA, AURICULÆFLORA.

a depth of about nine inches. When your seedlings have developed their fourth leaf, transplant into the prepared bed, choosing a dull day, or, better still, having the work done in the evening. Give plenty ot water at all stages of growth, and now and then a soaking with weak liquid manure. As the shoots become straggling, peg them down with wood pegs, made from forked twigs, and when in flower, remove the trusses as they go off, and thus prolong the flowering period.

VERBENA, CARNATION STRIPED.

There are numerous strains and varieties now to be had, and perhaps the best of the mixed strains is the one known as *American Mammoth*, the plants being of sturdy, vigorous habit, and yielding a profusion of immense trusses of flowers of all the colours known in this useful section of bedding plants, each flower being larger than an eight anna piece. This great improvement in size is certain to increase, in a very large measure, the popularity of this charming flower, this strain being altogether distinct and surprisingly beautiful. The colours present the same wide range as the ordinary varieties.

The following hybrids are all good and, in the case of the separate colours, provide splendid bedders, where special colours are required.

*Hybrida Auriculæflora.*—This superb and distinct section produces flowers in almost every shade of colour, with a large pure white eye. *Hybrida Auriculæflora Maxima*—Splendid large flowers. *Hybrida Candidissima*—A grand variety producing large trusses of flowers of the purest white. *Hybrida Carnation or Italian Striped*—This section is generally known as "Italian" Verbenas, from the striped kinds having first originated in Italy. Produce varieties with large trusses of flowers variously striped, blotched, and spotted. *Hybrida Grandiflora*—Produces very fine, richly coloured large flower trusses. *Hybrida Indigo Blue*—A

VERBENA, SCARLET DEFIANCE.

beautiful blue, with large white eye. *Hybrida Scarlet Defiance*—Intense fiery scarlet; a splendid variety for bedding. *Hybrida New Yellow*—Flowers beautiful creamy yellow; very distinct. *Hybrida Purple Mantle*—Beautiful rich purple; very fine.

## VERONICA.

### Nat Ord. SCROPHULARIACEÆ

### (Speedwell, or Cancerwort).

I do not think it would be possible to grow the Veronica with any degree of success on the Plains, but as all the known species of the plant are common in temperate and frigid regions, it should do well on the Hills, where the seed should be sown in October, and the seedlings planted out in the Spring, in beds of fairly rich soil. The best compost is made up of equal parts of loam, leaf mould and well rotted manure. The plants require plenty of root room, so the beds should be deeply trenched before planting.

## VIOLA ODORATA.

### *Sweet Violet.* (*Vern*—Bunufsheh) Nat. Ord.—Violaceæ.

The Sweet Violet is a popular favourite and requires no description, as it is much too well known to need any. The seed should be sown at the same time as the PANSY (Viola tricolor), and the after treatment of the plants is exactly the same. Plant out in a compost composed of turfy mould and thoroughly rotted cowdung "Do not use leaf mould." is the advice given by "Landolicus," as it is apt to attract insects which either feed on the leaves or use them as places of habitation. The seed will often take two or three months to germinate, and then very irregularly, so do not get impatient if you don't get your seedlings within this time. Where plants are obtainable it is much better to procure some, as they increase rapidly and save the trouble and delay of raising from seed.

## WAITZIA.

### Nat. Ord.—Compositæ.

A very pretty "Everlasting" which is useful for decorations, when fresh flowers are not available The large flowered variety, *Waitzia Grandiflora*, bears large bunches of fine, bright yellow flowers on plants from 1 to 2 feet high. Should be planted out in fairly large clumps, when they make a very fine effect. Sow on the Plains in October; Hills in October for Spring and early Summer flowering, and also from March to May.

# WALLFLOWER.

## Nat. Ord—Cruciferæ. (Cheiranthus Cheiri). (Vern Kurunful, Luhooa Shuboo, or Kheeree).

Hitherto it has been almost impossible to get the Wallflower to flower at all well in many places on the Plains, but growers now have provided for them an annual variety in *Early Paris Market*, which, if sown with other annuals in October on the Plains, will flower freely during the whole of the latter part of the cold weather. Seed of Wallflower should be sown on the Plains in October; Hills March to May and also in Autumn. When the seedlings are strong enough to handle, plant out in well drained beds of light, rich soil.

WALLFLOWER, DOUBLE GERMAN.

There are many colours, and varieties of this most useful, sweet scented flower, of which the following are amongst the best:—*Early Paris Market*, the variety referred to above, should be in every garden, more particularly on the Plains. *Ruby Gem.* This grand Novelty in certainly the most brilliant and effective variety of single Wallflower hitherto sent out. The colour is a beautiful clear shade of ruby violet, with a bluish satin-like sheen (quite unlike the old purple Wallflower, which is much more dark and dull in colour), and when seen in a mass, the effect produced is very striking. It has the habit of the ordinary dark blood Wallflower, of medium height, and the flowers are extra large and of good substance.

The following are all good colours of the *Single flowering* varieties:—*Blood Red*—A good old favourite sort. *Brown*—Very dark and sweet scented. *Feltham Blood Red*—An extra fine variety. Flowers

WALLFLOWER, SINGLE.

very dark and of wonderful size. A great improvement on the common Blood Red. *Purple*—Dark purplish violet. *Yellow*—A bright clear yellow.

Many people are fond of the *Double flowering* Wallflowers, but personally, I do not consider them in any way equal to the Singles. Those who prefer the Double varieties will find various strains offered by Seedsmen.

# WHITLAVIA.

Nat. Ord.—Hydrophyllaceæ.

This is a very pretty annual now more commonly known as *Phacelia Whitlavia.* Is of very easy culture and succeeds admirably all over India. Sow on the Plains in October; March to May on the Hills. The plants grow to a height of about 2 feet, and look extremely well if grown in masses. Will grow in any ordinary garden soil. There are several varieties, but for all practical purposes a packet or two of good mixed seed will be quite enough for any ordinary garden. *Gloxinioides* has very pretty Gloxinia-like flowers, blotched with blue and white. *Grandiflora* is a variety with very large, handsome blue flowers.

# WIGANDIA, CARACASANA.

Nat. Ord—Hydrophyllaceæ. (Caraccas Big-leaf.)

WIGANDIA, CARACASANA.

As shown in the illustration, this is a very handsome, large leaved, ornamental plant. Will not grow, except as a Winter Annual, on the Plains, where the seed should be sown in October, but on the Hills will grow on for years, attaining to a height of some 10 or 12 feet. On the Hills sow in October and also in March or April. Pot off the seedlings when large enough, into a light loamy soil, or plant out in the open garden. I find the plant perfectly hardy in Mussoorie at an altitude of 6,000 feet, and have a number of handsome plants, which have been growing in my garden for some six or eight years. The variety *Caracasana* is also known as *Macrophylla.*

# ZINNIAS.

Nat. Ord.—Compositæ.—(Youth-and-old-age).

Many people do not like the Zinnia on account of the stiffness of the flowers, but that complaint can hardly be made now, as for years past growers have been improving the various varieties to such an extent, that the flowers of to-day bear but slight resemblance to the stiff and unnatural looking flowers of only a few years ago

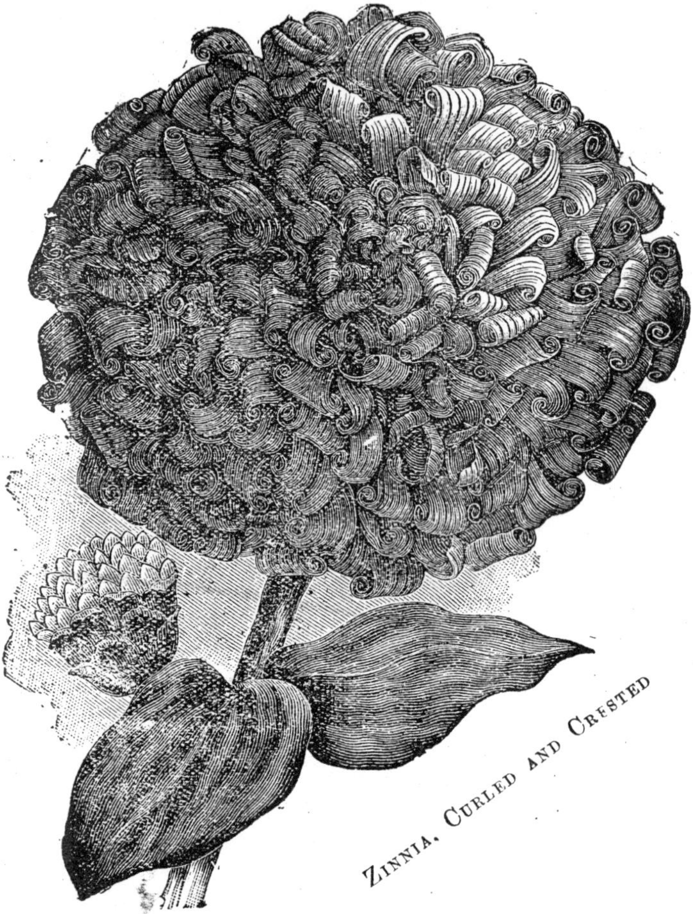

ZINNIA. CURLED AND CRESTED

A few years ago the double Zinnia was absolutely unknown in India. As the Zinnia can be had in flower at a time when but few other annuals can exist, it is particularly valuable for growing on the Plains.

Seed can be sown practically all the year round, but the best time is June and July. Sow in pots or pans and when about 4 inches high plant out in beds of fairly rich soil, fully exposed to the sun. The first flowers of even the best of the double flowering varieties are almost invariably single, and these should be carefully removed as they open. Until the rains start water freely.

There are now very many really fine strains in cultivation, and perhaps the best of all is the peculiarly beautiful *Curled and Crested.* The flowers are large and full, the petals being twisted, curled and crested into the most fantastic and graceful forms, rendering them free from the stiffness which was heretofore the characteristic of the family. The colours comprise orange, purple, pink, deep rose, yellow &c., and the form is beautifully shown in the illustration I give. The plants form compact bushes about 2 feet high by 2 feet through, and individual plants have been known to bear from 150 to 300 flowers, which are carried well above the foliage. Another extra fine sort is the popular *Zebra*, in which the flowers are of most perfect shape, and varied in colour, as will be found in the strain pure white and shades of orange, crimson, pink, yellow, violet, rose, scarlet &c., quite three-fourths of the flowers being beautifully striped and blotched with different shades. The plants are very compact and grow to a height of about 2 feet. One of the most popular strains is the *New Grand Mammoth* (Elegans Robusta Grandiflora Plenissima fl. pl.), a new very large flowering race, differing from the old variety in their most luxuriant robust growth, and in the larger, and more conical shape of the flowers, which have broader, and more petals. The plant forms a handsome bush, 3 feet in height, and the large, perfectly formed double flowers, measuring 5 to 6 inches across, are borne, in uninterrupted succession, on strong slender stems and well displayed above the foliage. The flowers are of the most intense and brilliant colours, and comprise several new and rich hues. The luxuriant growth and free flowering habit of this fine novelty render it particularly attractive for large groups or for flower borders.

ZINNIA, TOM THUMB,

Other good sorts are :—

*Haageana fl. pl.*—Splendid new varieties, specially suitabale for pot culture. *Pumila fl. pl.*—A fine dwarf variety, intermediate in height between the preceding and the ordinary Zinnia; flowers extra double and of the most distinct colours. *Tom Thumb*—These form charming, compact, free-flowering pigmy bushes, with small double flowers; they are specially suitable for edging small beds and groups, and also constitute very pretty objects when grown in pots.

A very good strain for bedding purposes is *Elegans fl. pl.* of which a number of separate colours are to be had from most Seedsmen. When beds of separate colours are wanted, these will be found useful. The colours usually comprise :—Crimson, Dark Purple, Flesh, Golden Yellow, Lilac, Purple, Rose, Scarlet, Sulphur Yellow, White.

ZINNIA, ELEGANS FL. PL.

# GARDENING CALENDARS

FOR

## HILLS & PLAINS

ARRANGED BY

W. W. JOHNSTONE.

# GARDENING CALENDARS.

In arranging Calendars of Gardening Operations for India, one is faced with the great difficulty of giving times for sowing &c, suitable for the very various climates prevailing in the different parts of the immense Indian Empire. In the following notes I have tried, with the assistance of gardeners in various parts of the country, to give information suited for as many places as possible but readers must be guided, more or less, by the sowing dates of the native malis, who generally know something about the most suitable times for gardening operations in their own districts. The Calendars I give should not be used as hard and fast rules, but should be taken as a basis on which to work. Gardening Calendars are useful in suggesting things that *may* be done, rather than for things that *must* be done.

# GARDENING CALENDAR.

## FOR THE PLAINS.

### JANUARY.

*Vegetable Garden:*—Make successional sowings of Peas, Beans, Lettuces, Cress, Mustard, Radishes, Spinach, Celery, Beet, Squash, Turnips, &c. The first sowings of Celery should be earthed up this month. Keep weeds down by free use of the hoe. Although in some parts, Bengal for instance, the soil will still be fairly moist, in most places watering will have to be carefully seen to. An occasional application of weak liquid manure will be found of great benefit. Plant out seedlings of Cauliflower, Cabbage and Kohl Rabi.

*Flower Garden* :—Make a final sowing of Nasturtiums, Candytuft, Mignonette, Marigold, Convolvulus &c. Pot off Asters, Cinerarias, Pansies, Stocks &c. Divide Chrysanthemums, which will have finished flowering by now Some growers prefer to plant out the divided plants into beds, but I advise potting them off singly in 3 inch pots. Many plants should be pruned this month, such as :—Bignonias, Hibiscus, Tecomas &c., &c., while cuttings of Aloysia Citriodora, Carnations, Geraniums, Heliotrope, Pansies &c., strike readily if put in now.

### FEBRUARY.

*Vegetable Garden* :—Sow a few seeds of American Water Melons. Successional sowings may also be made of Cress, Mustard and Lettuce. Drench late Peas, also Runner Beans, with water every day. A good top dressing of fresh stable manure will be found of great benefit, more particularly if the manure is laid down previous to watering. Celery also will need plenty of water. See that the seed pods are picked off Dwarf Beans as soon as they are ready for use. and give the plants frequent drenchings with weak liquid manure. Thin out late sown Turnips. Also thin out Carrots and Onions to give them plenty of room to develope.

*Flower Garden* :—The Chrysanthemum plants which were divided and potted off into 3 inch pots last month, should now be shifted on into 6 inch ones, taking care to use a very rich compost. Caladiums and all other tuberous, fibrous or bulbous rooted plants that have been dormant during the cold season, should now be re-planted or re-potted.

Plant out late seedlings of such things as Dianthus, Petunias, Phlox, Salpiglossis &c. See that your plants are not stinted with water, as the weather will now be warming up considerably. A sowing of Tecoma Radicans may now be put in. Budding and layering Roses is always successful this month, and also in March.

## MARCH.

*Vegetable Garden* :--Garden Herbs should be cut as soon as the flowers begin to open. Dry in an open shed or in a room where plenty of air can be given. When thoroughly dry, put in paper bags and hang where they will be free from damp. See to your Asparagus beds and top-dress them with a compost enriched with well rotted manure. The surface of the beds should be carefully removed before top-dressing with the fresh compost. Beet, Carrots, Onions and Parsnips should be lifted and stored for future use. The Beet, Carrots and Parsnips keep best if stored in dry sand. In Upper India sowings of Cucumber and Squash may now be made. Small sowing of Parsley should be made in a shady situation. Musk Melons should be sown now.

*Flower Garden* :—Allow Dahlias to die down by witholding water, and when dried off store in dry sand. If the roots of your Chrysanthemums have filled the 6 inch pots, give the plants another shift into 8 inch ones, using fresh rich compost. Allow Gloxinias, Callas, Lilies and any other bulbs that have flowered, to die down gradually. Prune shrubs that have flowered. Any plants of choice Petunias and Verbenas that you may wish to preserve, should now be lifted, potted and kept under shelter from the sun. Any repotting that is required should be done this month, and any plants which you do not wish to repot should have the top soil removed and a top-dressing of fresh compost given. Carefully see to watering.

## APRIL.

*Vegetable Garden* :—English Vegetables will almost all be finished now, but any left should be carefully watered. Your Asparagus beds will require plenty of water. Sow some Sâgs and Okra in a sheltered spot. Sow Cucumbers and Squashes, and see that Melons are treated liberally with water. All empty beds should be ploughed or dug.

*Flower Garden* :—Start a few Achimines for early flowering. Prune Passifloras and other climbing plants which flower on the young wood they make. Store away bulbous plants which have died down; leave in pots, storing in a dry go-down.

## MAY.

*Vegetable Garden* :—Asparagus will now be ready for cutting, and the beds should be very frequently watered. About the middle or end of the month sow Native Vegetable seeds, such as :—Egg Plant, Okra, Maize, Seems, Cucumbers, Squash, Vegetable Marrow, Sâg &c., &c. Plant tubers of Jerusalem Artichokes, if not done earlier. A little acclimatised Lettuce seed may be sown.

*Flower Garden* :—There will be few, if any, annuals alive now, but any there may be should be carefully watered morning and evening. See to your Chrysanthemums, giving plenty of water. Many of the Japanese and other Lilies do well if potted this month See that the leaves of fine foliage plants are frequently sponged. Any Ferns not potted earlier in the season should now be seen to. Top dress pot Roses with rich compost, and give frequent drenchings with liquid manure.

### JUNE.

*Vegetable Garden* :—Successional sowings of Maize and other Vegetables sown last month may still be put in. Sow Tipari.

*Flower Garden* :—About the beginning of the month, sowings of Amaranthus, Balsams, Celosia, Datura, Gomphrena, Helianthus, Ipomea, Marigolds, Nicotiana, Torenias, Zinnias &c. &c., should be made, placing the seed pans in a shady place till the seed germinates Palms and any other ornamental plants that have not been repotted or top-dressed should be seen to at once. Plant Dahlia tubers and sow seed. Pot Gloxinia tubers. Make cuttings of Roses, also of most hard wooded and soft wooded tropical plants.

### JULY.

*Vegetable Garden* :—Make successional sowings of Egg Plants, Okra, Cucumbers and the different kinds of Runner Beans and Gourds. See that all vacant ground is frequently turned over Earth up Jerusalem Artichokes. Continue to make sowings of Native Vegetable seeds.

*Flower Garden* :—Bud Roses. Seedlings of most of the Annuals sown last month will now be ready for planting out. Plant on well raised beds, as the plants will not thrive in a water-logged soil Chrysanthemums will be ready for shifting into their flowering pots. Pot any Gloxinias that were not ready last month. Continue sowings of Annuals mentioned last month.

### AUGUST.

*Vegetable Garden* :—In the United Provinces and Upper Bengal, small sowings of the early varieties of Cauliflower such as, Primus, Early London, Early Paris, Early Como &c., should be made. A small sowing of Celery should be made to provide plants for early planting allowed to grow larger before the operation. Earth up any Celery plants that are large enough, and give frequent supplies of liquid manure. See that plenty of water is given to Squashes, Asparagus &c. Transplant Endive a foot or 15 inches apart. Give Spinach plenty of room by thinning to 6 or 8 inches apart. See that the mali uses his hoe frequently, well stirring the soil to a depth of 2 or 3 inches, and leaving the top as open and loose as possible.

*Flower Garden*:—Larkspur and Nemophila may be sown now. A final sowing of Annuals can still be made, but late sown plants will require to be pushed on well by frequent applications of liquid manure, to get them ready for flowering before the end of the cold weather. Thin out seedlings sown in the open. Prick out seedlings of Asters, Pansies, Wallflowers, Stocks, Sweet Williams &c. Plant out any transplanted seedlings of Antirrhinums, Phlox, Pinks &c. which were not planted last month, and give liberal supplies of liquid manure every ten days.

# GARDENING CALENDAR.

## FOR THE HILLS.

### JANUARY

*Vegetable Garden*: —There is not very much that can be done this month on the Hills, unless the weather is very open, when small so · ings of Horn Carrots, Peas and Beans may be made, but these sowings must be very carefully protected with straw or litter. Small sowings of Lettuces, Broccoli, Cauliflow:r, Parsley and Radishes may be made in glass frames with bottom heat.

*Flower Garden* :—Be careful not to give your plants much water while the soil is at all moist, too little is infinitely better than too much at this time of the year. Seedlings of Primulas, Cinerarias, Petunias &c, should now be ready for transplanting, and should be pricked out into boxes or potted off singly in pots and kept under cover. Give choice shrubs and plants a good top-dressing with litter, to protect the roots. If the weather is open, plant hardy bulbs, such as Hyacinths, Crocuses, Snowdrops, Tulips, Ranunculi, Anemones, Gladioli &c Make a sowing of Gloxinias, and seed of other gesneraceous plants. Sow Primulas and Cinerarias for plants to flower in succession to those sown in December. Chrysanthemum cuttings may be made towards the end of the month Sow Sweet Peas about the end of the month.

### FEBRUARY.

*Vegetable Garden :*—Make small sowings in pots or boxes, or better still, in frames, of Asparagus, Beet, Broccoli, Cabbage, Carrots, Cauliflower, Cress, Endive, Lettuce, Parsnips, Salsify, Spinach and Turnips. If you have not got frames, these sowings should be made in pots or boxes in a warm verandah. Peas sown last month should be earthed up and protected with a top dressing of litter or manure.

*Flower Garden* :—Antirrhinums, Asters, Cinerarias, Calceolarias, Daisies, Pansies, Phlox, Petunias and other species requiring a long time to perfect their growth, should be sown now under shelter. Primula Sinensis should now be in full flower and the plants should be kept in a fairly warm verandah. Pot on Cinerarias which were sown earlier, as they require it. Transplant layers of Carnations and Picotees. Repot Geraniums, Pelargoniums, Roses, and Fuchsias. Continue making cuttings of Chrysanthemums, and pot on those struck in December.

watering
protect
not exc
be sown

*Veg*
of the M
be sown
during t
Spring a
in bearin
&c. To
well rott
*Flo*
entirely
exposed
bulbs ar
lifted sh
potted
which ha
leaves &c
mould.
with stra

*Vege*
should be
before the
a rush c
orders pr
night afte
following
a few wee
in rotatio
During t
seen to.
rotted ma
up with
should be
*Flowe*
now be r
plants, ex
very spari
or less deli
verandah,
even end, o

First Edition: 2010 (Saka 1932)

Second Edition: 2021 (Saka 1942)

ISBN 978-93-5409-147-6
HIS-ENG-REP-006-2021-22

Price : ₹ 180.00

Published by the Director General,
Publications Division, Ministry of Information and Broadcasting,
Government of India, Soochna Bhawan,
CGO Complex, Lodhi Road, New Delhi-110003

http://www.publicationsdivision.nic.in

**Sales Centres** : • **Delhi** l Soochna Bhawan, C.G.O. Complex, Lodhi Road, New Delhi-110003 • Hall No. 196, Old Secretariat, Delhi-110054 • **Mumbai** - 701, B-Wing, 7th Floor, Kendriya Sadan, Belapur, Navi Mumbai-400614 • **Kolkata** - 8, Esplanade East, Kolkata-700069 • **Chennai** - 'A' Wing, Rajaji Bhawan, Besant Nagar, Chennai-600090 • **Patna** - 'Bihar State Co-operative Bank Building, Ashoka Rapath, Patna-800004 • **Thiruvananthapuram** - Press Road, Near Govt. Press, Thiruvananthapuram-695001 • **Lucknow** - Hall No. 1, 2nd Floor, Kendriya Bhawan, Sector H, Aliganj, Lucknow-226024 • **Hyderabad** - Block 4, 1st Floor, Gruhakalpa Complex, M.G. Road, Nampally Hyderabad-500001 • **Bengaluru** - 1st Floor, 'F' Wing, Kendriya Sadan, Koramangala, Bangalore-560034

---

**RAJGURU THE INVINCIBLE REVOLUTIONARY (ENGLISH)**

Translation : Dr. Yashvant Verma & Anil Verma from original (Hindi) Ek Ajeya Krantikari by Anil Verma

Editor : Nitima Shiv Charan

Cover Design : R.K. Tandon

---

Typesetter : Quick Prints, Naraina, New Delhi-110 028.

Printed at : J.K Offset Graphics Pvt. Ltd., New Delhi -110 020